THE SHIELD™

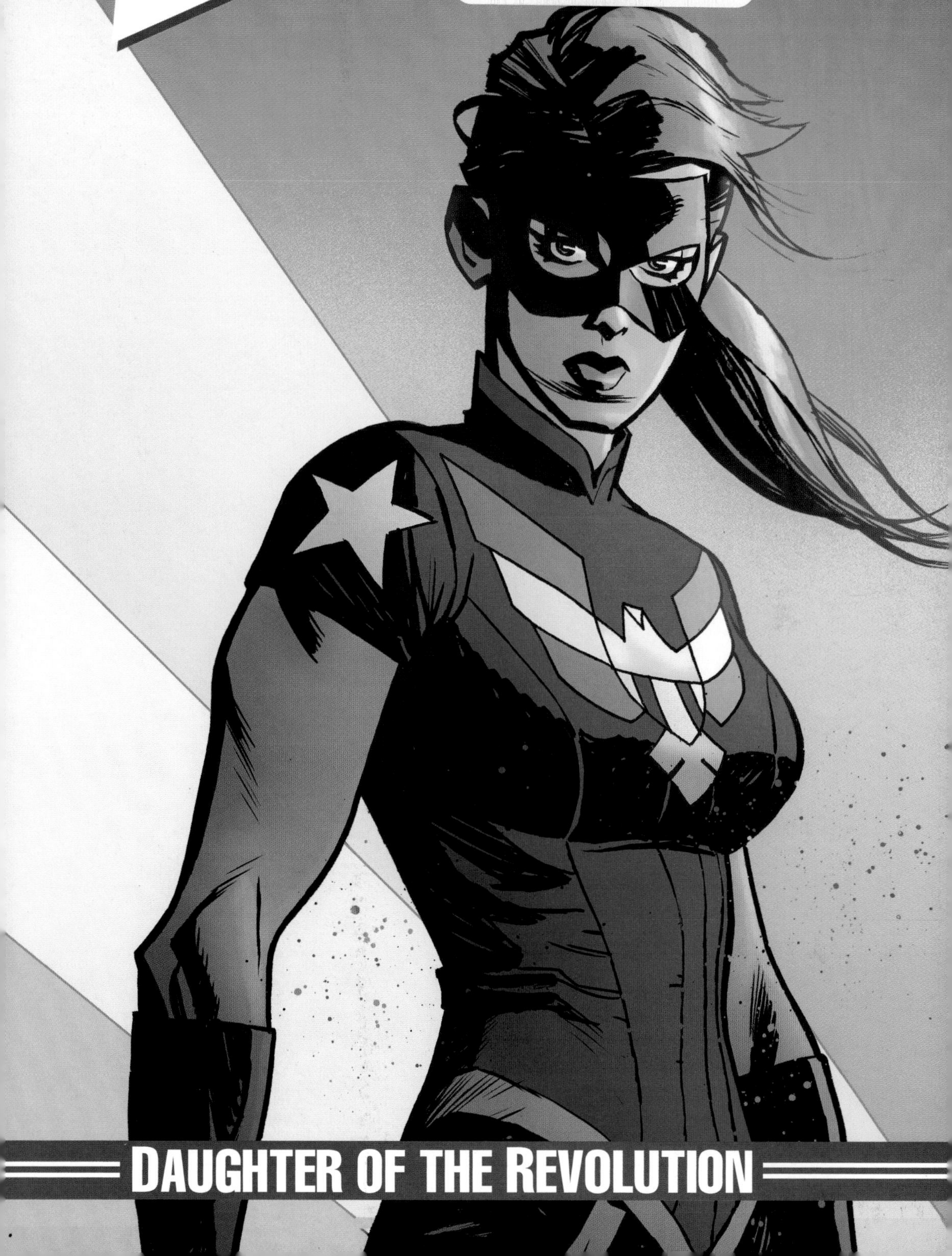

DAUGHTER OF THE REVOLUTION

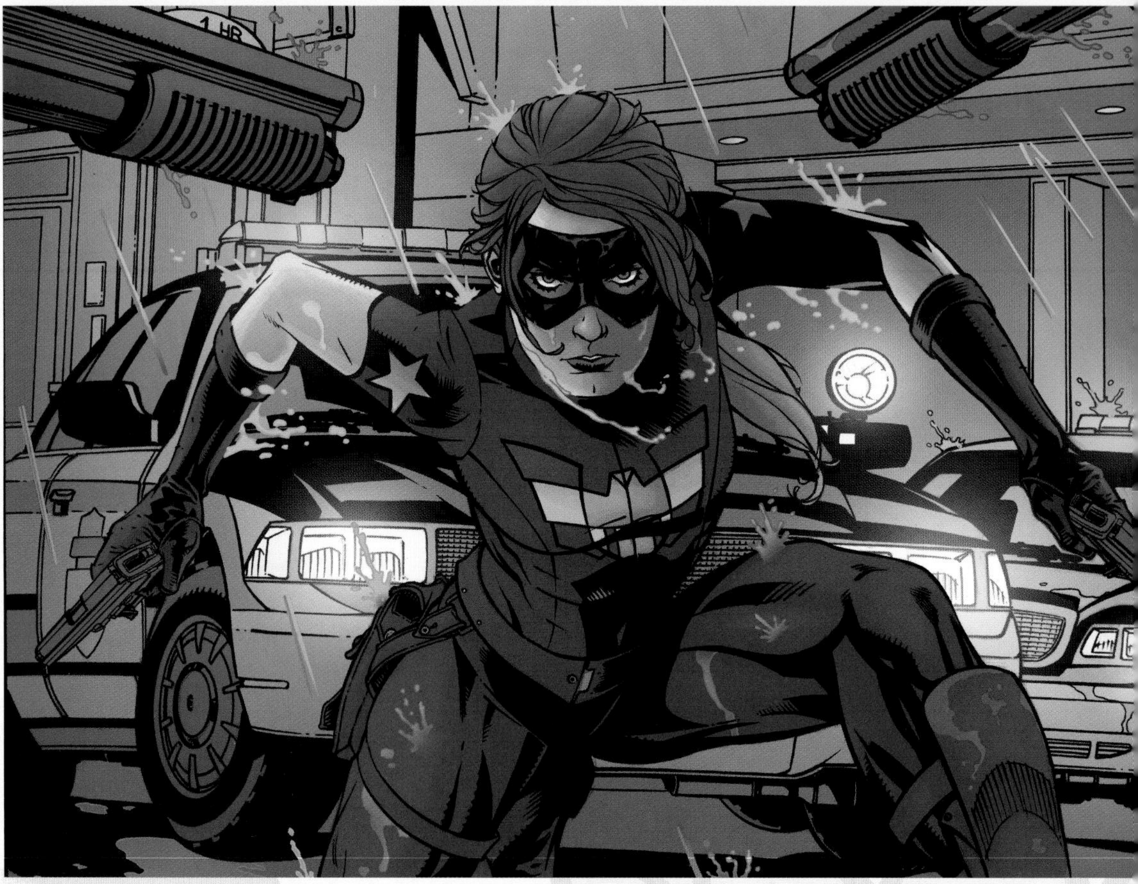
1 HR

STORY
ADAM CHRISTOPHER & CHUCK WENDIG

ART
DREW JOHNSON
ISSUES 1, 2 (PGS 1-12) & 3
RAY SNYDER
INKS ISSUE 2 (PGS 1-12)
AL BARRIONUEVO
ISSUE 2 (PGS 13-22)
GREG SCOTT
ISSUE 4

COLORING
KELLY FITZPATRICK

LETTERING
RACHEL DEERING
SPECIAL THANKS TO JACK MORELLI - ISSUE 3

EDITOR
ALEX SEGURA

ASSISTANT EDITOR
JAMIE LEE ROTANTE

GRAPHIC DESIGN
VINCENT LOVALLO

PUBLISHER
JON GOLDWATER

INTRODUCTION BY ALEX SEGURA

REIMAGINING AN ICON

The task our CEO/Publisher, Jon Goldwater, gave me when I came back to Archie Comics was simple–shock some life into our superhero characters.

It was a daunting task. The Dark Circle heroes are iconic–but have also been through various iterations and long, dormant periods. The idea was to dust them off and present them in a way that would not only appeal to their small but fanatic followers, but to new readers looking for something different.

I knew The Shield would be one of the first heroes we took a look at. I just didn't think it'd be the hero we ended up with.

The email from Jon was clear–"The Shield should be a new person. A woman. Strong, heroic." For decades, despite being the first patriotic hero, The Shield has been saddled with the "Captain America clone" tag. It was time to change that.

With that mandate, I knew I needed creative minds who were not only comfortable with taking major risks, but also well-versed in comics and how they work. I got really lucky with our first choice: writers Adam Christopher and Chuck Wendig. They're both bombastically creative, savvy and not scared to push buttons. Who better to reshape an iconic hero that was riddled with preconceptions?

Adam and Chuck also played off each other well, with Adam as the student of comic book history and Red Circle in particular, able to layer their pitch with hat tips and nods to the past while still making sure the story felt vibrant and new. Chuck brought a manic energy to the plotting and deft touch to the dialogue that gave the comic a sense of spark and energy that felt new. But that would come later.

First, though, allow me to pull back the curtain a bit and let you, dear reader, know a truth about comics: it's a lot of work. The first idea isn't always the idea you see on the page and it's very much about compromise. Reinventing a character like The Shield was not easy, and the process involved a lot of brainstorming, revisions and–at least once, that I can recall–complete overhauls. It had to be perfect. Just right.

To their credit, Adam and Chuck took everything in stride, poking and tinkering with their concept and watching it evolve into something different, more compelling and, as you'll soon find out, memorable. Paired with a supremely iconic costume design by artist Wilfredo Torres plus stupendous, craftsman-like interior artwork from veterans like Drew Johnson, Al Barrionuevo and Greg Scott, and you're left with a comic that is planted in the real world, but evokes the energy of the most beloved superhero adventures. A patriotic hero for today, that's been around since the beginning.

Mission accomplished.

Alex Segura,
Editor, *The Shield*

ISSUE ONE

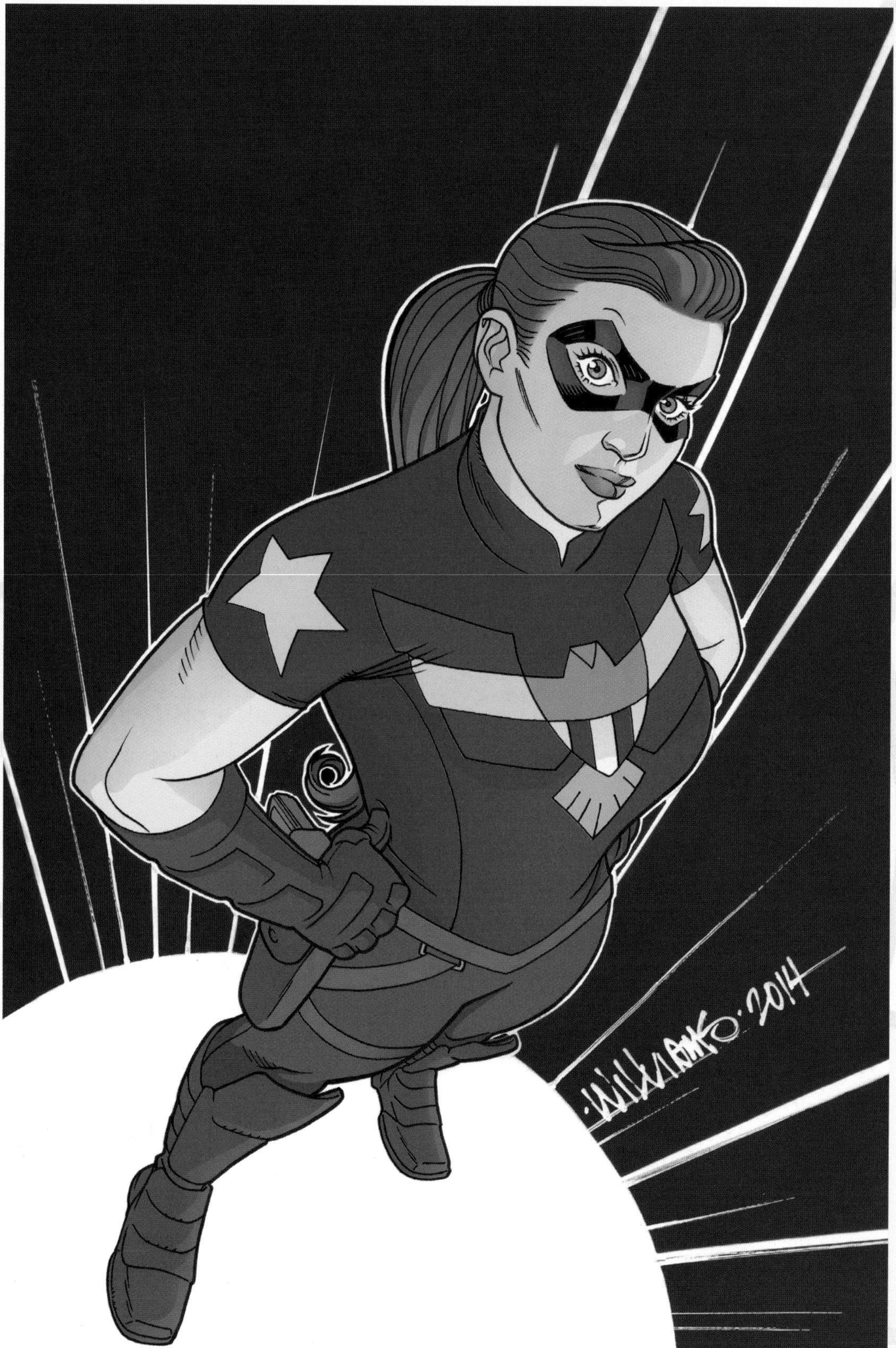

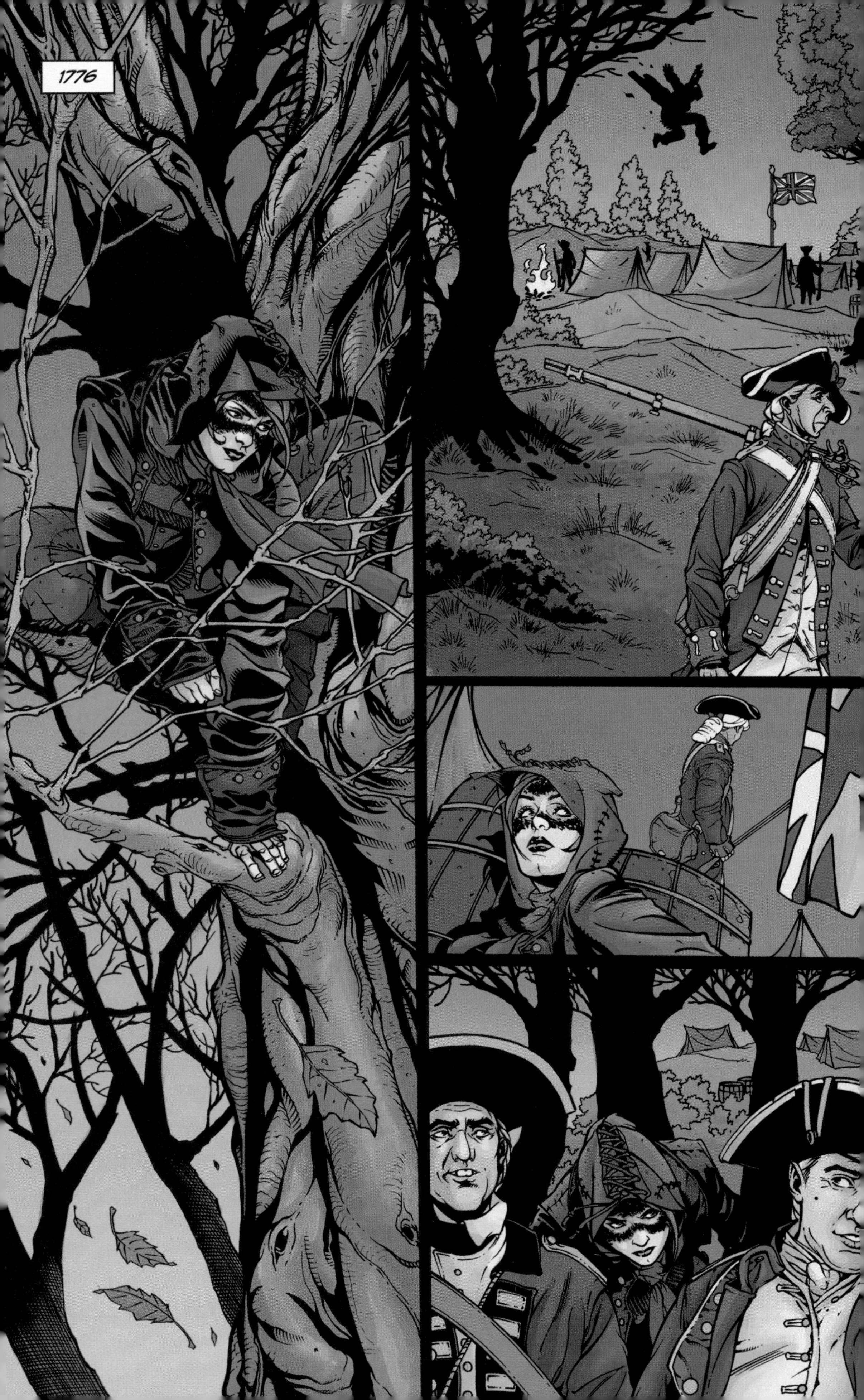
1776

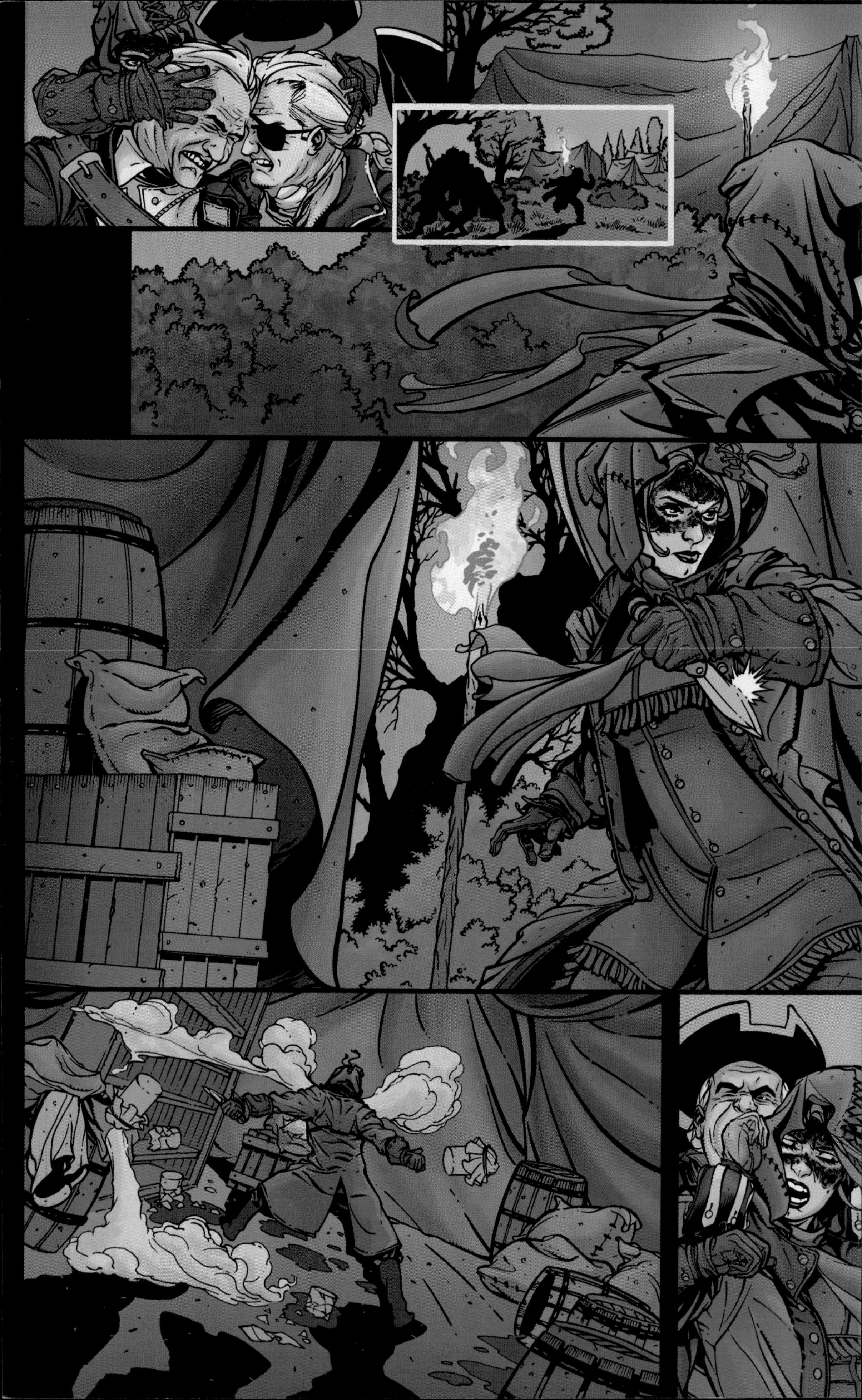

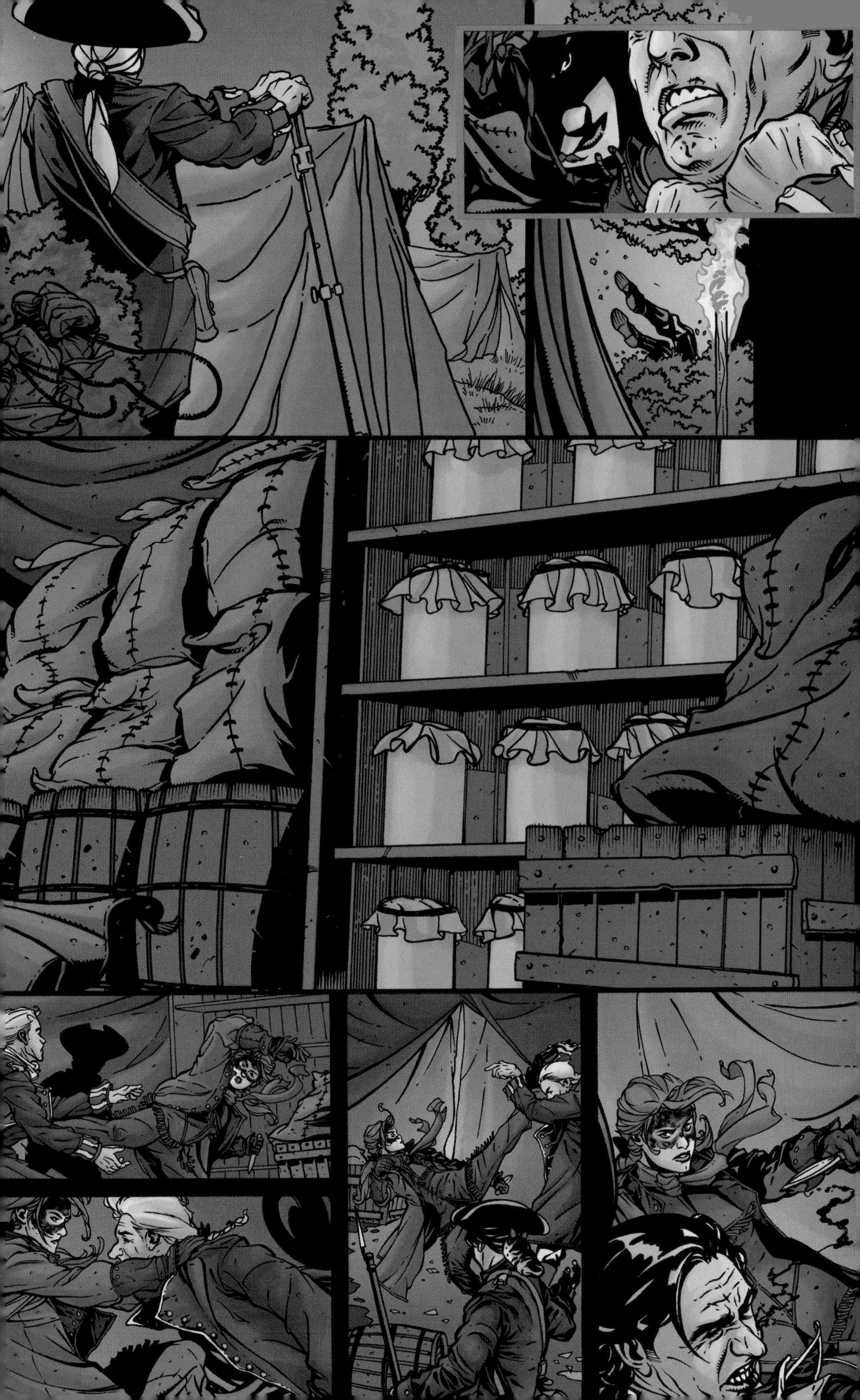

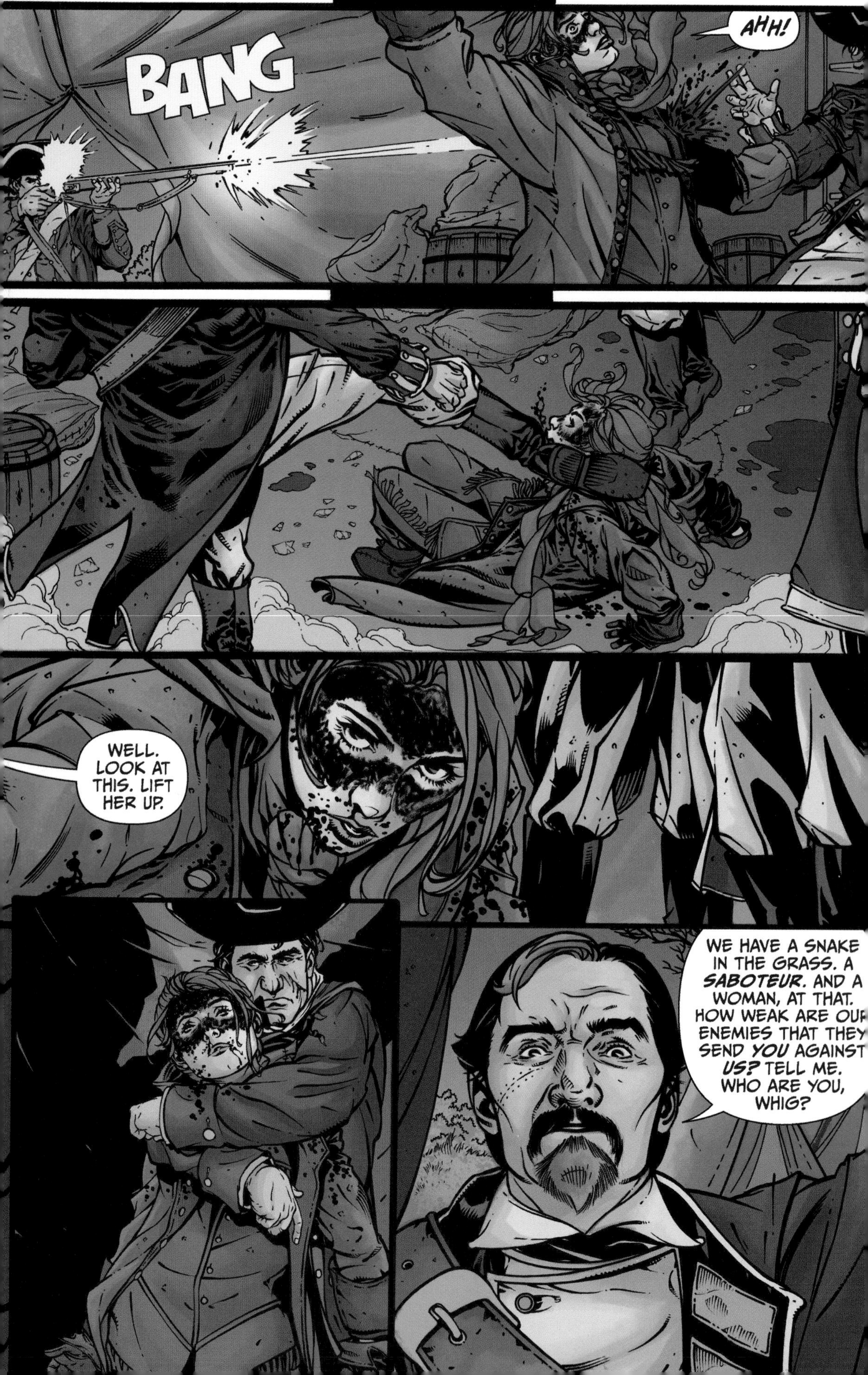
BANG
AHH!
WELL. LOOK AT THIS. LIFT HER UP.
WE HAVE A SNAKE IN THE GRASS. A SABOTEUR. AND A WOMAN, AT THAT. HOW WEAK ARE OUR ENEMIES THAT THEY SEND YOU AGAINST US? TELL ME. WHO ARE YOU, WHIG?

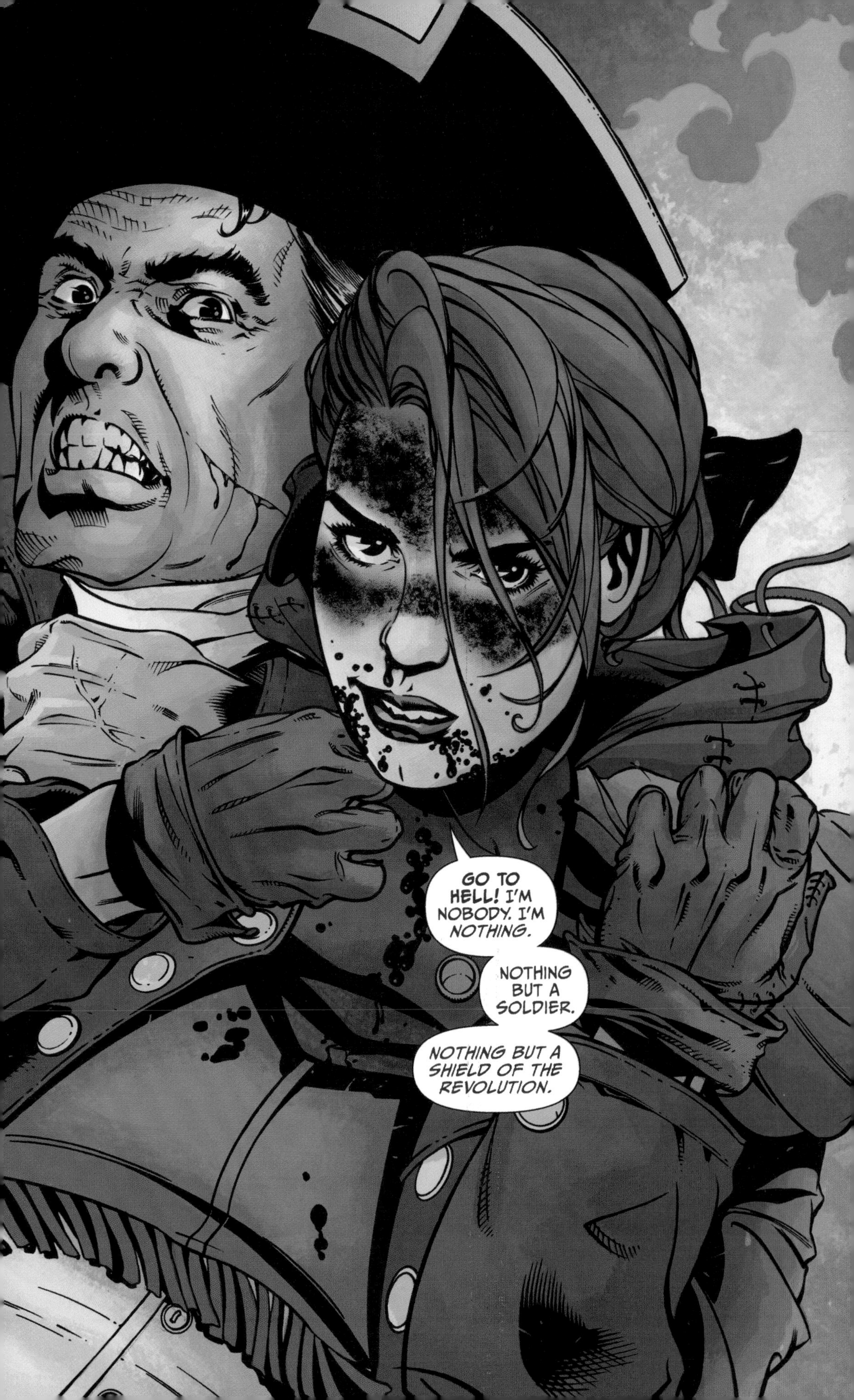
GO TO **HELL!** I'M NOBODY. I'M *NOTHING.*
NOTHING BUT A SOLDIER.
NOTHING BUT A SHIELD OF THE REVOLUTION.

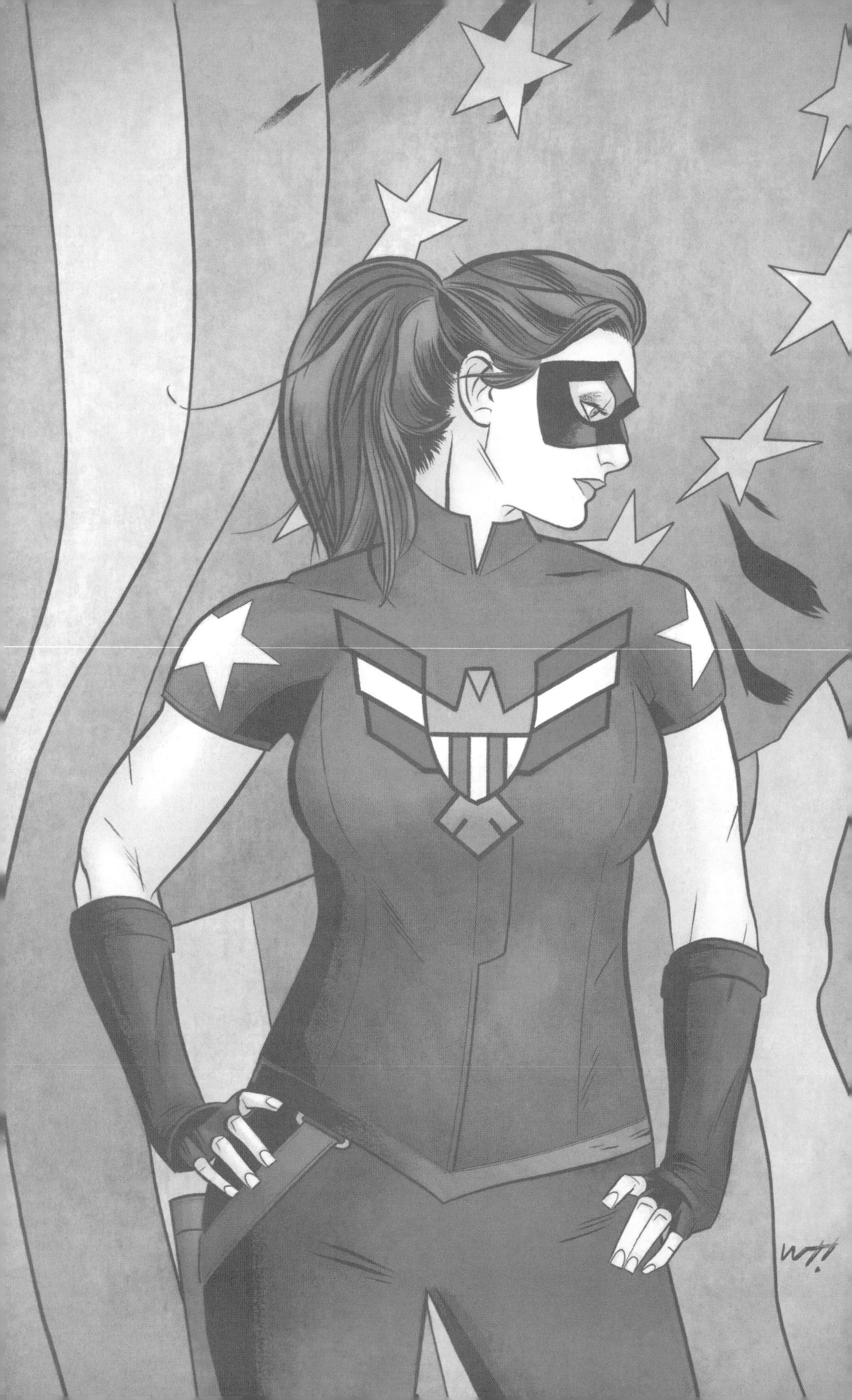

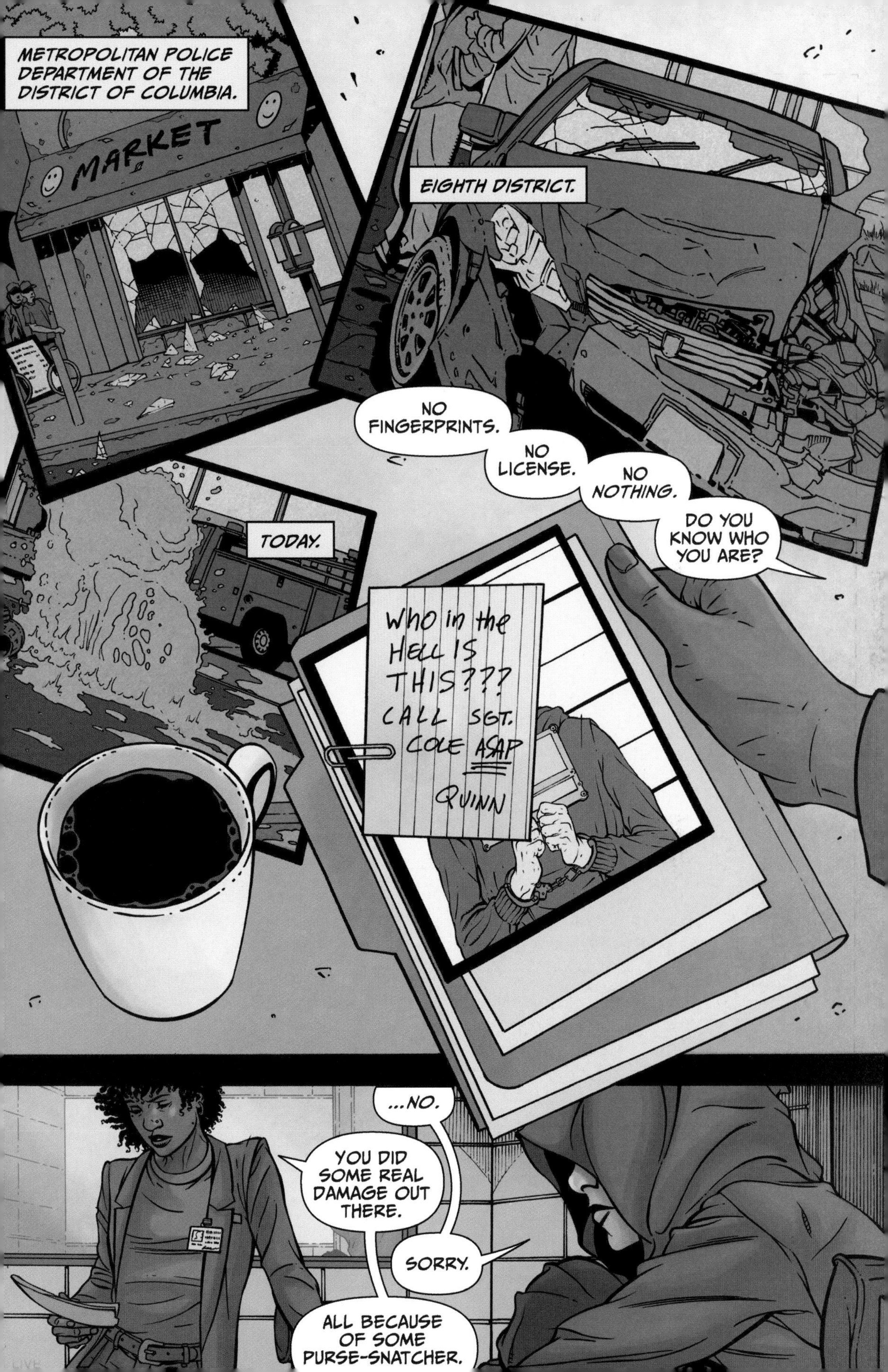
METROPOLITAN POLICE DEPARTMENT OF THE DISTRICT OF COLUMBIA.
MARKET
EIGHTH DISTRICT.
NO FINGERPRINTS.
NO LICENSE.
NO NOTHING.
DO YOU KNOW WHO YOU ARE?
TODAY.
Who in the HELL IS THIS??? CALL SGT. COLE ASAP
QUINN
...NO.
YOU DID SOME REAL DAMAGE OUT THERE.
SORRY.
ALL BECAUSE OF SOME PURSE-SNATCHER.

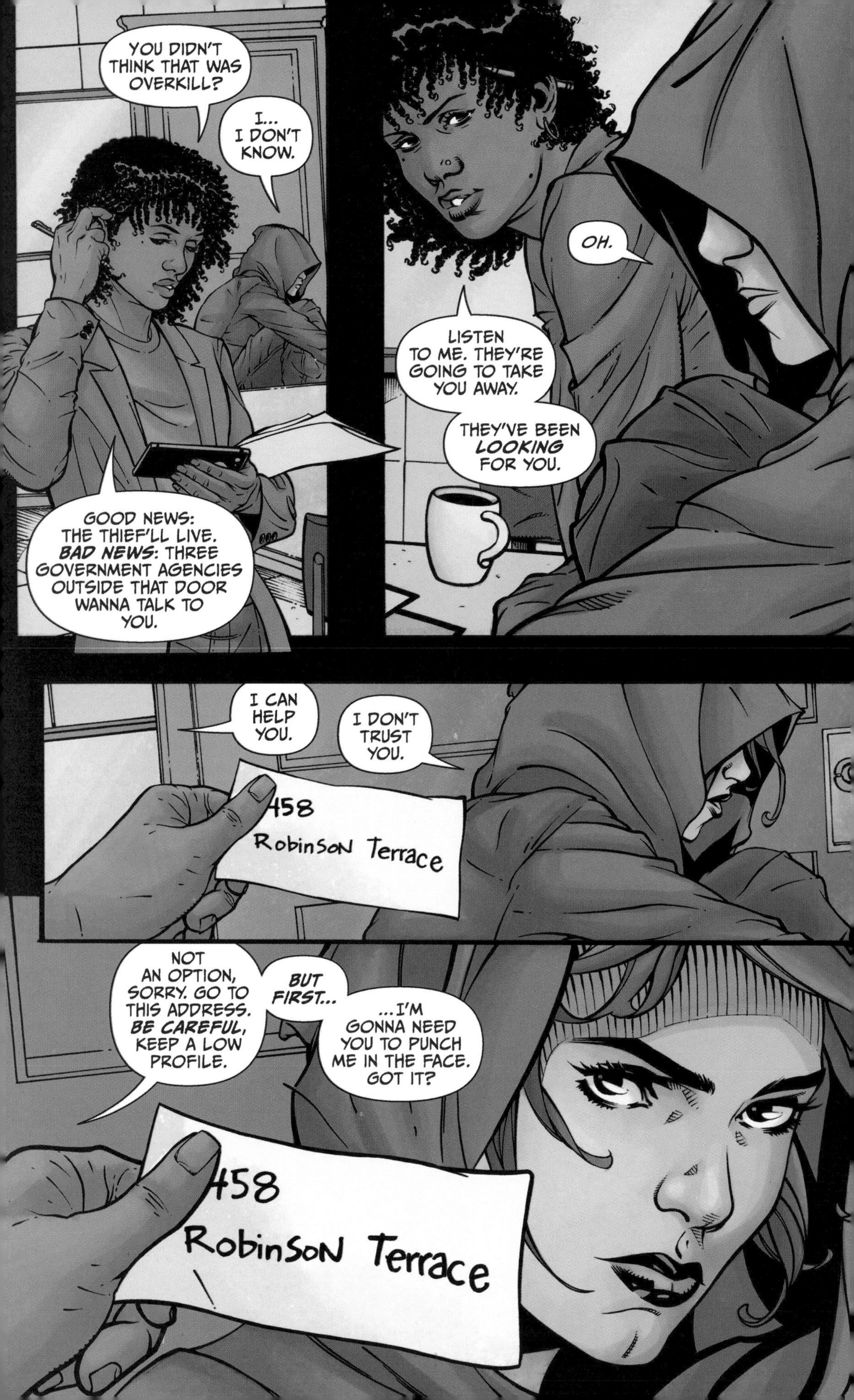

YOU DIDN'T THINK THAT WAS OVERKILL?
I... I DON'T KNOW.
GOOD NEWS: THE THIEF'LL LIVE. ***BAD NEWS***: THREE GOVERNMENT AGENCIES OUTSIDE THAT DOOR WANNA TALK TO YOU.
OH.
LISTEN TO ME. THEY'RE GOING TO TAKE YOU AWAY.
THEY'VE BEEN ***LOOKING*** FOR YOU.
I CAN HELP YOU.
I DON'T TRUST YOU.
458 Robinson Terrace
NOT AN OPTION, SORRY. GO TO THIS ADDRESS. ***BE CAREFUL***, KEEP A LOW PROFILE.
BUT FIRST...
...I'M GONNA NEED YOU TO PUNCH ME IN THE FACE. GOT IT?
458 Robinson Terrace

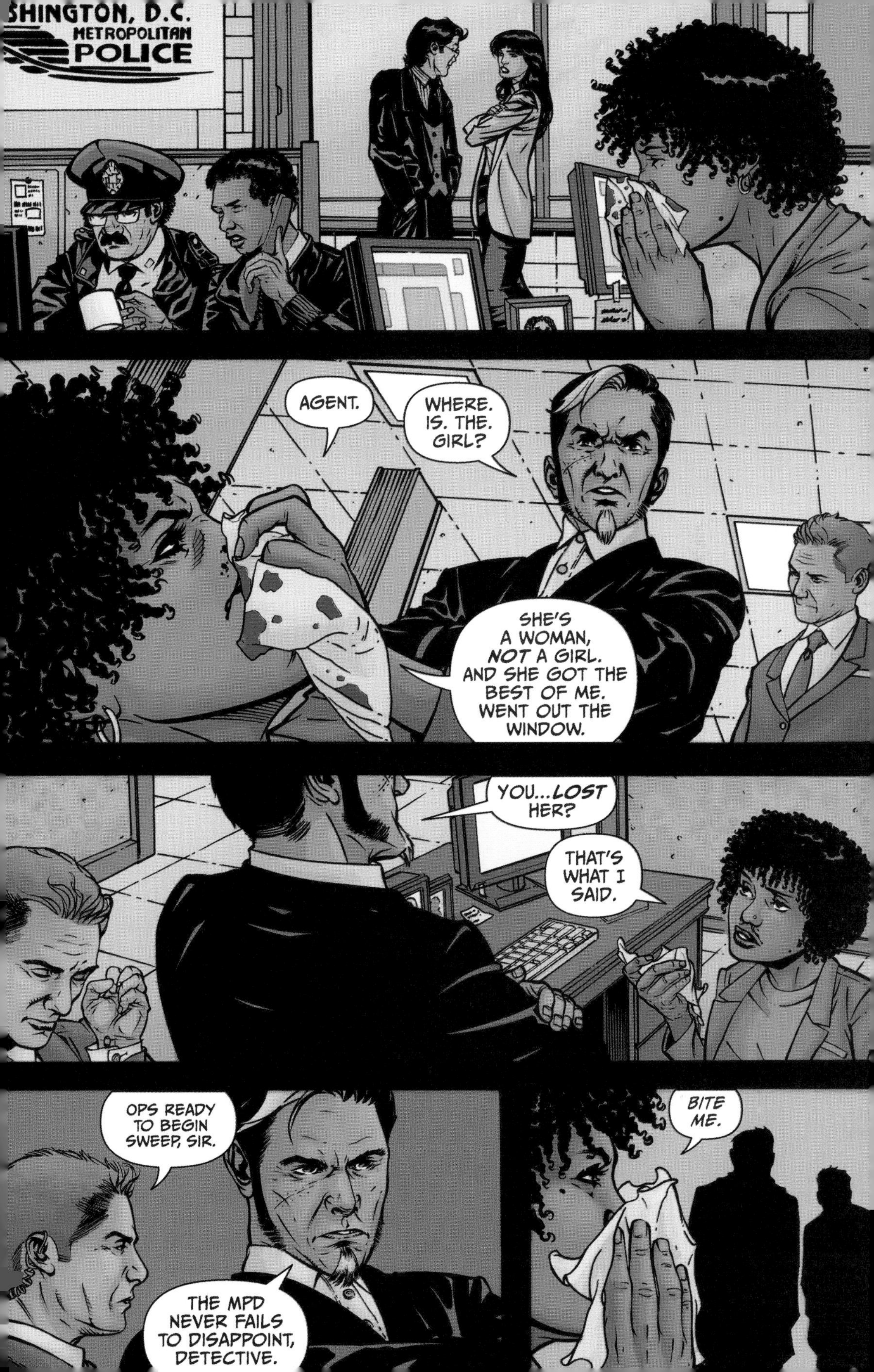
SHINGTON, D.C. METROPOLITAN POLICE
AGENT.
WHERE. IS. THE. GIRL?
SHE'S A WOMAN, NOT A GIRL. AND SHE GOT THE BEST OF ME. WENT OUT THE WINDOW.
YOU...LOST HER?
THAT'S WHAT I SAID.
OPS READY TO BEGIN SWEEP, SIR.
THE MPD NEVER FAILS TO DISAPPOINT, DETECTIVE.
BITE ME.

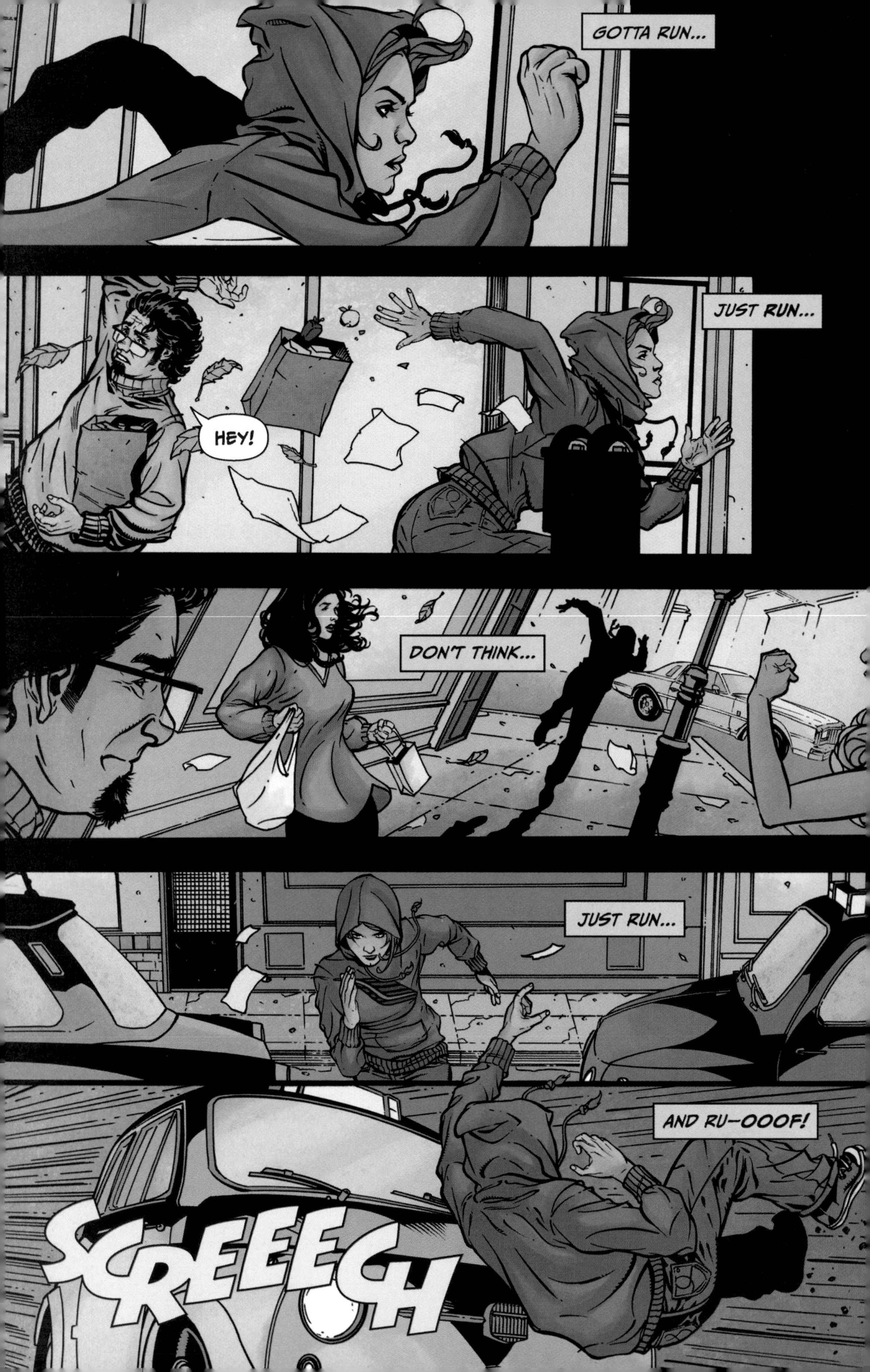
GOTTA RUN...
JUST RUN...
HEY!
DON'T THINK...
JUST RUN...
AND RU–OOOF!
SCREEECH

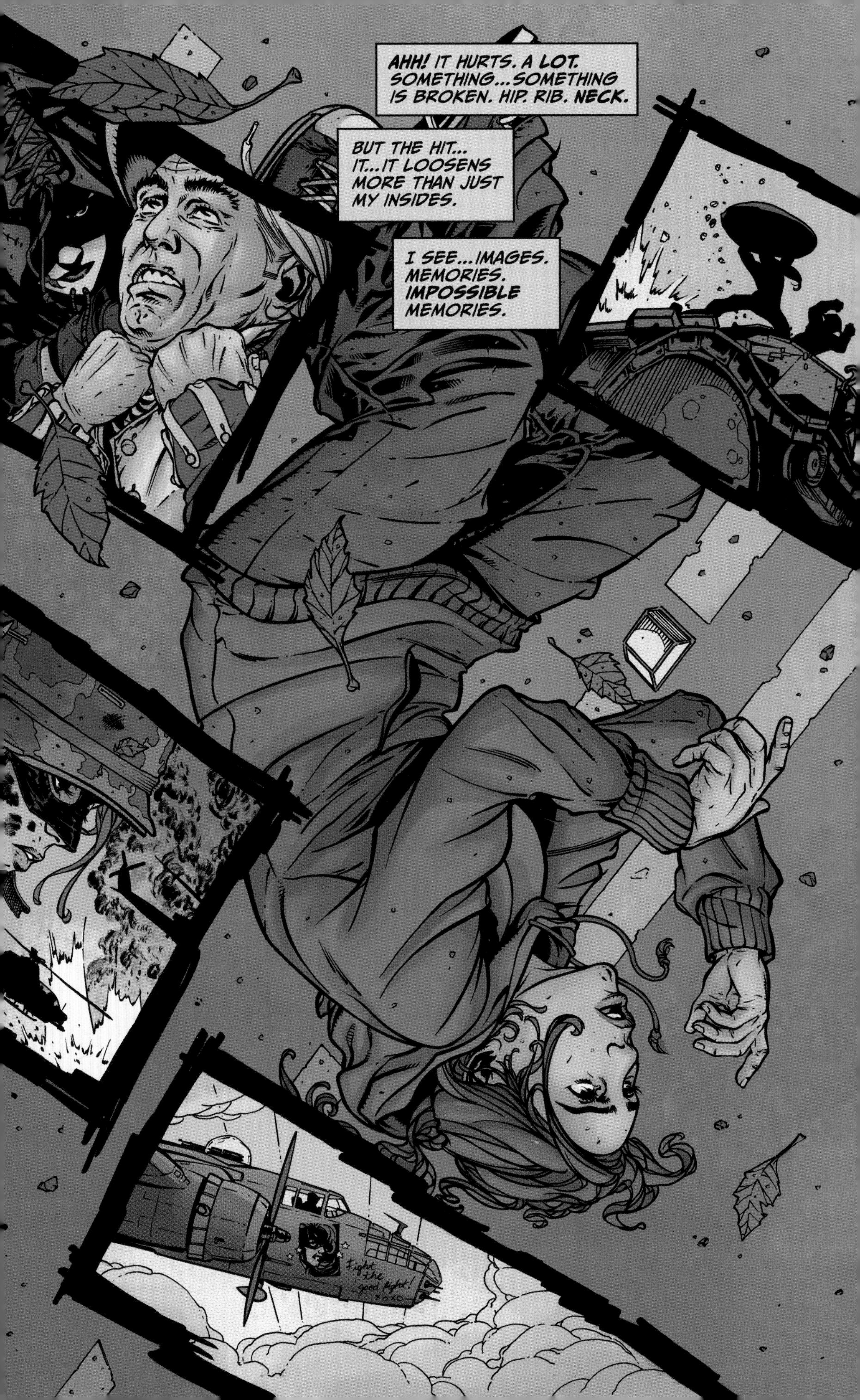
AHH! IT HURTS. A LOT. SOMETHING...SOMETHING IS BROKEN. HIP. RIB. NECK.
BUT THE HIT... IT...IT LOOSENS MORE THAN JUST MY INSIDES.
I SEE...IMAGES. MEMORIES. IMPOSSIBLE MEMORIES.
Fight the good fight! XOXO

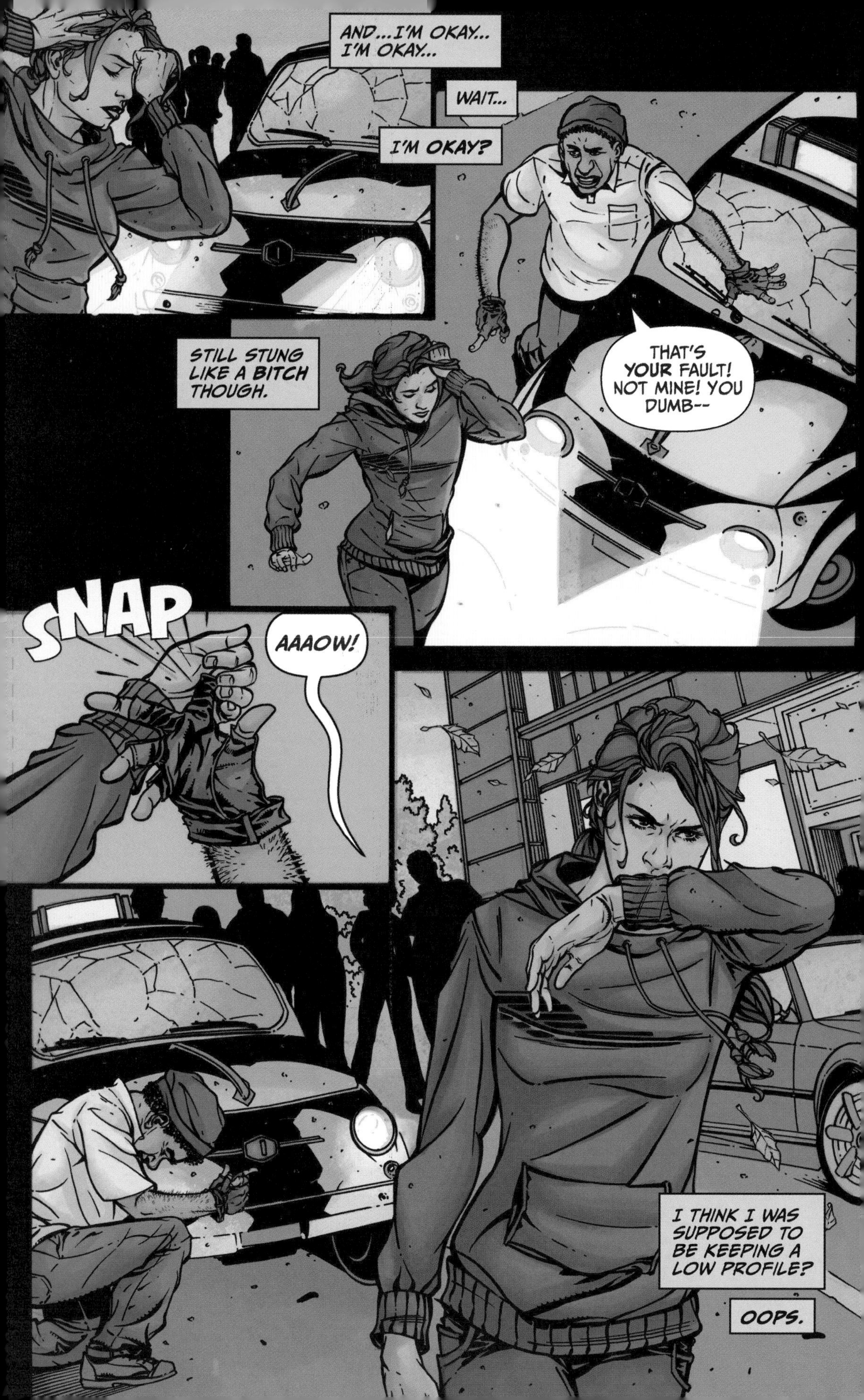

AND...I'M OKAY... I'M OKAY...
WAIT...
I'M OKAY?
STILL STUNG LIKE A BITCH THOUGH.
THAT'S YOUR FAULT! NOT MINE! YOU DUMB--
SNAP
AAAOW!
I THINK I WAS SUPPOSED TO BE KEEPING A LOW PROFILE?
OOPS.

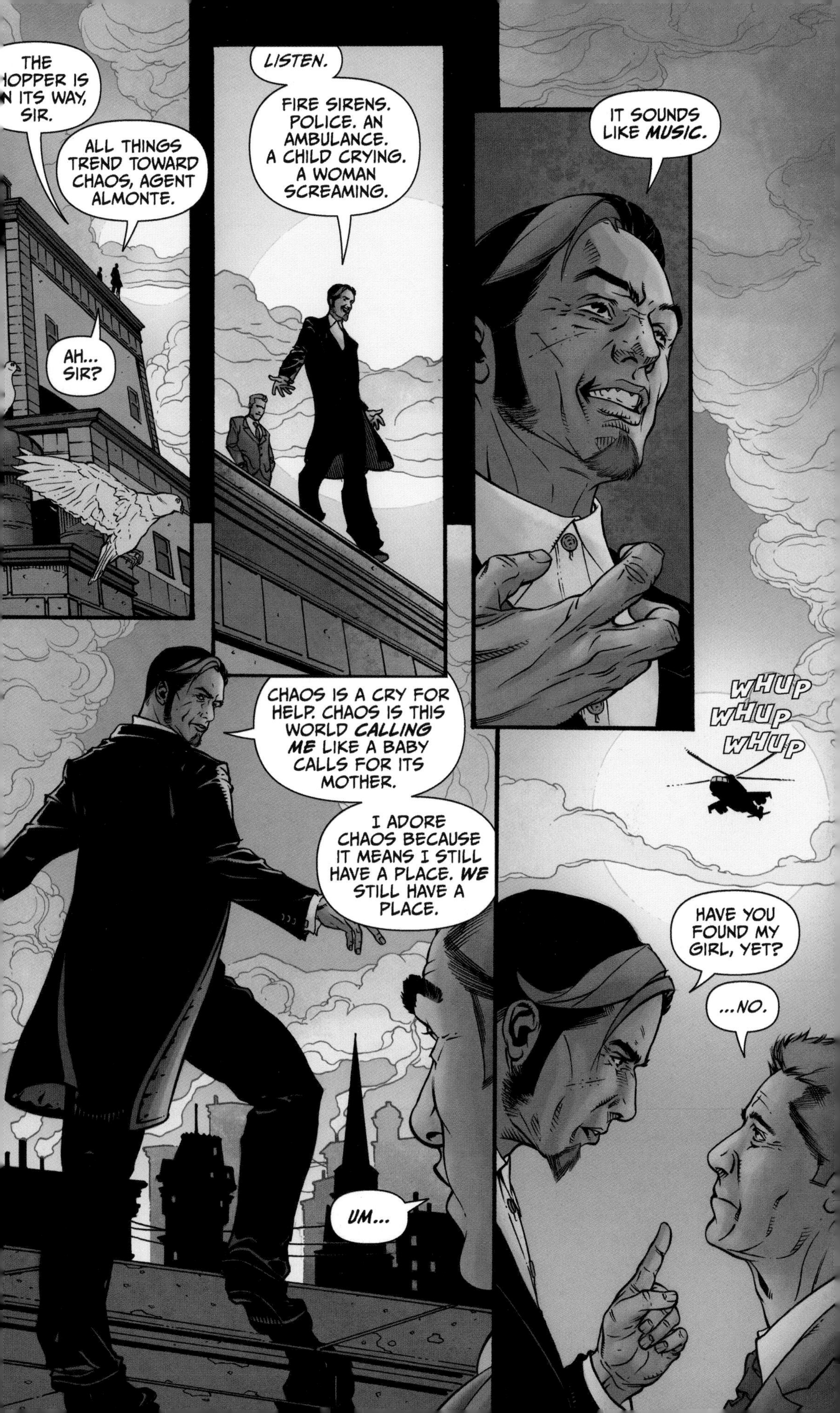
THE HOPPER IS N ITS WAY, SIR.
ALL THINGS TREND TOWARD CHAOS, AGENT ALMONTE.
AH... SIR?
LISTEN.
FIRE SIRENS. POLICE. AN AMBULANCE. A CHILD CRYING. A WOMAN SCREAMING.
IT SOUNDS LIKE MUSIC.
CHAOS IS A CRY FOR HELP. CHAOS IS THIS WORLD CALLING ME LIKE A BABY CALLS FOR ITS MOTHER.
I ADORE CHAOS BECAUSE IT MEANS I STILL HAVE A PLACE. WE STILL HAVE A PLACE.
UM...
WHUP WHUP WHUP
HAVE YOU FOUND MY GIRL, YET?
...NO.

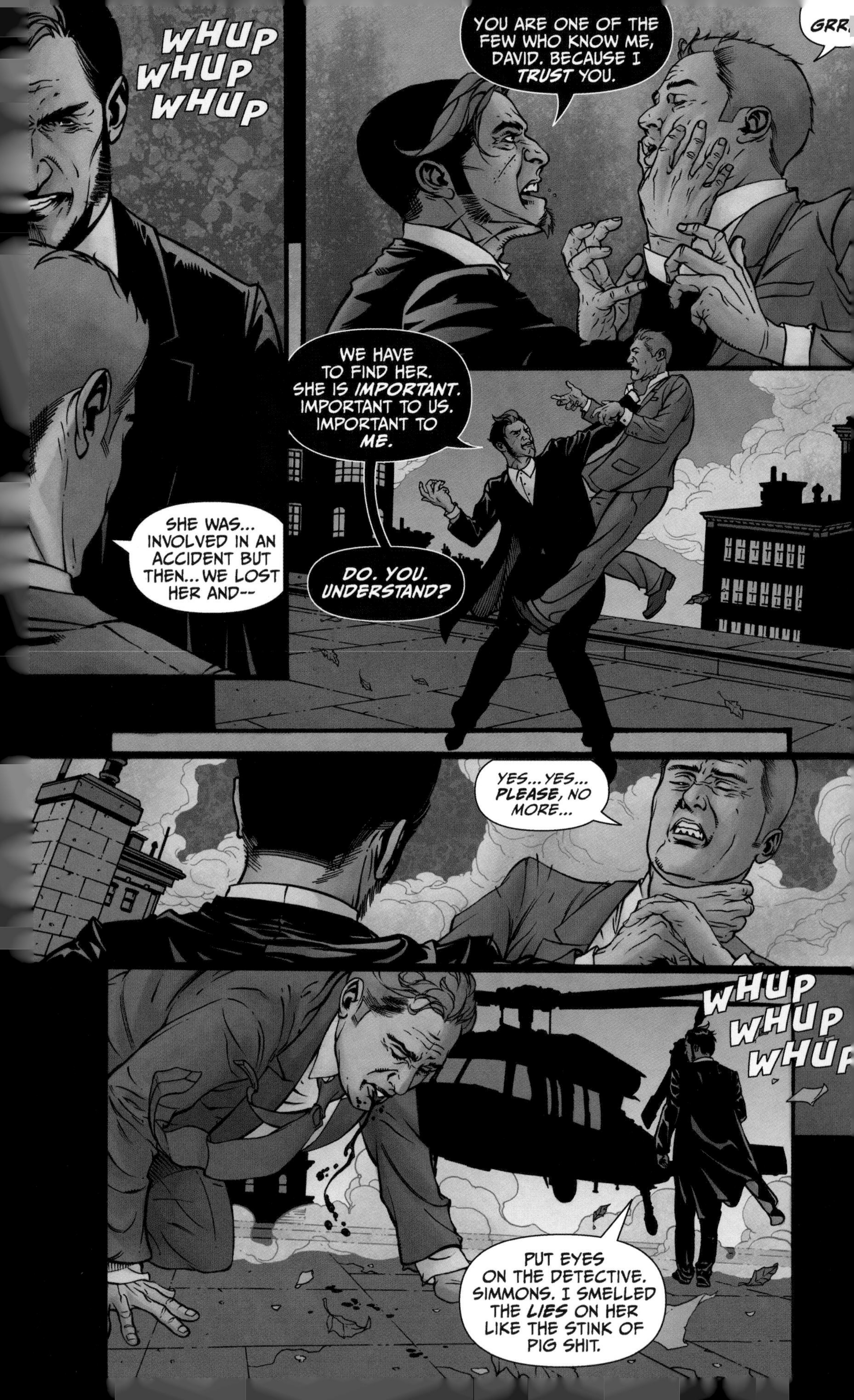
WHUP
WHUP
WHUP
YOU ARE ONE OF THE FEW WHO KNOW ME, DAVID. BECAUSE I *TRUST* YOU.
GRR
SHE WAS... INVOLVED IN AN ACCIDENT BUT THEN...WE LOST HER AND--
WE HAVE TO FIND HER. SHE IS *IMPORTANT.* IMPORTANT TO US. IMPORTANT TO *ME.*
DO. YOU. UNDERSTAND?
YES...YES... PLEASE, NO MORE...
WHUP
WHUP
WHUP
PUT EYES ON THE DETECTIVE. SIMMONS. I SMELLED THE *LIES* ON HER LIKE THE STINK OF PIG SHIT.

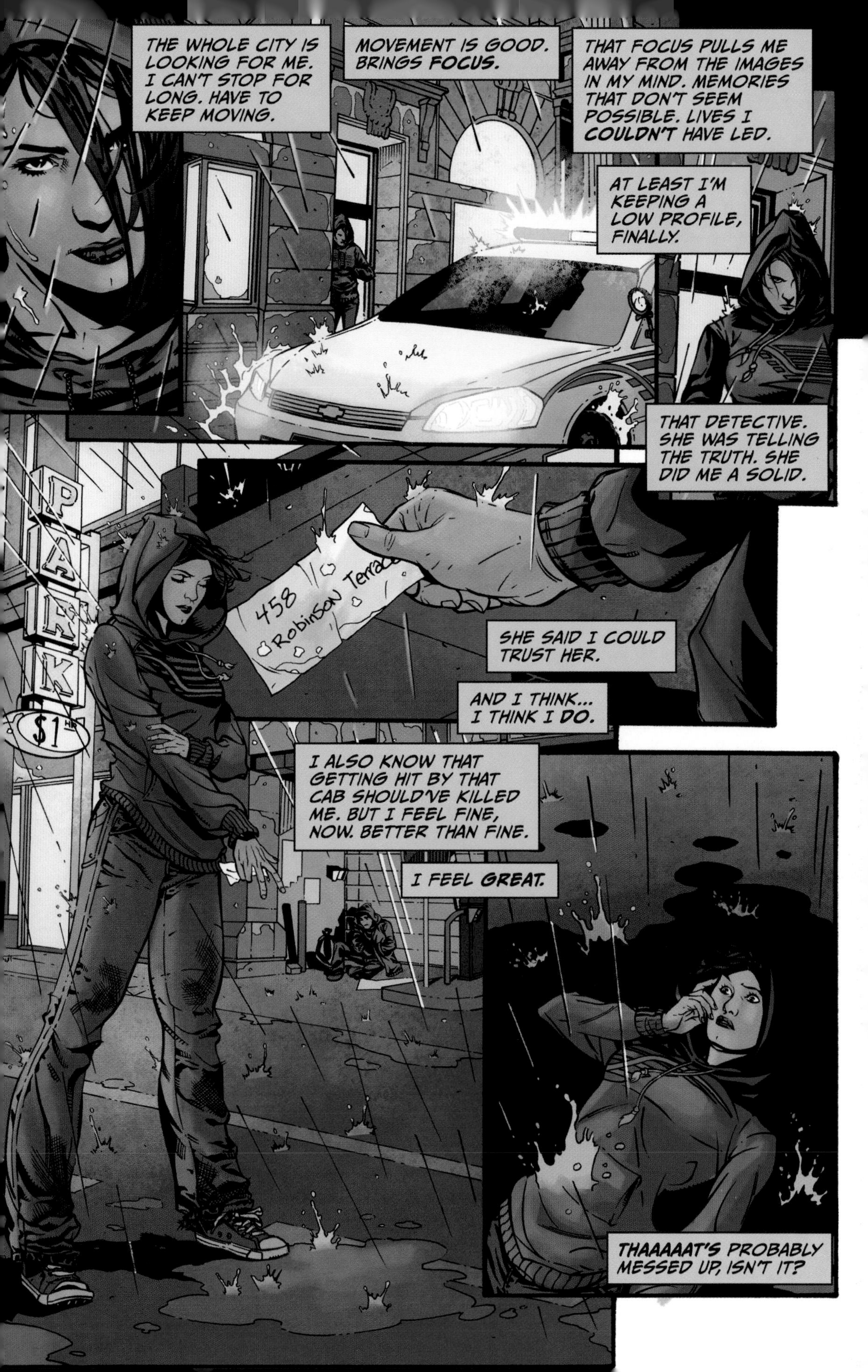
THE WHOLE CITY IS LOOKING FOR ME. I CAN'T STOP FOR LONG. HAVE TO KEEP MOVING.
MOVEMENT IS GOOD. BRINGS FOCUS.
THAT FOCUS PULLS ME AWAY FROM THE IMAGES IN MY MIND. MEMORIES THAT DON'T SEEM POSSIBLE. LIVES I COULDN'T HAVE LED.
AT LEAST I'M KEEPING A LOW PROFILE, FINALLY.
THAT DETECTIVE. SHE WAS TELLING THE TRUTH. SHE DID ME A SOLID.
PARK
$1 HR
458 RobinSON Terrace
SHE SAID I COULD TRUST HER.
AND I THINK... I THINK I DO.
I ALSO KNOW THAT GETTING HIT BY THAT CAB SHOULD'VE KILLED ME. BUT I FEEL FINE, NOW. BETTER THAN FINE.
I FEEL GREAT.
THAAAAAT'S PROBABLY MESSED UP, ISN'T IT?

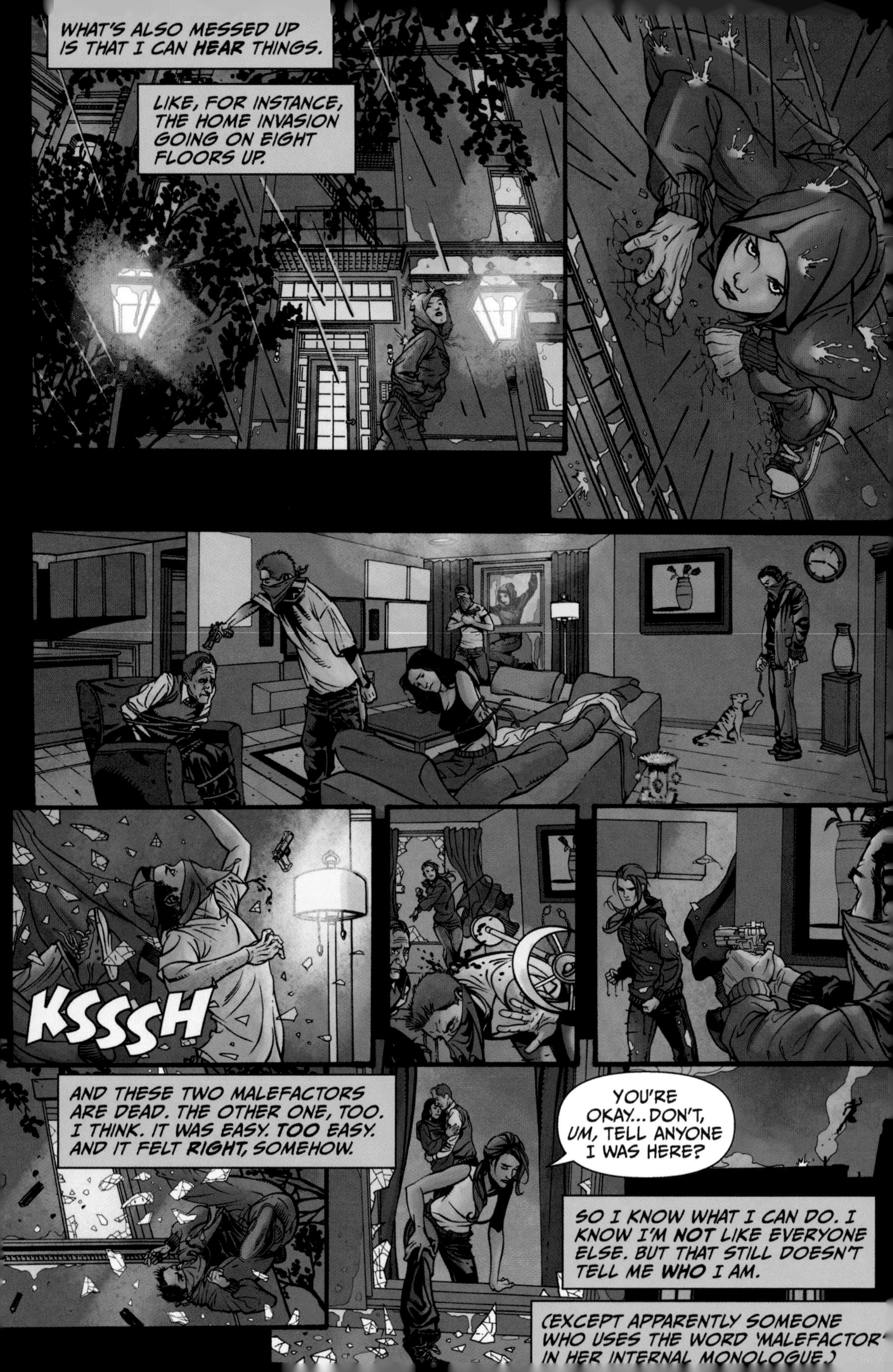
WHAT'S ALSO MESSED UP IS THAT I CAN HEAR THINGS.
LIKE, FOR INSTANCE, THE HOME INVASION GOING ON EIGHT FLOORS UP.
KSSSH
AND THESE TWO MALEFACTORS ARE DEAD. THE OTHER ONE, TOO. I THINK. IT WAS EASY. TOO EASY. AND IT FELT RIGHT, SOMEHOW.
YOU'RE OKAY...DON'T, UM, TELL ANYONE I WAS HERE?
SO I KNOW WHAT I CAN DO. I KNOW I'M NOT LIKE EVERYONE ELSE. BUT THAT STILL DOESN'T TELL ME WHO I AM.
(EXCEPT APPARENTLY SOMEONE WHO USES THE WORD 'MALEFACTOR' IN HER INTERNAL MONOLOGUE.)

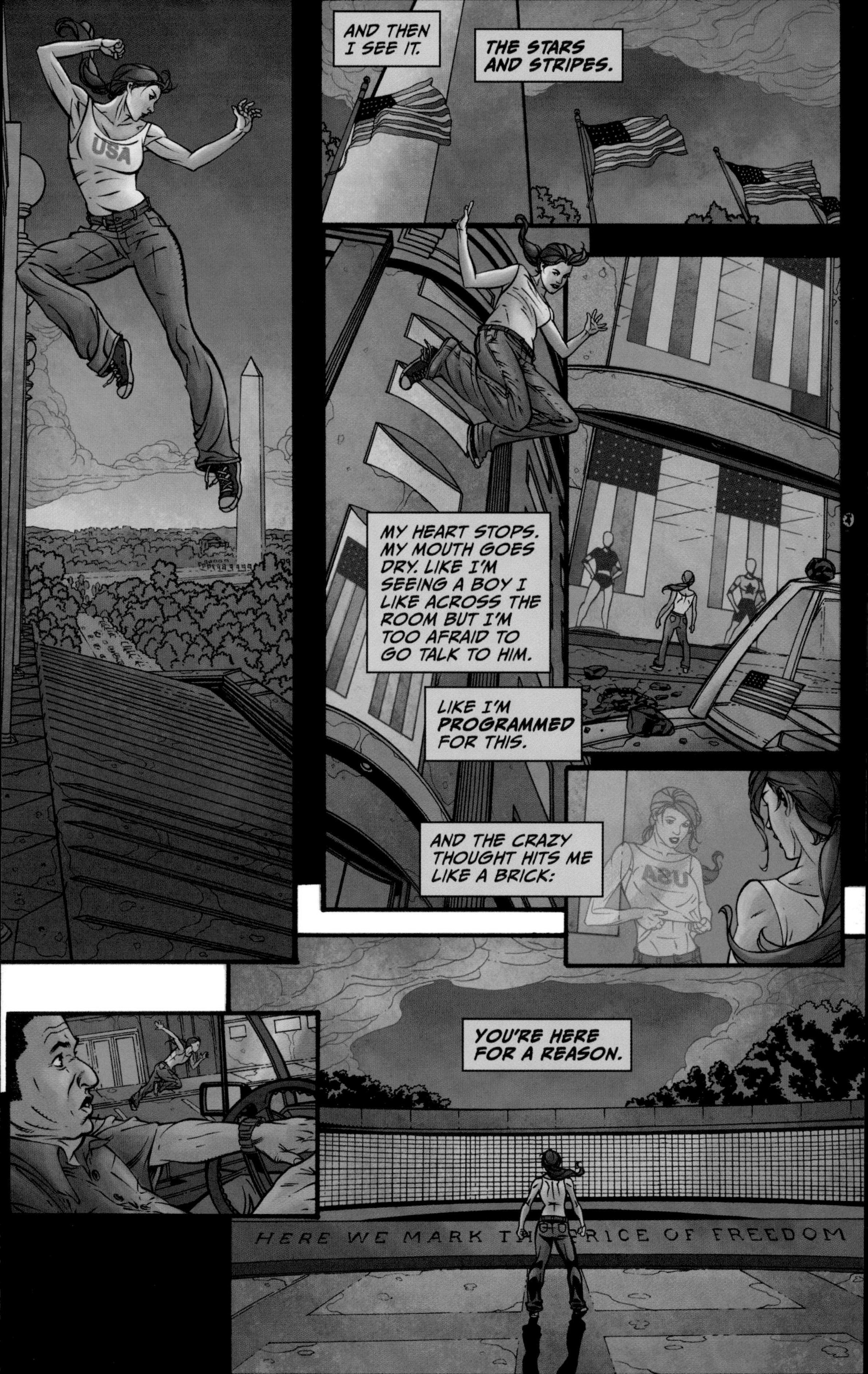
AND THEN I SEE IT.
THE STARS AND STRIPES.
MY HEART STOPS. MY MOUTH GOES DRY. LIKE I'M SEEING A BOY I LIKE ACROSS THE ROOM BUT I'M TOO AFRAID TO GO TALK TO HIM.
LIKE I'M PROGRAMMED FOR THIS.
AND THE CRAZY THOUGHT HITS ME LIKE A BRICK:
YOU'RE HERE FOR A REASON.
HERE WE MARK TH PRICE OF FREEDOM

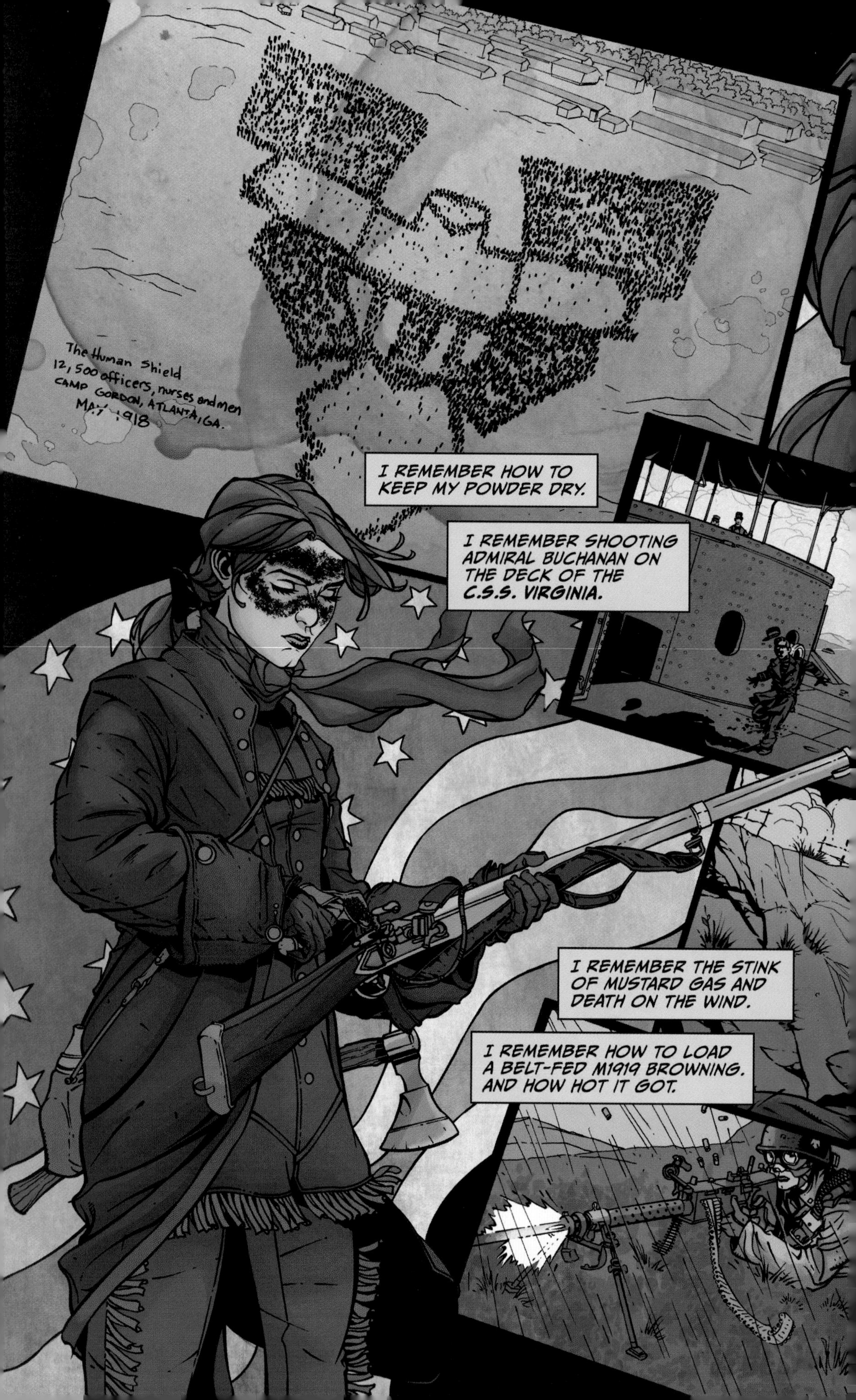
The Human Shield
12,500 officers, nurses and men
CAMP GORDON, ATLANTA, GA.
MAY, 1918
I REMEMBER HOW TO KEEP MY POWDER DRY.
I REMEMBER SHOOTING ADMIRAL BUCHANAN ON THE DECK OF THE C.S.S. VIRGINIA.
I REMEMBER THE STINK OF MUSTARD GAS AND DEATH ON THE WIND.
I REMEMBER HOW TO LOAD A BELT-FED M1919 BROWNING. AND HOW HOT IT GOT.

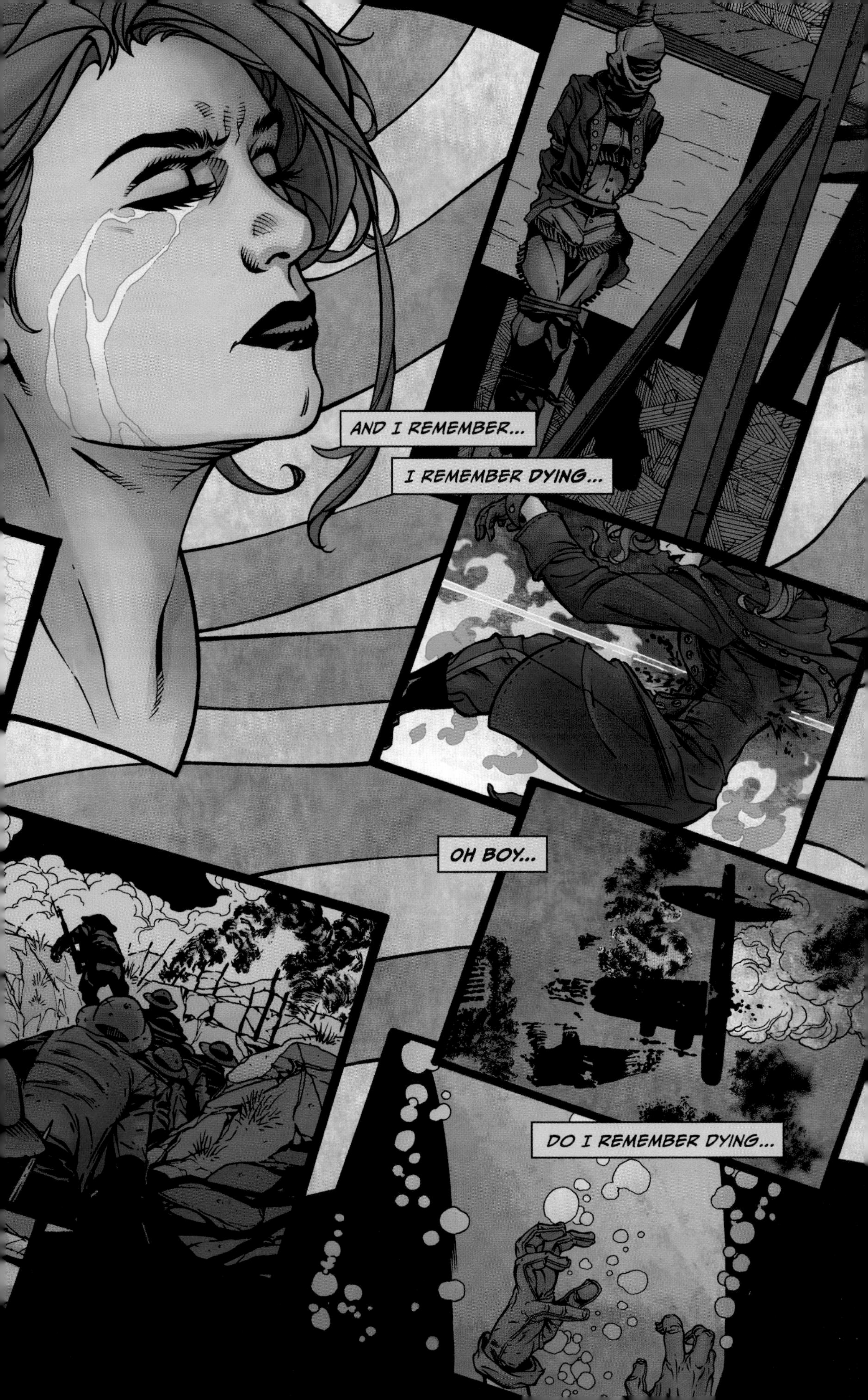
AND I REMEMBER...
I REMEMBER DYING...
OH BOY...
DO I REMEMBER DYING...

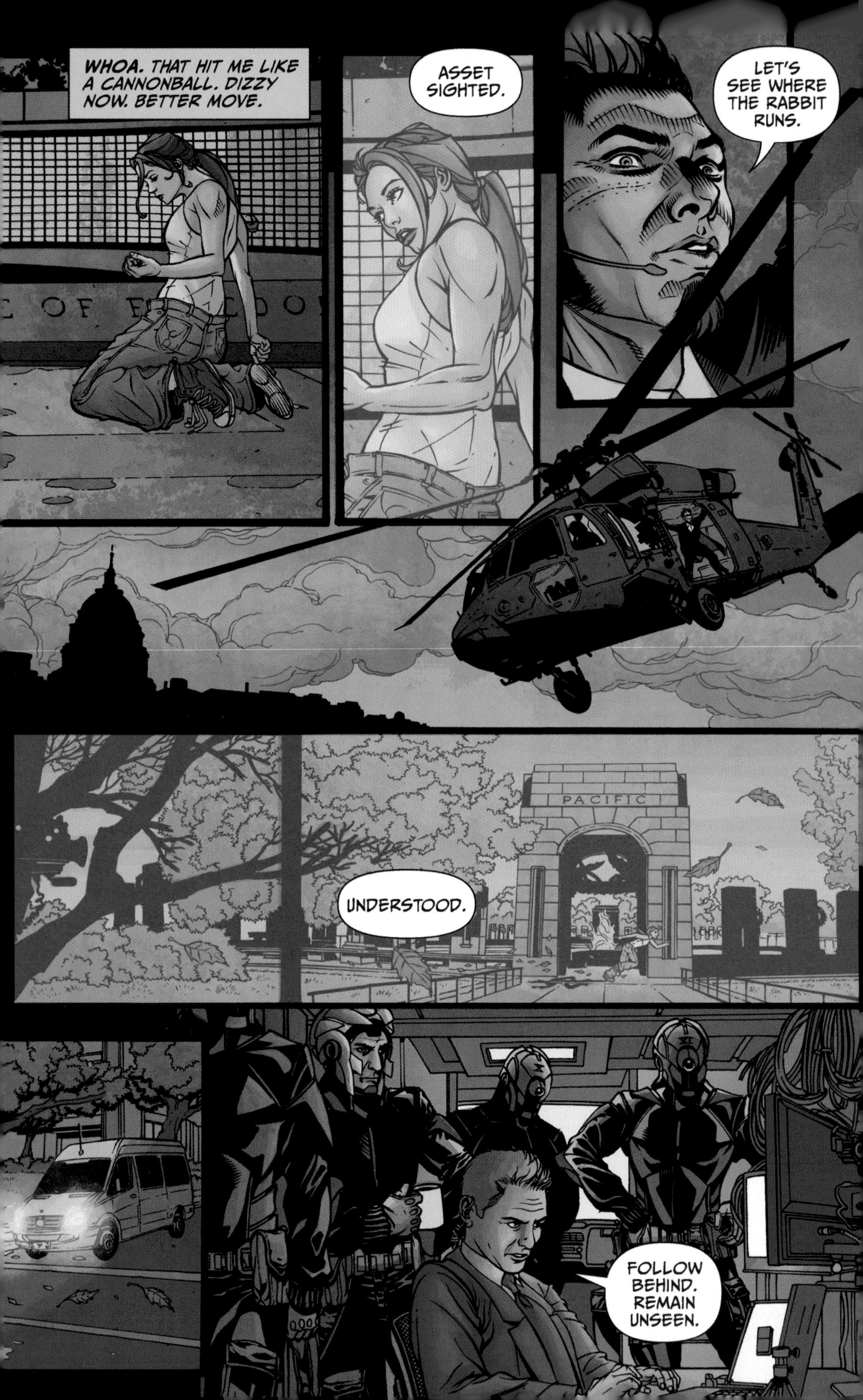
WHOA. THAT HIT ME LIKE A CANNONBALL. DIZZY NOW. BETTER MOVE.
ASSET SIGHTED.
LET'S SEE WHERE THE RABBIT RUNS.
PACIFIC
UNDERSTOOD.
FOLLOW BEHIND. REMAIN UNSEEN.

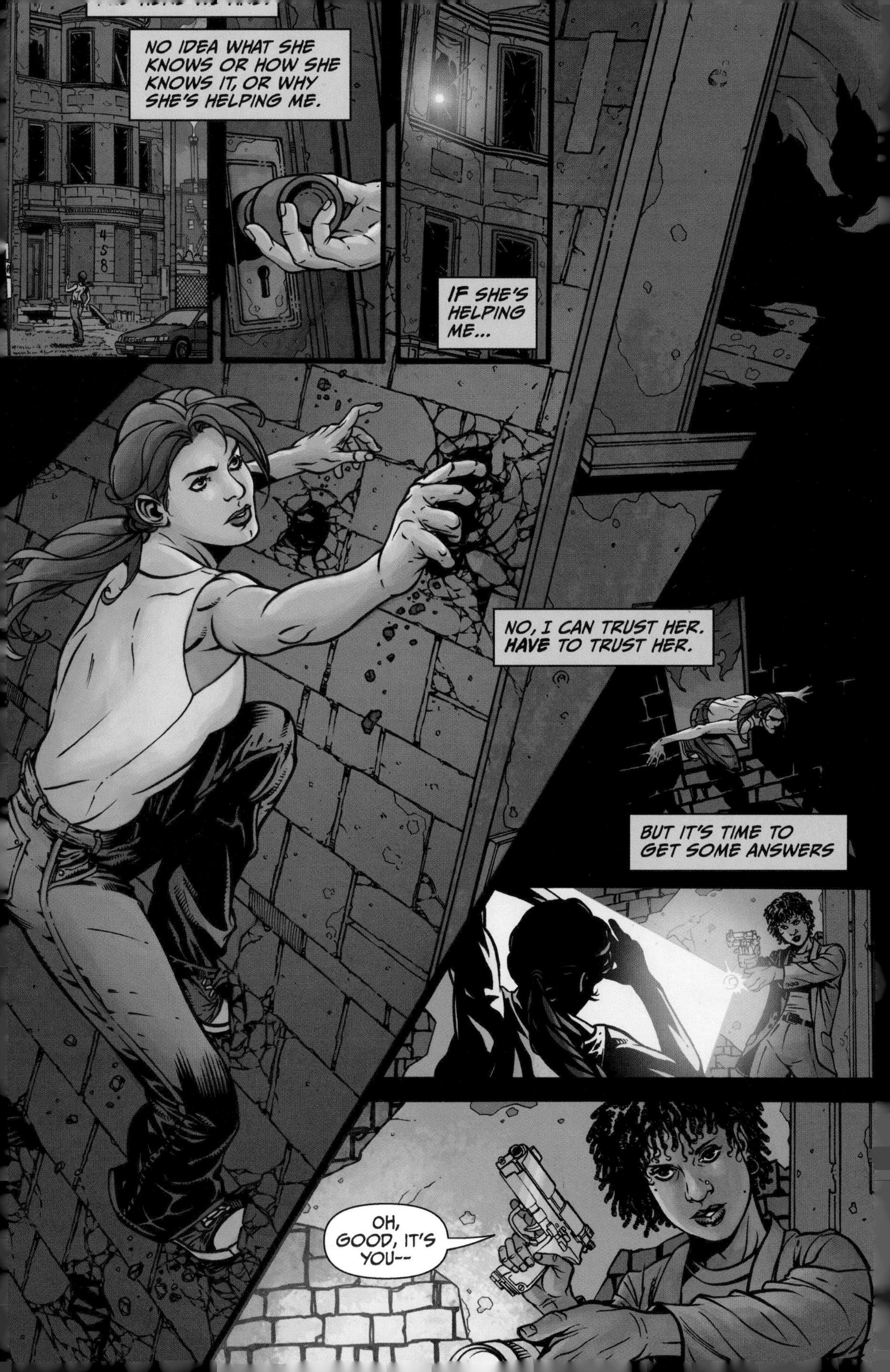
NO IDEA WHAT SHE KNOWS OR HOW SHE KNOWS IT, OR WHY SHE'S HELPING ME.
IF SHE'S HELPING ME...
NO, I CAN TRUST HER. HAVE TO TRUST HER.
BUT IT'S TIME TO GET SOME ANSWERS
OH, GOOD, IT'S YOU--

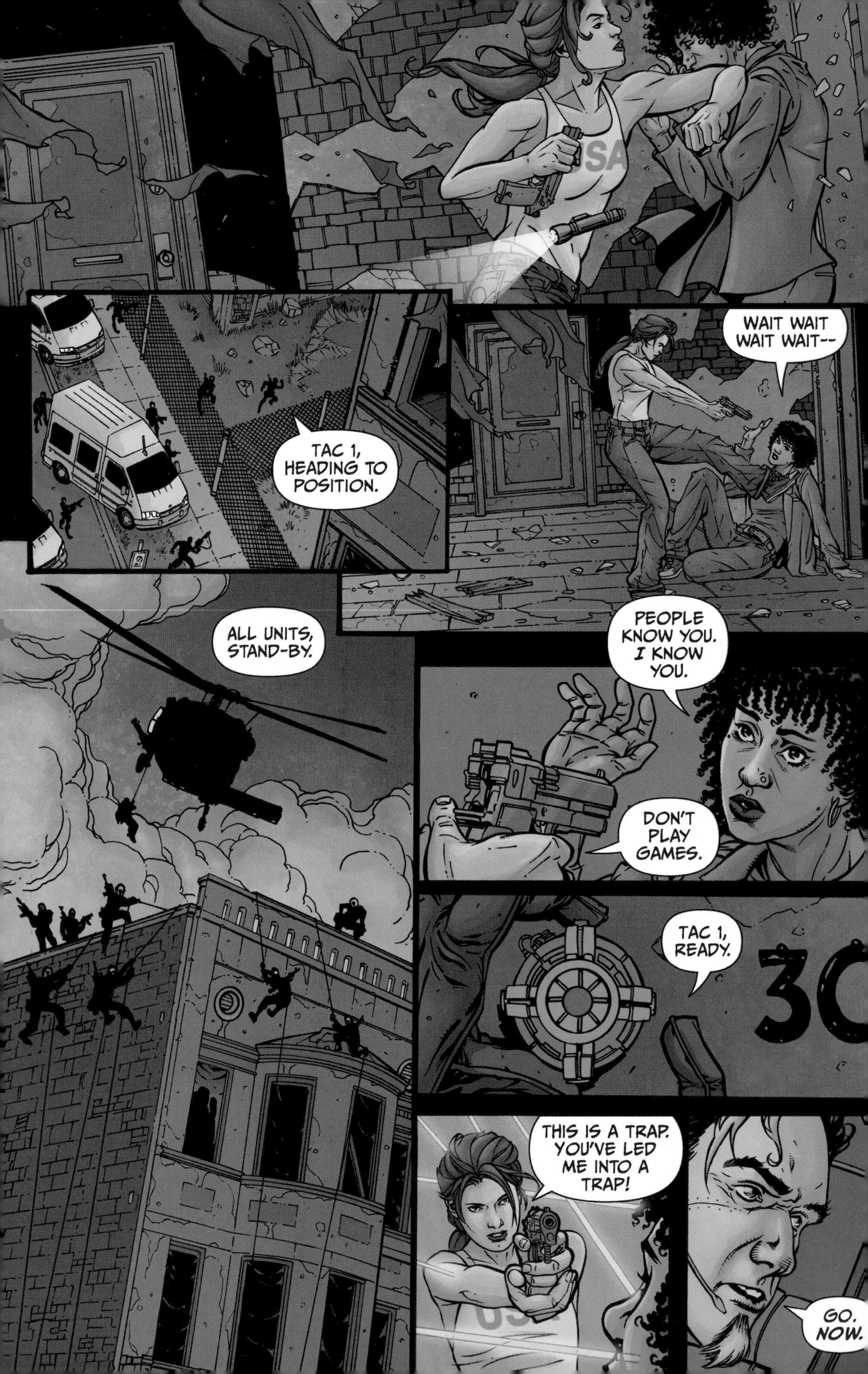
TAC 1, HEADING TO POSITION.
WAIT WAIT WAIT WAIT--
ALL UNITS, STAND-BY.
PEOPLE KNOW YOU. I KNOW YOU.
DON'T PLAY GAMES.
TAC 1, READY.
30
THIS IS A TRAP. YOU'VE LED ME INTO A TRAP!
GO. NOW.

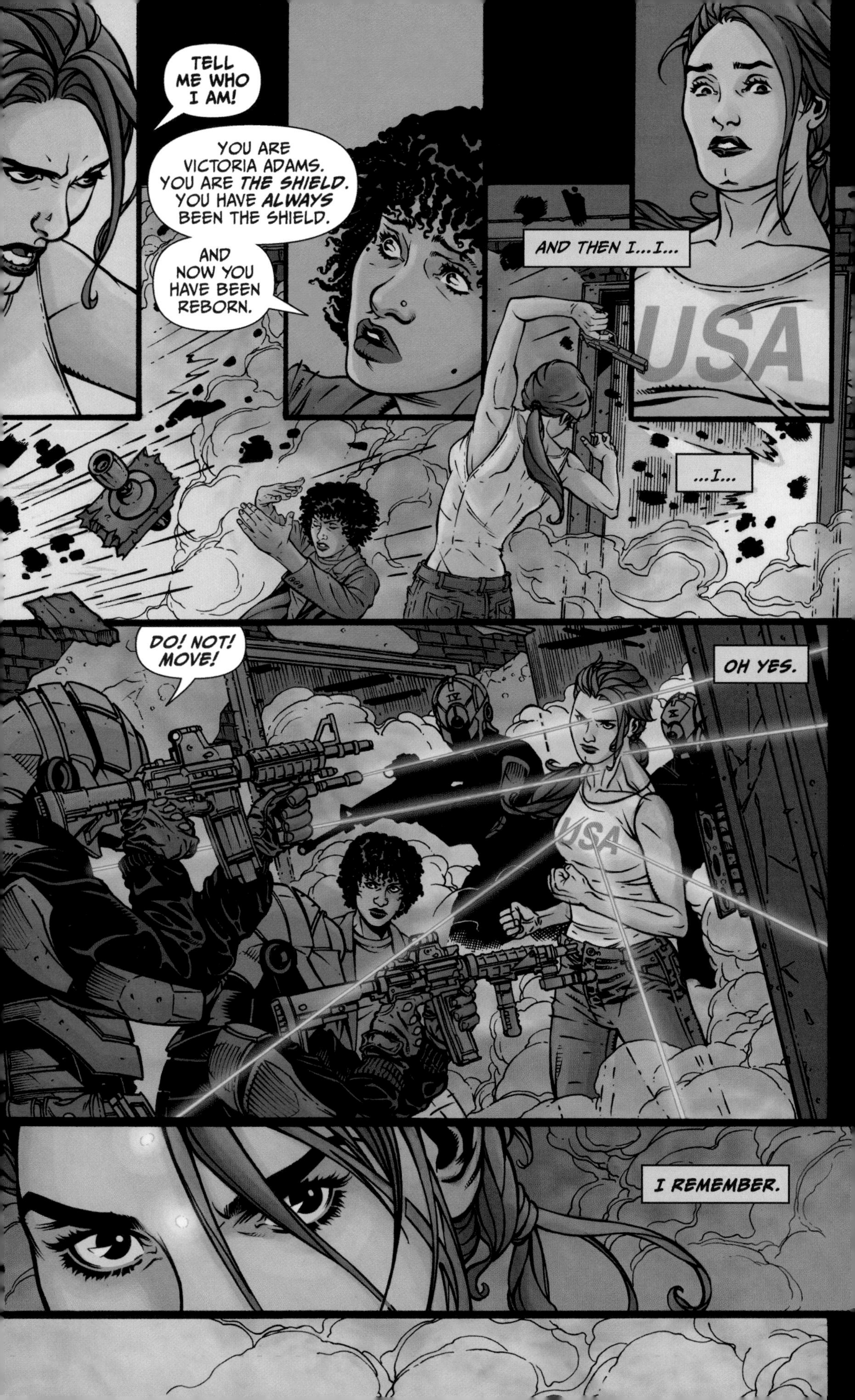
TELL ME WHO I AM!
YOU ARE VICTORIA ADAMS. YOU ARE THE SHIELD. YOU HAVE ALWAYS BEEN THE SHIELD.
AND NOW YOU HAVE BEEN REBORN.
AND THEN I...I...
USA
...I...
DO! NOT! MOVE!
OH YES.
USA
I REMEMBER.

ISSUE TWO

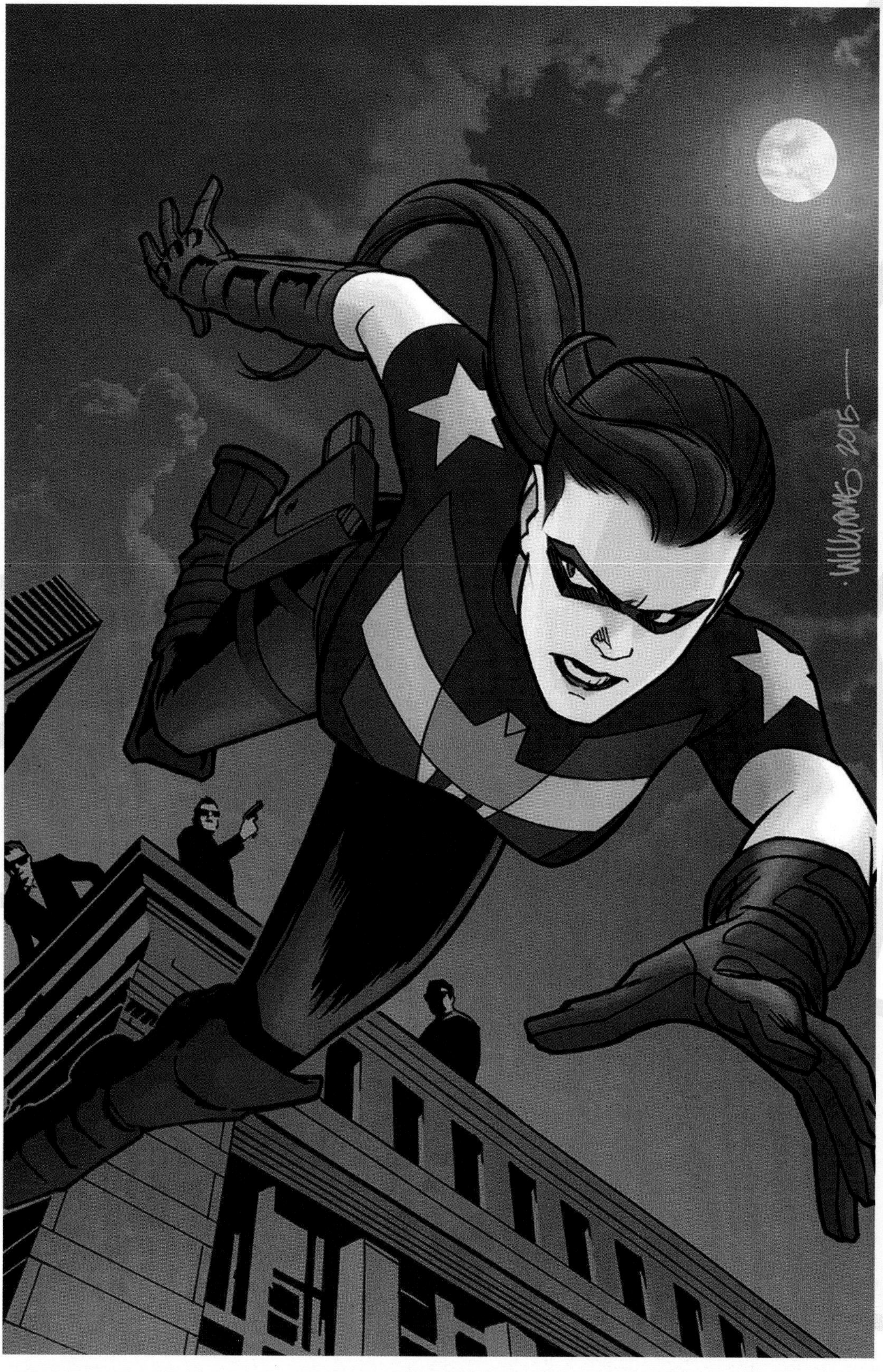

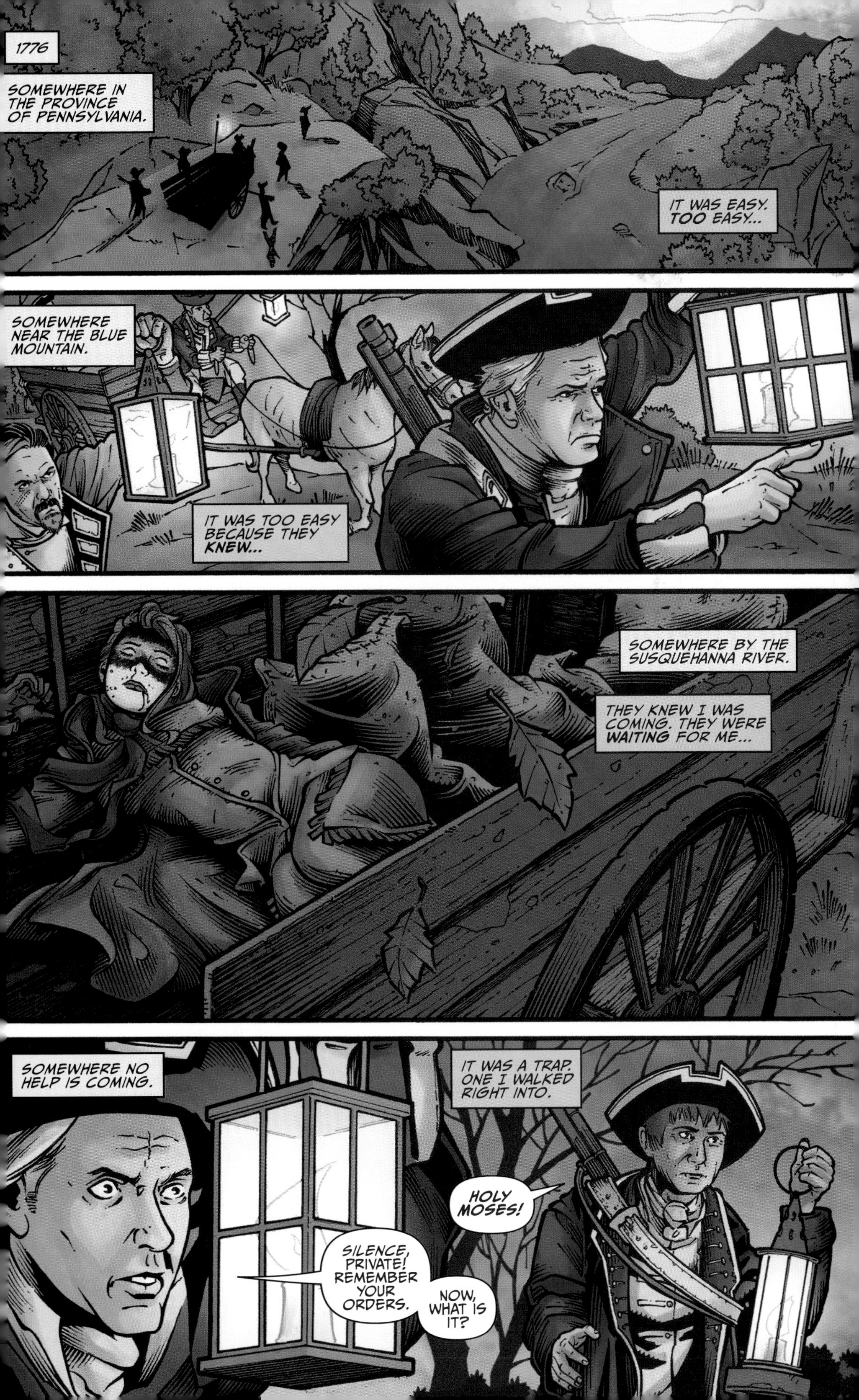
1776
SOMEWHERE IN THE PROVINCE OF PENNSYLVANIA.
IT WAS EASY. TOO EASY...
SOMEWHERE NEAR THE BLUE MOUNTAIN.
IT WAS TOO EASY BECAUSE THEY KNEW...
SOMEWHERE BY THE SUSQUEHANNA RIVER.
THEY KNEW I WAS COMING. THEY WERE WAITING FOR ME...
SOMEWHERE NO HELP IS COMING.
IT WAS A TRAP. ONE I WALKED RIGHT INTO.
HOLY MOSES!
SILENCE, PRIVATE! REMEMBER YOUR ORDERS.
NOW, WHAT IS IT?

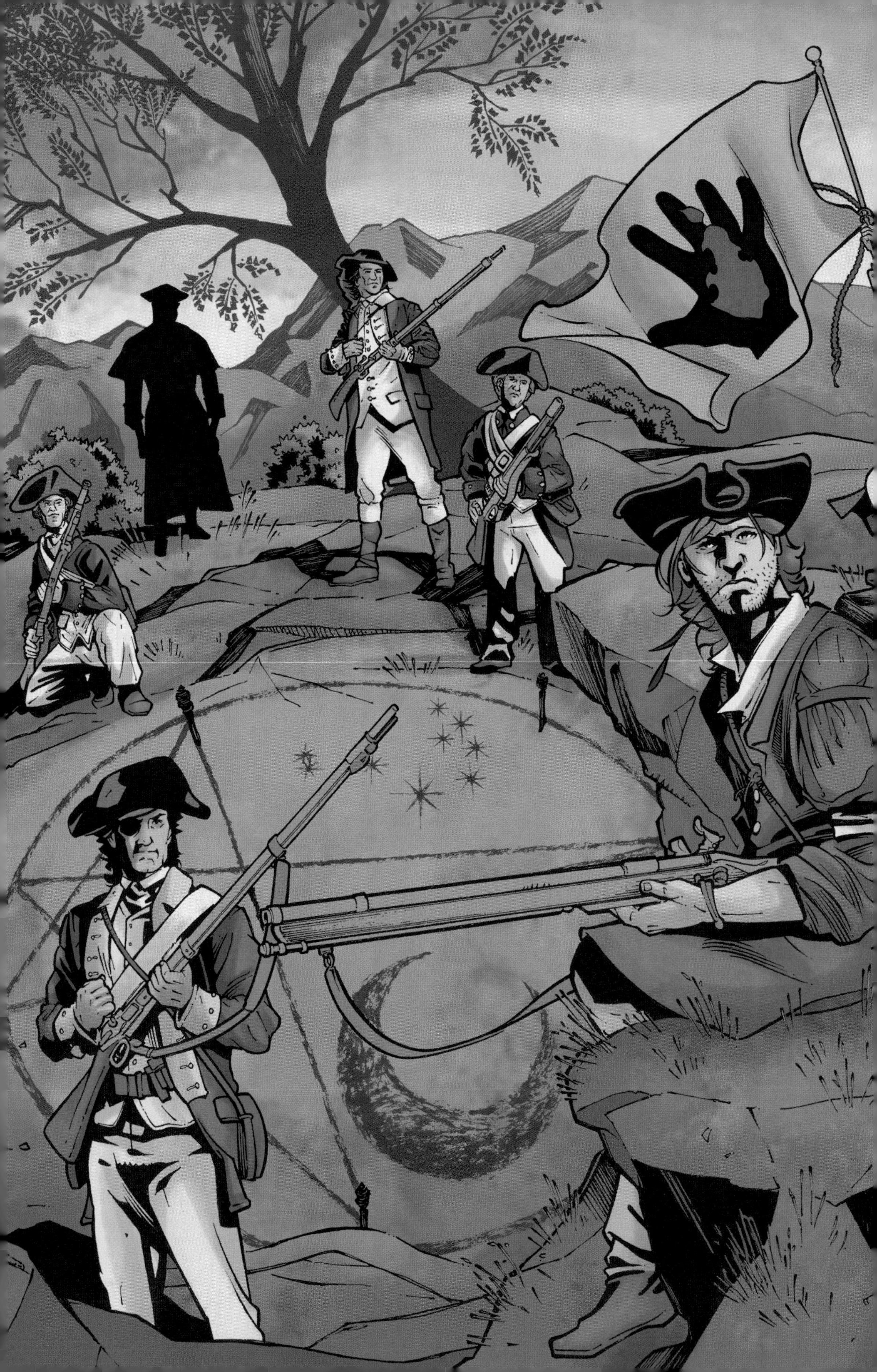

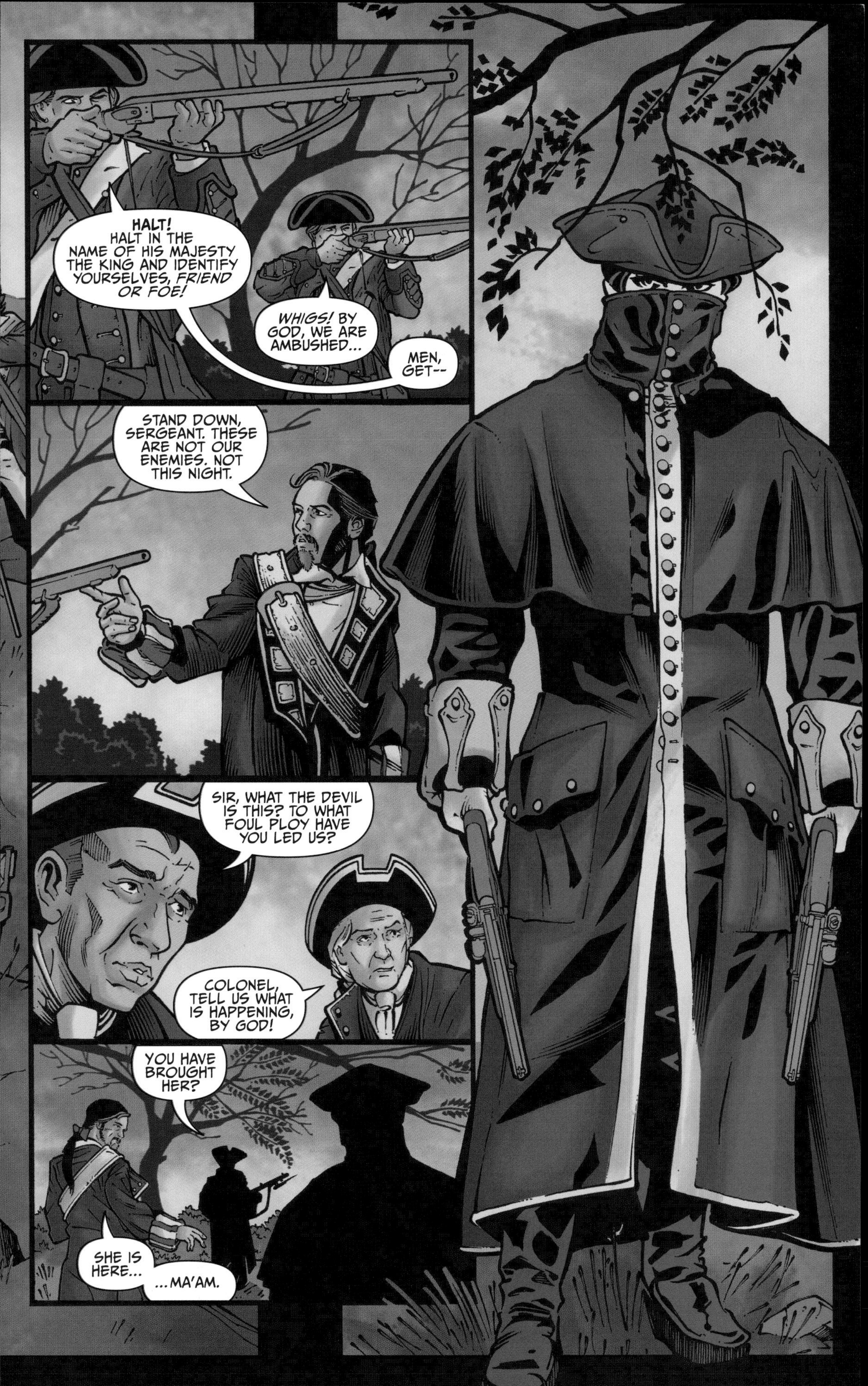
HALT! HALT IN THE NAME OF HIS MAJESTY THE KING AND IDENTIFY YOURSELVES, FRIEND OR FOE!
WHIGS! BY GOD, WE ARE AMBUSHED...
MEN, GET--
STAND DOWN, SERGEANT. THESE ARE NOT OUR ENEMIES. NOT THIS NIGHT.
SIR, WHAT THE DEVIL IS THIS? TO WHAT FOUL PLOY HAVE YOU LED US?
COLONEL, TELL US WHAT IS HAPPENING, BY GOD!
YOU HAVE BROUGHT HER?
SHE IS HERE...
...MA'AM.

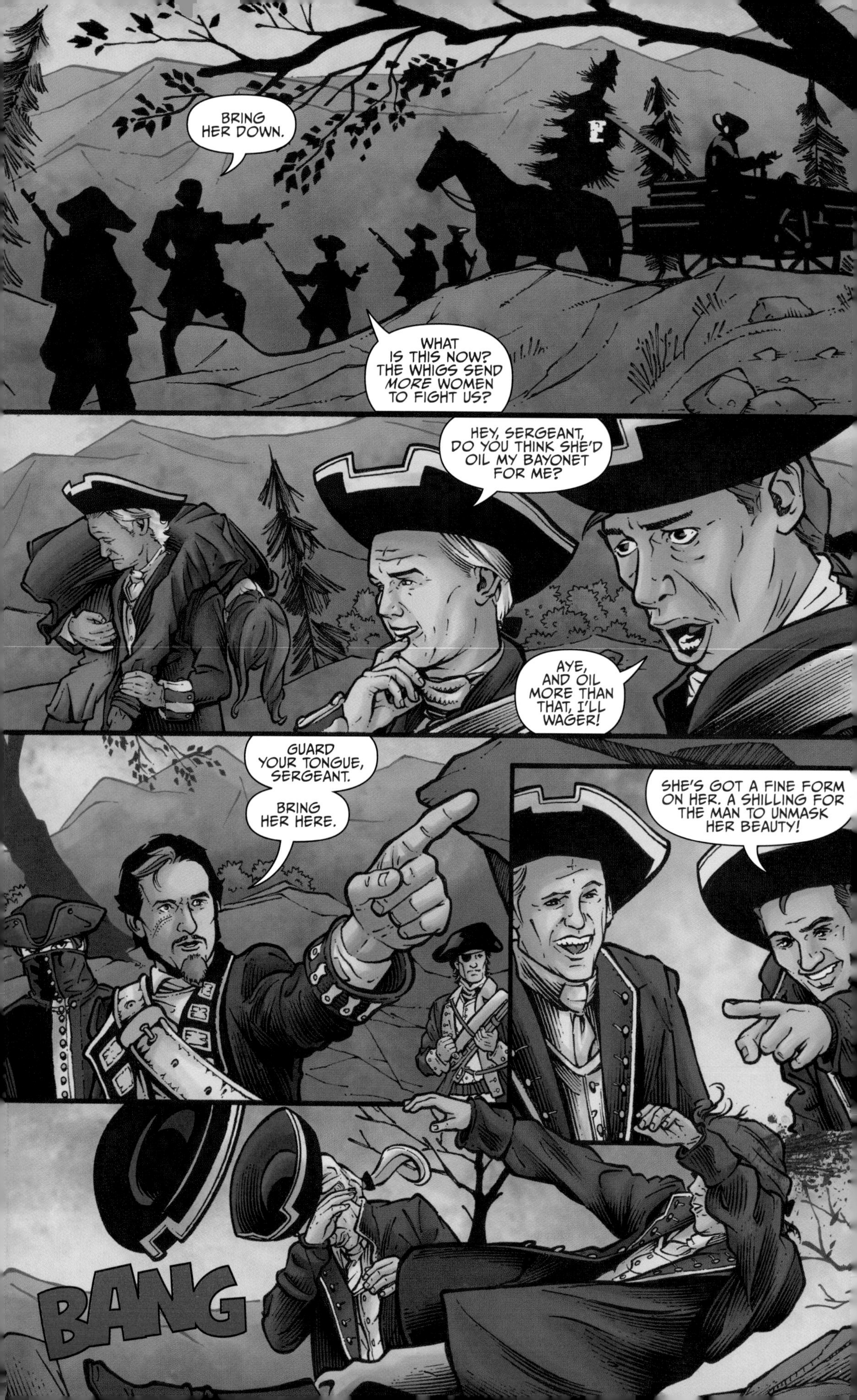
BRING HER DOWN.
WHAT IS THIS NOW? THE WHIGS SEND *MORE* WOMEN TO FIGHT US?
HEY, SERGEANT, DO YOU THINK SHE'D OIL MY BAYONET FOR ME?
AYE, AND OIL MORE THAN THAT, I'LL WAGER!
GUARD YOUR TONGUE, SERGEANT.
BRING HER HERE.
SHE'S GOT A FINE FORM ON HER. A SHILLING FOR THE MAN TO UNMASK HER BEAUTY!
BANG

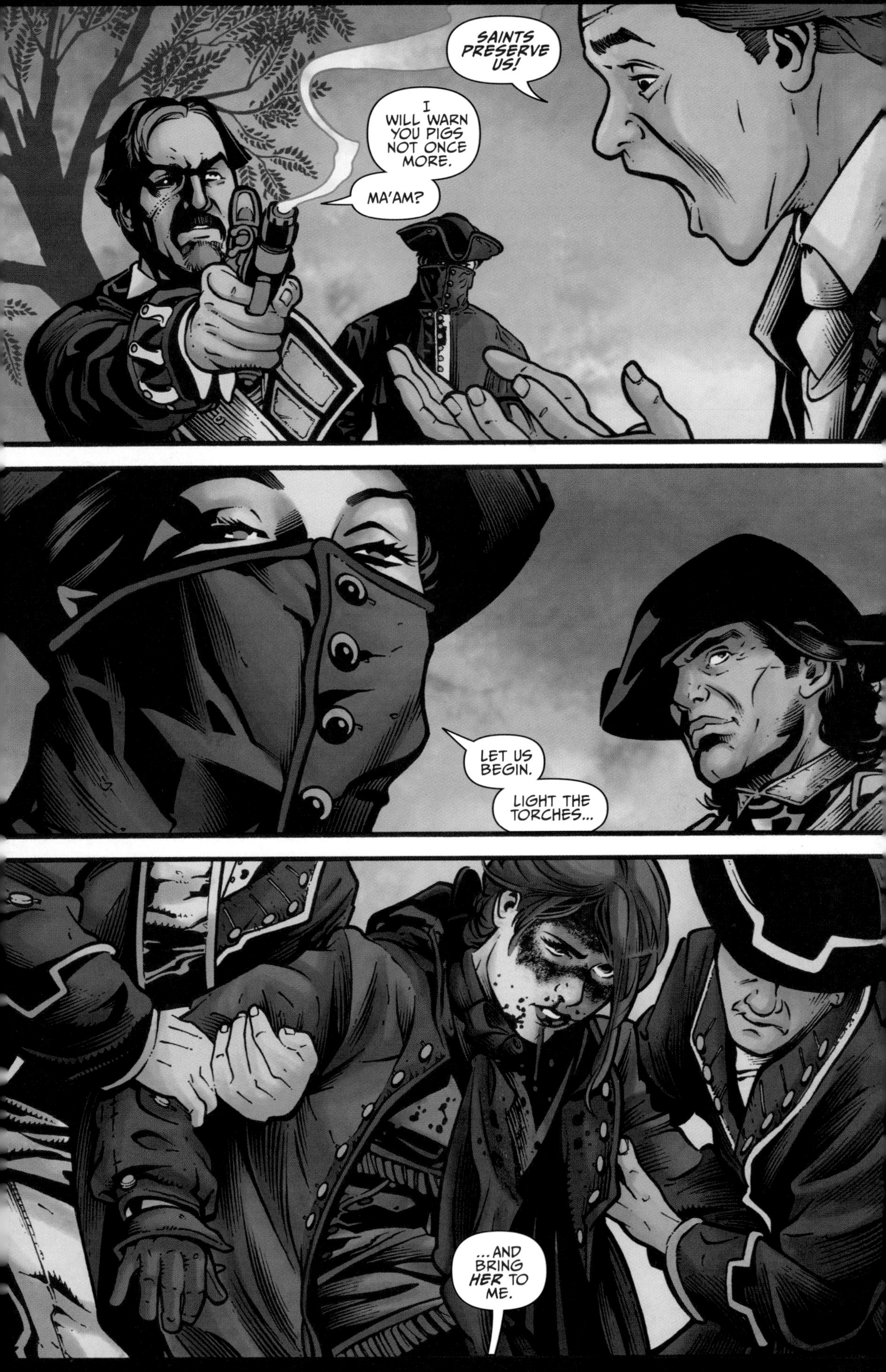
SAINTS PRESERVE US!
I WILL WARN YOU PIGS NOT ONCE MORE.
MA'AM?
LET US BEGIN.
LIGHT THE TORCHES...
...AND BRING *HER* TO ME.

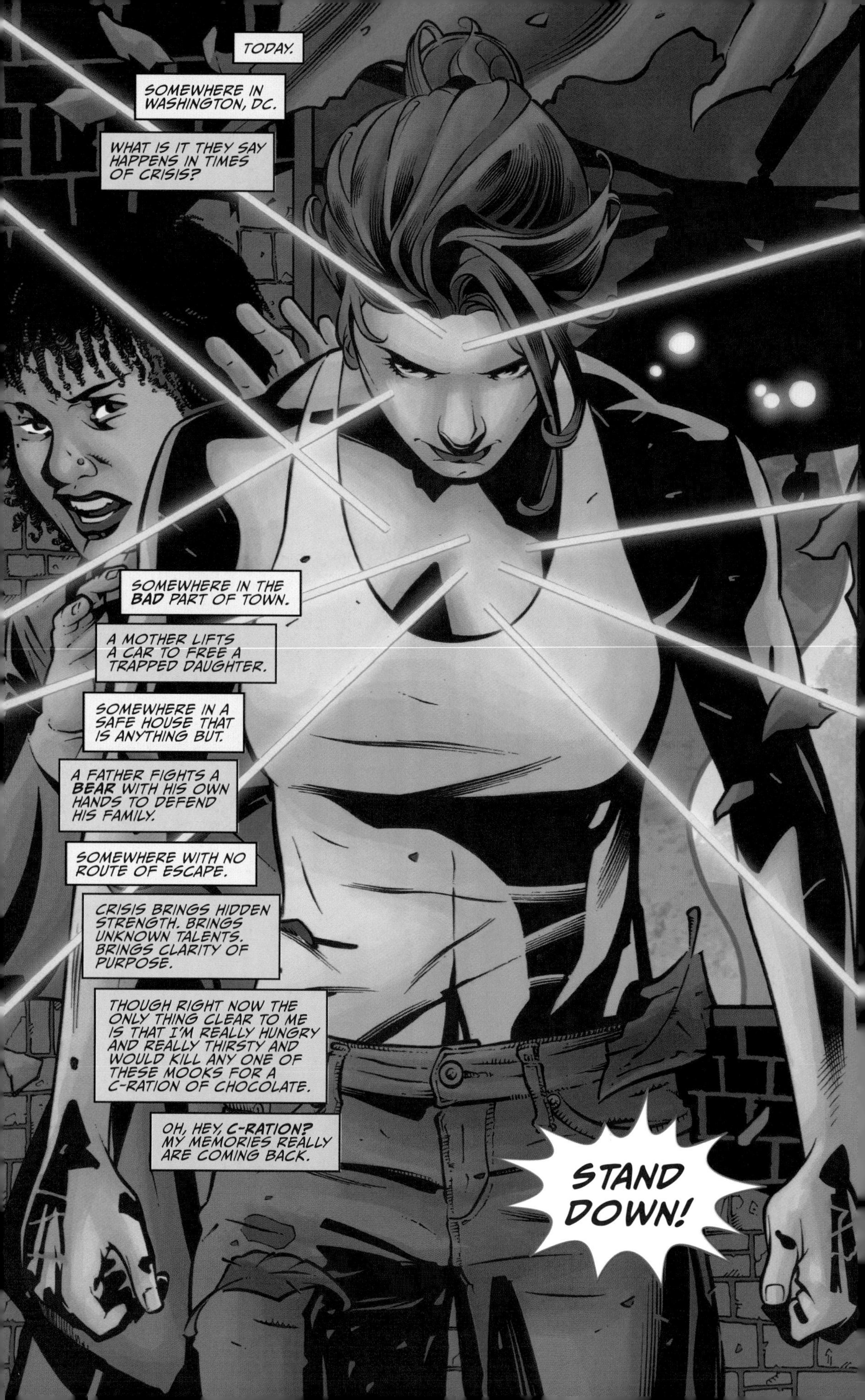
TODAY.
SOMEWHERE IN WASHINGTON, DC.
WHAT IS IT THEY SAY HAPPENS IN TIMES OF CRISIS?
SOMEWHERE IN THE **BAD** PART OF TOWN.
A MOTHER LIFTS A CAR TO FREE A TRAPPED DAUGHTER.
SOMEWHERE IN A SAFE HOUSE THAT IS ANYTHING BUT.
A FATHER FIGHTS A **BEAR** WITH HIS OWN HANDS TO DEFEND HIS FAMILY.
SOMEWHERE WITH NO ROUTE OF ESCAPE.
CRISIS BRINGS HIDDEN STRENGTH. BRINGS UNKNOWN TALENTS. BRINGS CLARITY OF PURPOSE.
THOUGH RIGHT NOW THE ONLY THING CLEAR TO ME IS THAT I'M REALLY HUNGRY AND REALLY THIRSTY AND WOULD KILL ANY ONE OF THESE MOOKS FOR A C-RATION OF CHOCOLATE.
OH, HEY, **C-RATION?** MY MEMORIES REALLY ARE COMING BACK.
STAND DOWN!

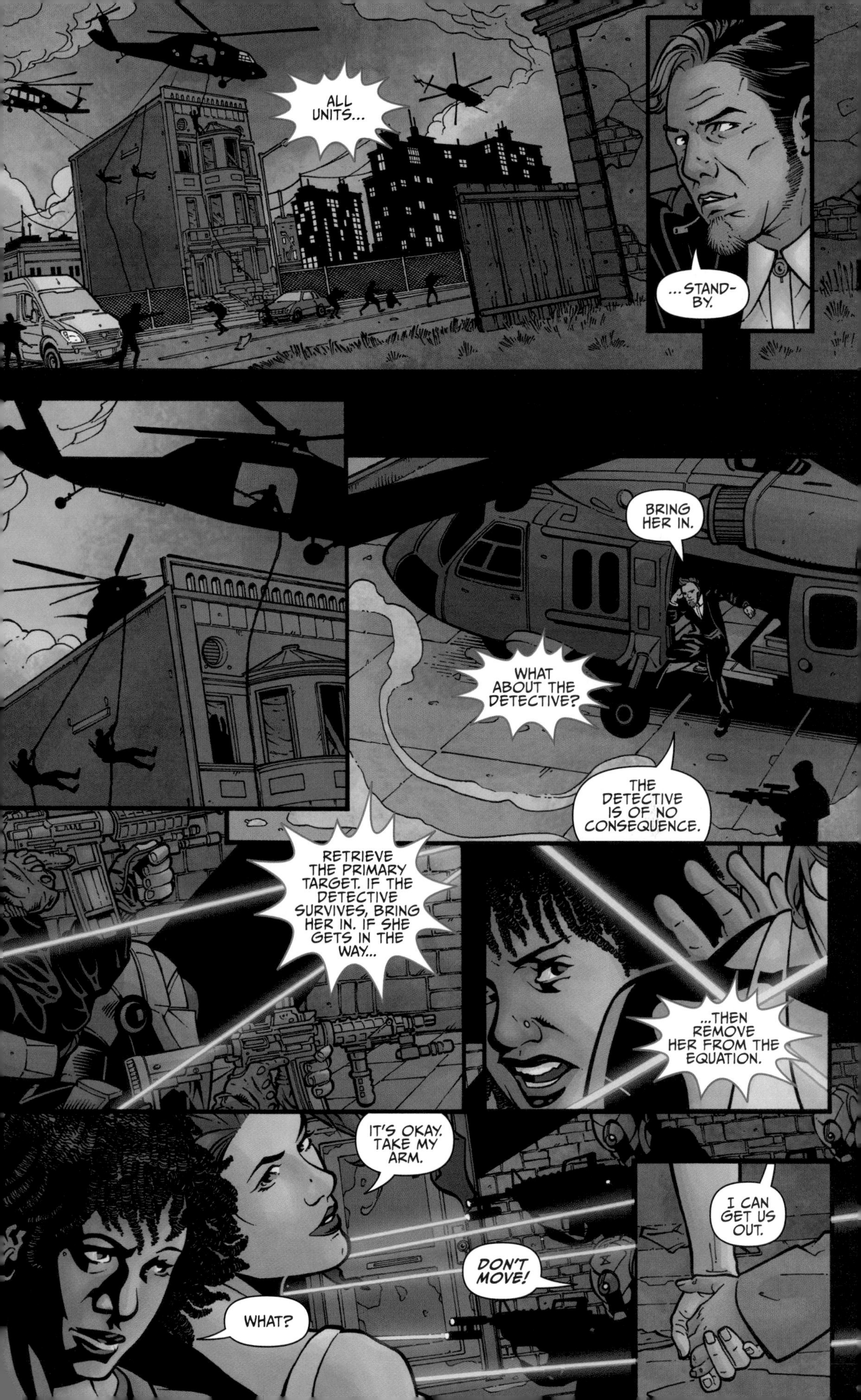
ALL UNITS...
...STAND-BY.
BRING HER IN.
WHAT ABOUT THE DETECTIVE?
THE DETECTIVE IS OF NO CONSEQUENCE.
RETRIEVE THE PRIMARY TARGET. IF THE DETECTIVE SURVIVES, BRING HER IN. IF SHE GETS IN THE WAY...
...THEN REMOVE HER FROM THE EQUATION.
IT'S OKAY. TAKE MY ARM.
I CAN GET US OUT.
WHAT?
DON'T MOVE!

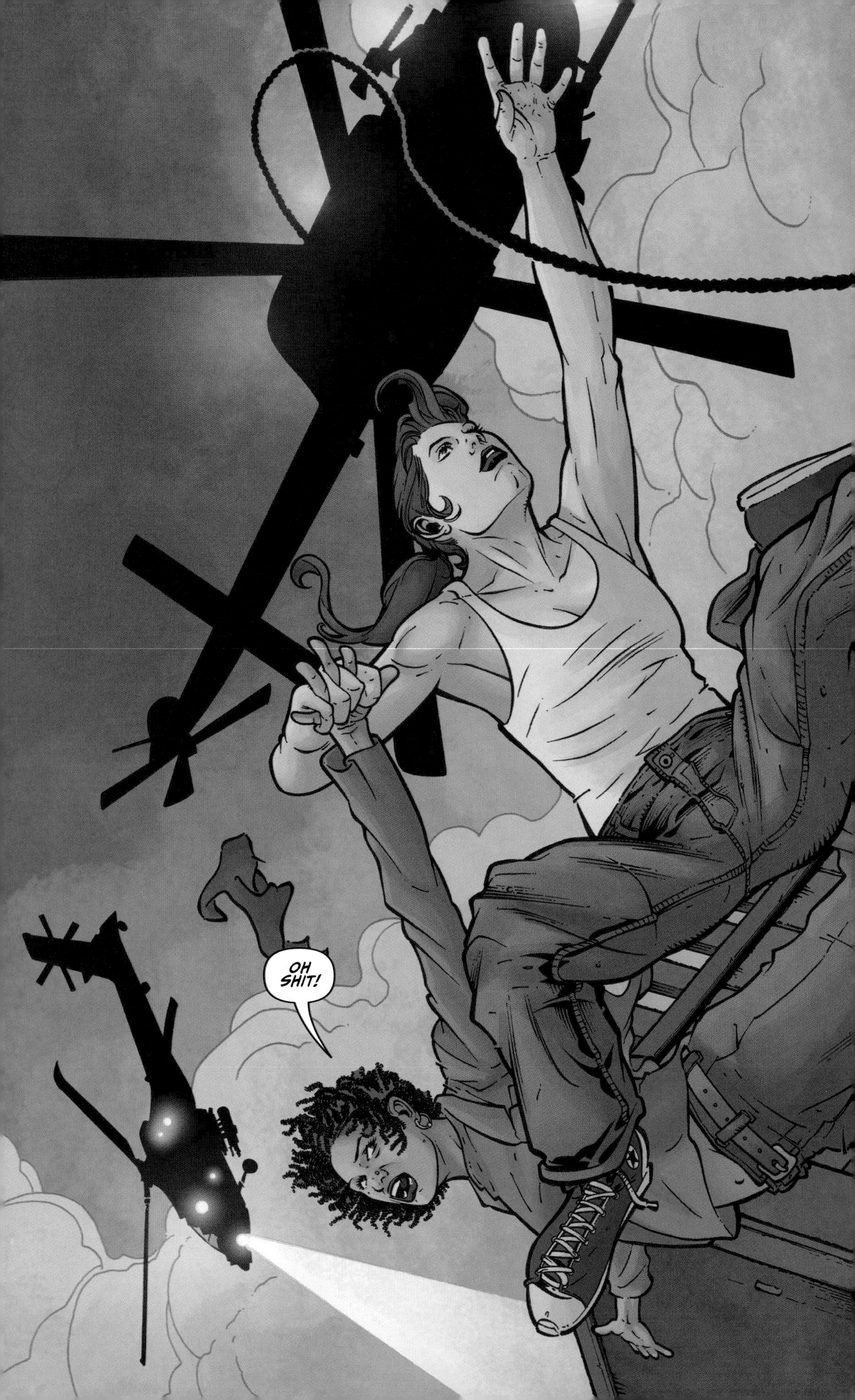
OH
SHIT!

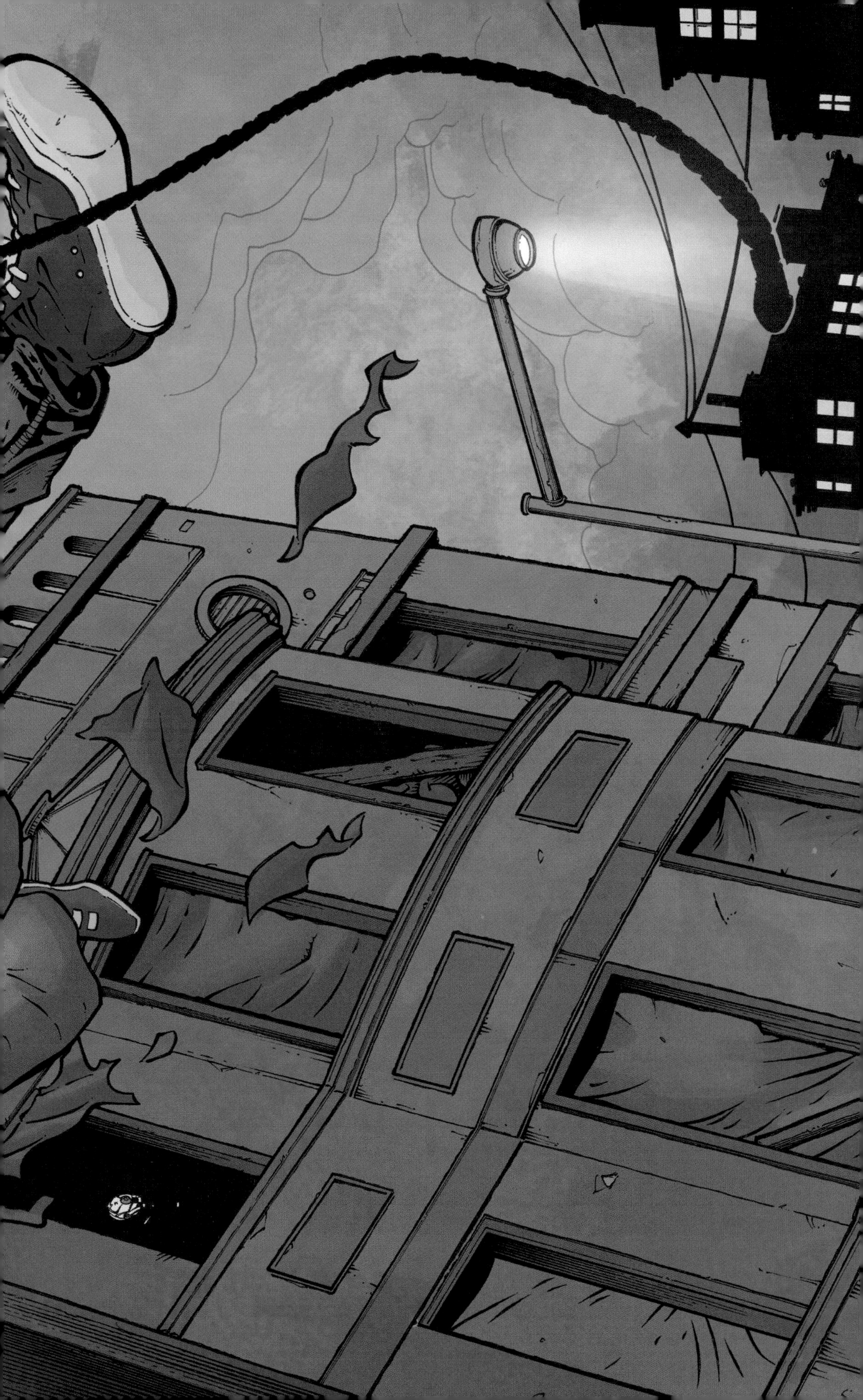

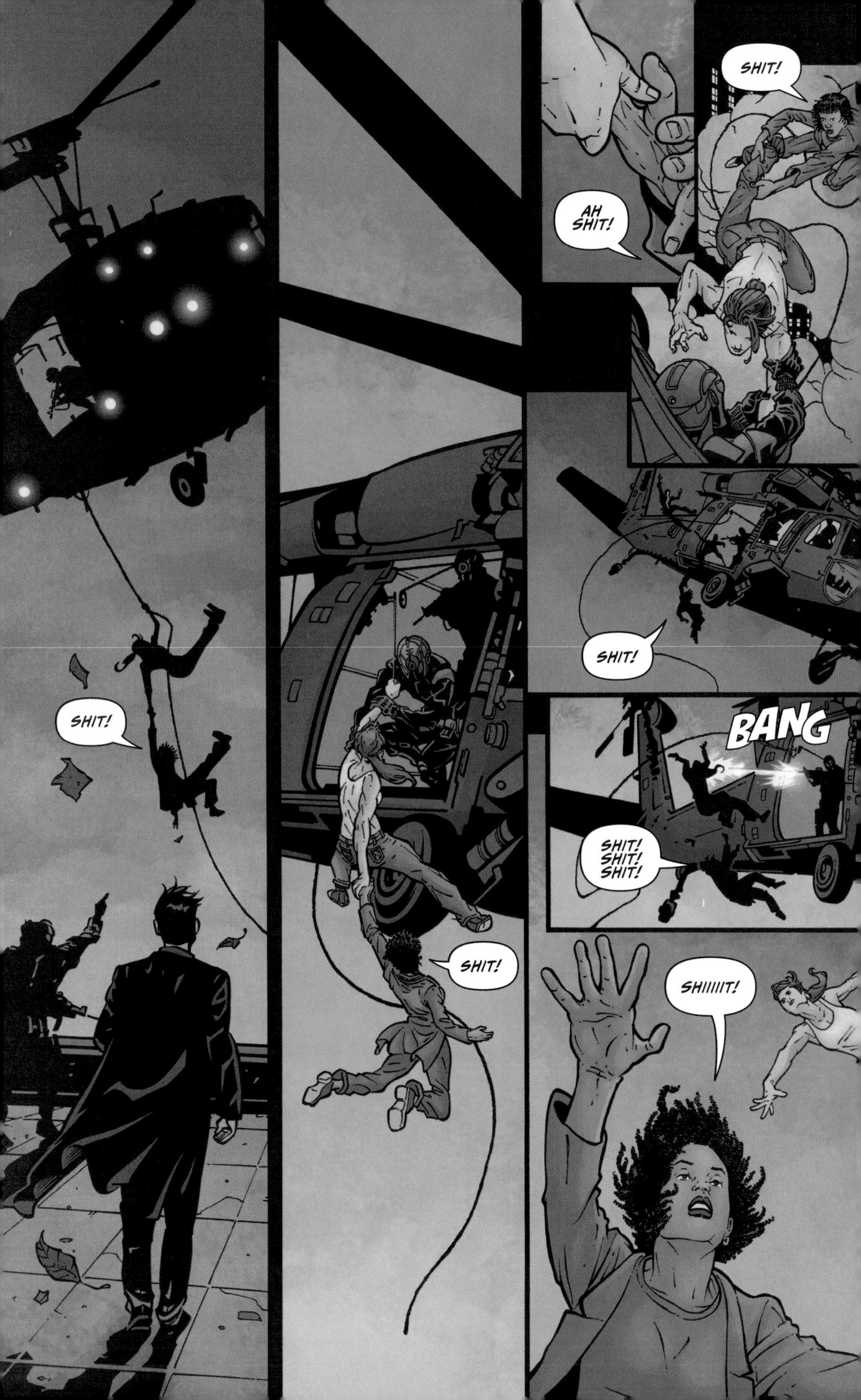
SHIT!
SHIT!
AH SHIT!
SHIT!
SHIT!
BANG
SHIT! SHIT! SHIT!
SHIIIIIT!

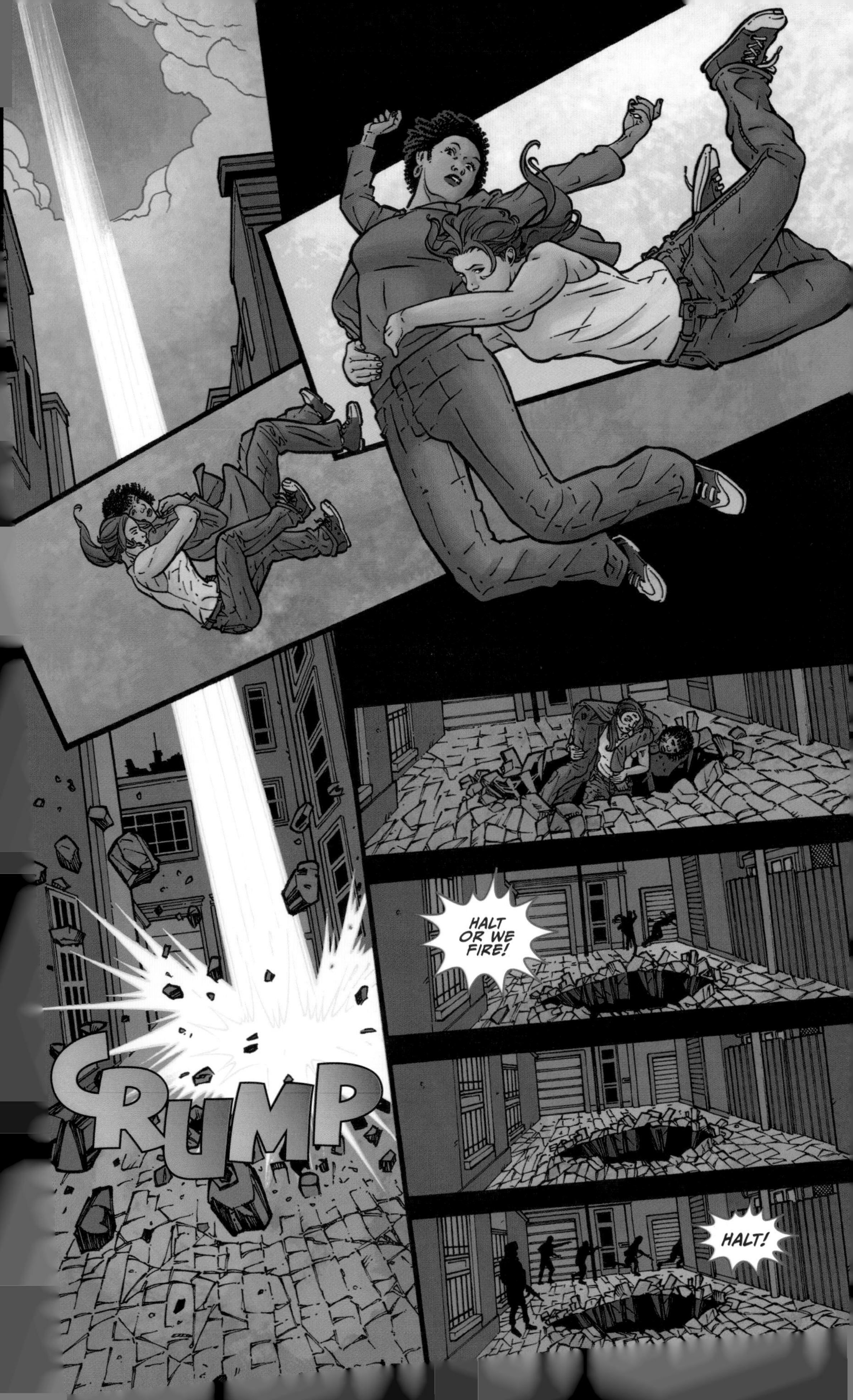
CRUMP
HALT OR WE FIRE!
HALT!

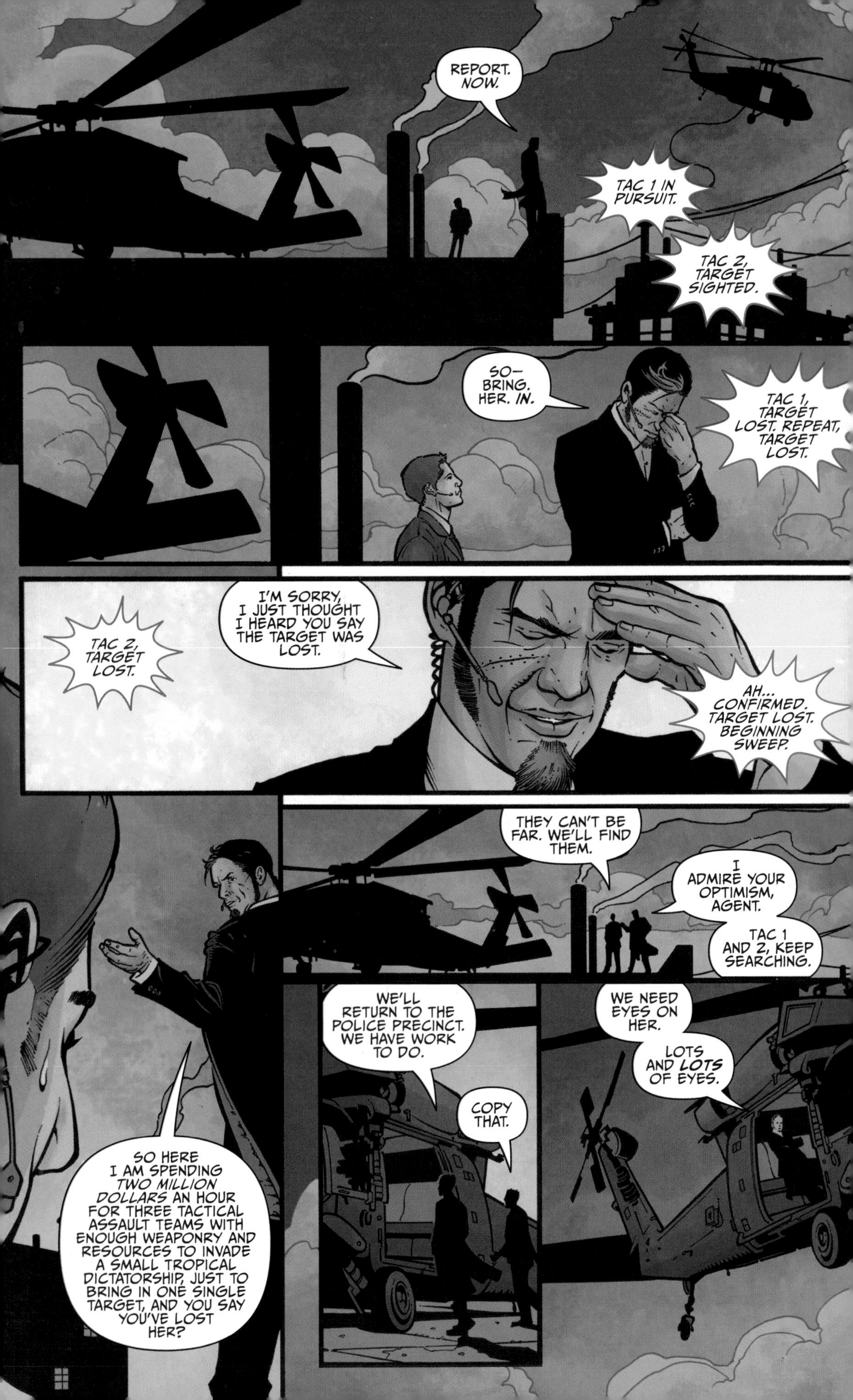
REPORT. NOW.
TAC 1 IN PURSUIT.
TAC 2, TARGET SIGHTED.
SO— BRING. HER. IN.
TAC 1, TARGET LOST. REPEAT, TARGET LOST.
TAC 2, TARGET LOST.
I'M SORRY, I JUST THOUGHT I HEARD YOU SAY THE TARGET WAS LOST.
AH... CONFIRMED. TARGET LOST. BEGINNING SWEEP.
SO HERE I AM SPENDING TWO MILLION DOLLARS AN HOUR FOR THREE TACTICAL ASSAULT TEAMS WITH ENOUGH WEAPONRY AND RESOURCES TO INVADE A SMALL TROPICAL DICTATORSHIP, JUST TO BRING IN ONE SINGLE TARGET, AND YOU SAY YOU'VE LOST HER?
THEY CAN'T BE FAR. WE'LL FIND THEM.
I ADMIRE YOUR OPTIMISM, AGENT.
TAC 1 AND 2, KEEP SEARCHING.
WE'LL RETURN TO THE POLICE PRECINCT. WE HAVE WORK TO DO.
COPY THAT.
WE NEED EYES ON HER.
LOTS AND LOTS OF EYES.

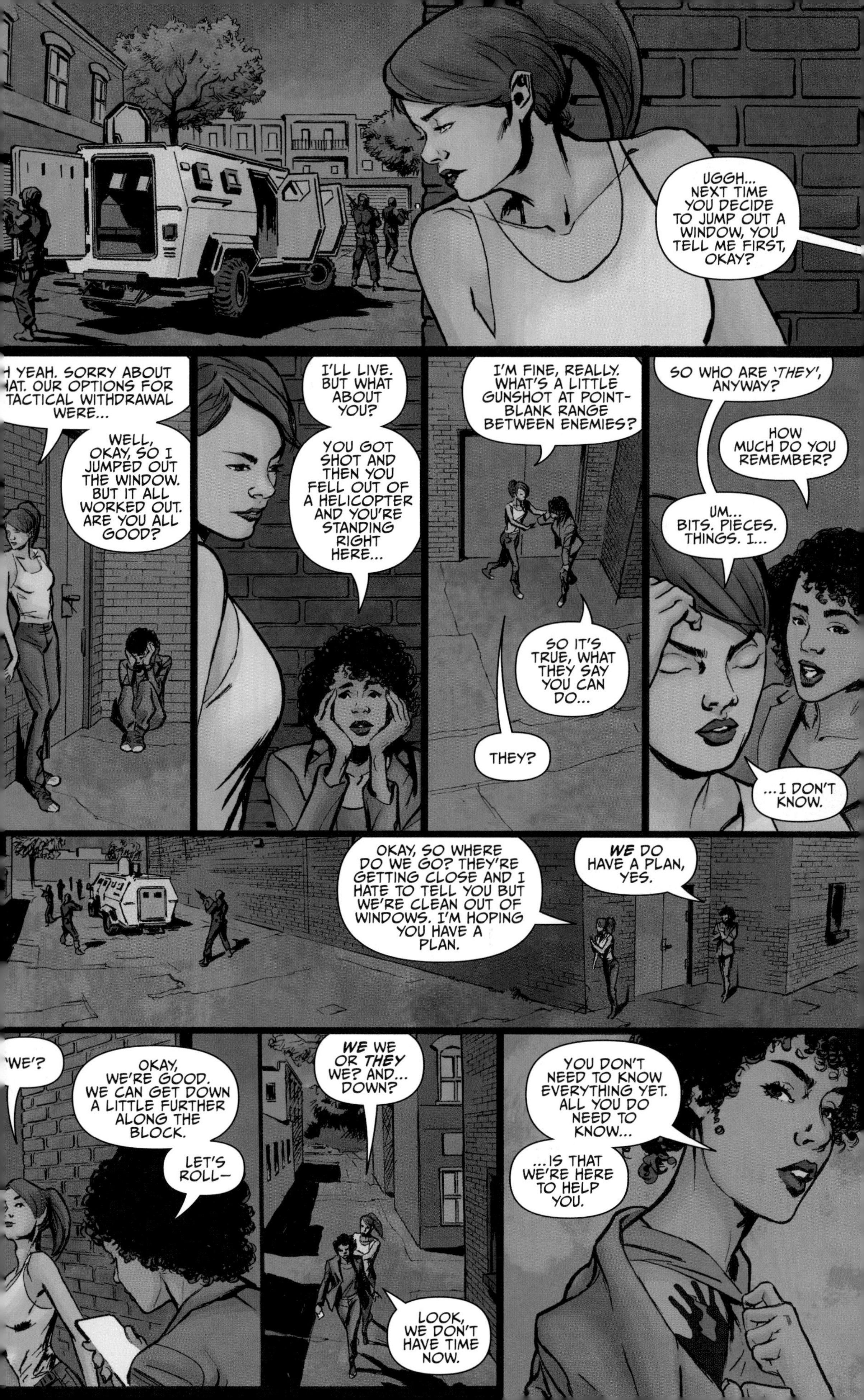
UGGH... NEXT TIME YOU DECIDE TO JUMP OUT A WINDOW, YOU TELL ME FIRST, OKAY?
H YEAH. SORRY ABOUT HAT. OUR OPTIONS FOR TACTICAL WITHDRAWAL WERE...
WELL, OKAY, SO I JUMPED OUT THE WINDOW. BUT IT ALL WORKED OUT. ARE YOU ALL GOOD?
I'LL LIVE. BUT WHAT ABOUT YOU?
YOU GOT SHOT AND THEN YOU FELL OUT OF A HELICOPTER AND YOU'RE STANDING RIGHT HERE...
I'M FINE, REALLY. WHAT'S A LITTLE GUNSHOT AT POINT-BLANK RANGE BETWEEN ENEMIES?
SO IT'S TRUE, WHAT THEY SAY YOU CAN DO...
THEY?
SO WHO ARE 'THEY', ANYWAY?
HOW MUCH DO YOU REMEMBER?
UM... BITS. PIECES. THINGS. I...
...I DON'T KNOW.
OKAY, SO WHERE DO WE GO? THEY'RE GETTING CLOSE AND I HATE TO TELL YOU BUT WE'RE CLEAN OUT OF WINDOWS. I'M HOPING YOU HAVE A PLAN.
WE DO HAVE A PLAN, YES.
'WE'?
OKAY, WE'RE GOOD. WE CAN GET DOWN A LITTLE FURTHER ALONG THE BLOCK.
LET'S ROLL—
WE WE OR THEY WE? AND... DOWN?
LOOK, WE DON'T HAVE TIME NOW.
YOU DON'T NEED TO KNOW EVERYTHING YET. ALL YOU DO NEED TO KNOW...
...IS THAT WE'RE HERE TO HELP YOU.

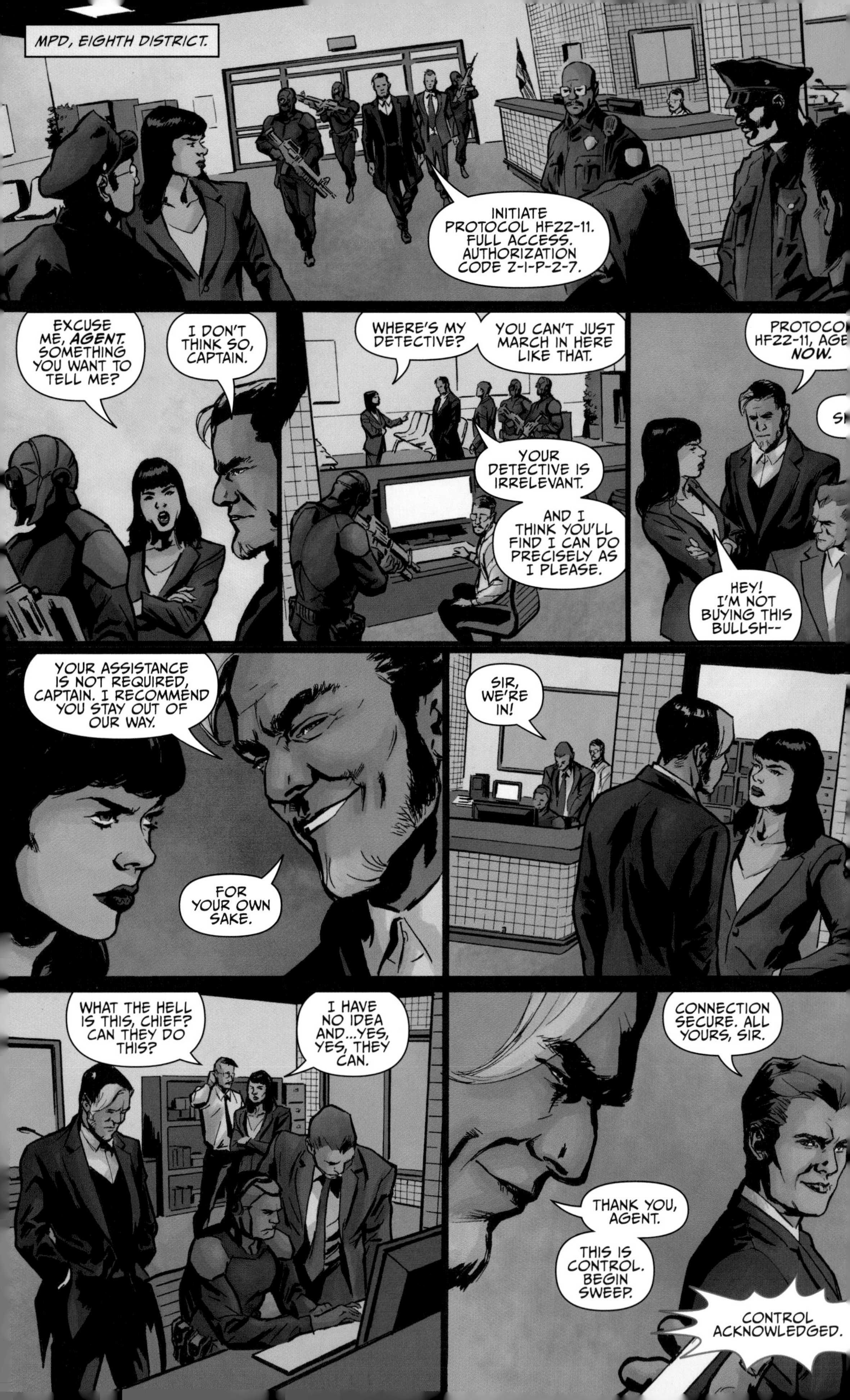
MPD, EIGHTH DISTRICT.
INITIATE PROTOCOL HF22-11. FULL ACCESS. AUTHORIZATION CODE Z-1-P-2-7.
EXCUSE ME, AGENT. SOMETHING YOU WANT TO TELL ME?
I DON'T THINK SO, CAPTAIN.
WHERE'S MY DETECTIVE?
YOU CAN'T JUST MARCH IN HERE LIKE THAT.
YOUR DETECTIVE IS IRRELEVANT.
AND I THINK YOU'LL FIND I CAN DO PRECISELY AS I PLEASE.
HEY! I'M NOT BUYING THIS BULLSH--
YOUR ASSISTANCE IS NOT REQUIRED, CAPTAIN. I RECOMMEND YOU STAY OUT OF OUR WAY.
FOR YOUR OWN SAKE.
SIR, WE'RE IN!
WHAT THE HELL IS THIS, CHIEF? CAN THEY DO THIS?
I HAVE NO IDEA AND...YES, YES, THEY CAN.
CONNECTION SECURE. ALL YOURS, SIR.
THANK YOU, AGENT.
THIS IS CONTROL. BEGIN SWEEP.
CONTROL ACKNOWLEDGED.

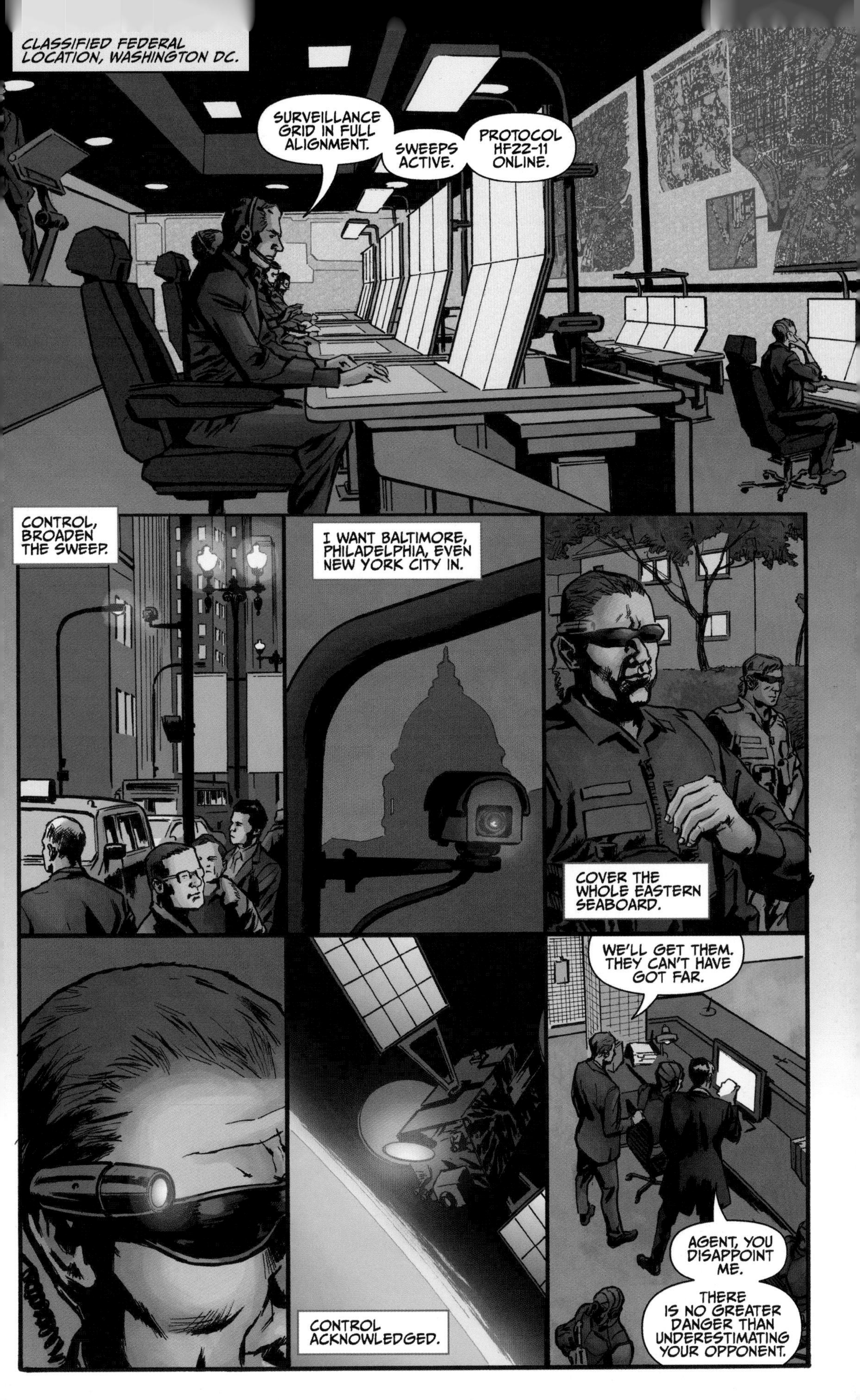
CLASSIFIED FEDERAL LOCATION, WASHINGTON DC.
SURVEILLANCE GRID IN FULL ALIGNMENT.
SWEEPS ACTIVE.
PROTOCOL HF22-11 ONLINE.
CONTROL, BROADEN THE SWEEP.
I WANT BALTIMORE, PHILADELPHIA, EVEN NEW YORK CITY IN.
COVER THE WHOLE EASTERN SEABOARD.
CONTROL ACKNOWLEDGED.
WE'LL GET THEM. THEY CAN'T HAVE GOT FAR.
AGENT, YOU DISAPPOINT ME.
THERE IS NO GREATER DANGER THAN UNDERESTIMATING YOUR OPPONENT.

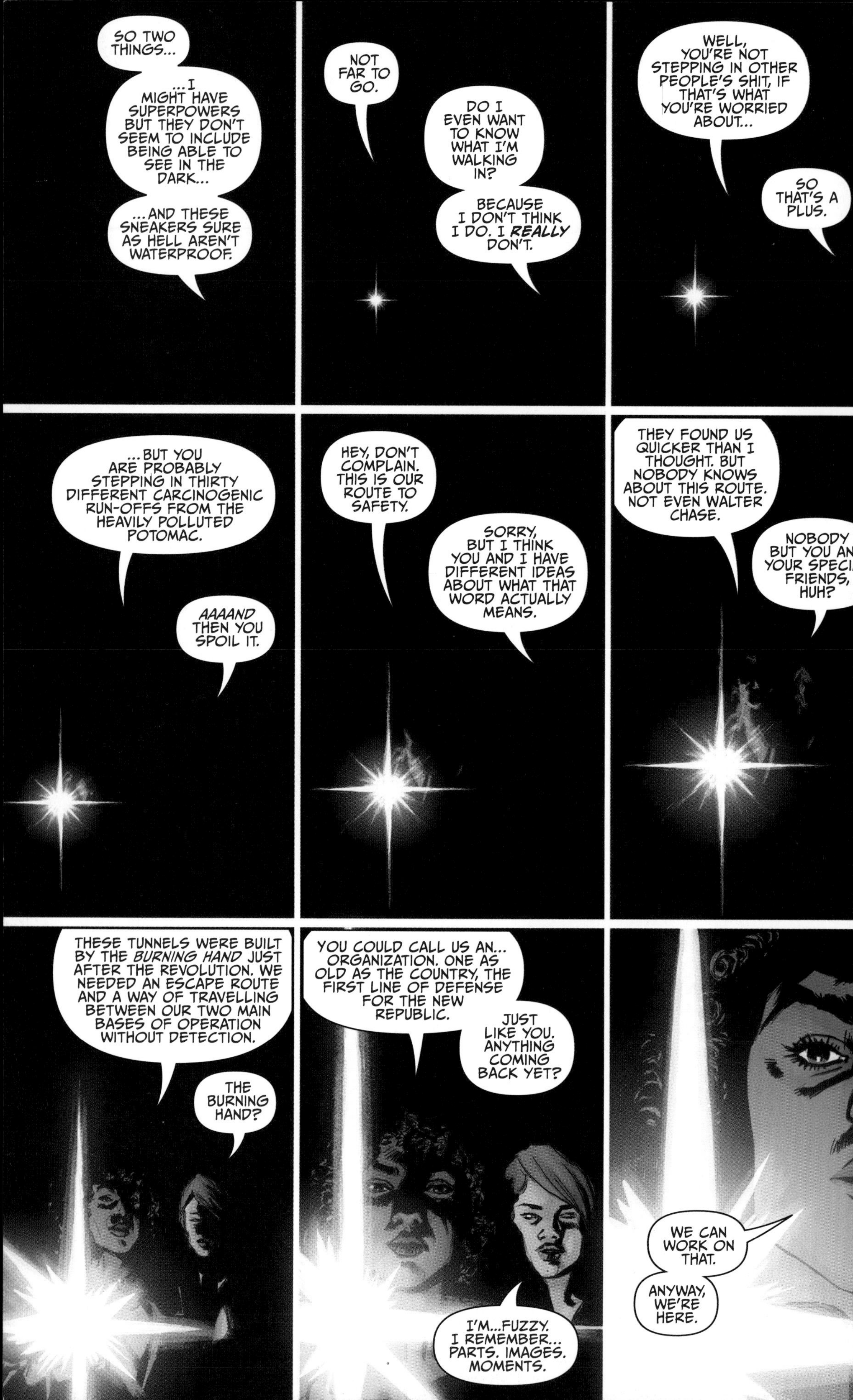
SO TWO THINGS...
...I MIGHT HAVE SUPERPOWERS BUT THEY DON'T SEEM TO INCLUDE BEING ABLE TO SEE IN THE DARK...
...AND THESE SNEAKERS SURE AS HELL AREN'T WATERPROOF.
NOT FAR TO GO.
DO I EVEN WANT TO KNOW WHAT I'M WALKING IN?
BECAUSE I DON'T THINK I DO. I *REALLY* DON'T.
WELL, YOU'RE NOT STEPPING IN OTHER PEOPLE'S SHIT, IF THAT'S WHAT YOU'RE WORRIED ABOUT...
SO THAT'S A PLUS.
...BUT YOU ARE PROBABLY STEPPING IN THIRTY DIFFERENT CARCINOGENIC RUN-OFFS FROM THE HEAVILY POLLUTED POTOMAC.
AAAAND THEN YOU SPOIL IT.
HEY, DON'T COMPLAIN. THIS IS OUR ROUTE TO SAFETY.
SORRY, BUT I THINK YOU AND I HAVE DIFFERENT IDEAS ABOUT WHAT THAT WORD ACTUALLY MEANS.
THEY FOUND US QUICKER THAN I THOUGHT. BUT NOBODY KNOWS ABOUT THIS ROUTE. NOT EVEN WALTER CHASE.
NOBODY BUT YOU AN YOUR SPECI FRIENDS, HUH?
THESE TUNNELS WERE BUILT BY THE *BURNING HAND* JUST AFTER THE REVOLUTION. WE NEEDED AN ESCAPE ROUTE AND A WAY OF TRAVELLING BETWEEN OUR TWO MAIN BASES OF OPERATION WITHOUT DETECTION.
THE BURNING HAND?
YOU COULD CALL US AN... ORGANIZATION. ONE AS OLD AS THE COUNTRY, THE FIRST LINE OF DEFENSE FOR THE NEW REPUBLIC.
JUST LIKE YOU. ANYTHING COMING BACK YET?
I'M...FUZZY. I REMEMBER... PARTS. IMAGES. MOMENTS.
WE CAN WORK ON THAT.
ANYWAY, WE'RE HERE.

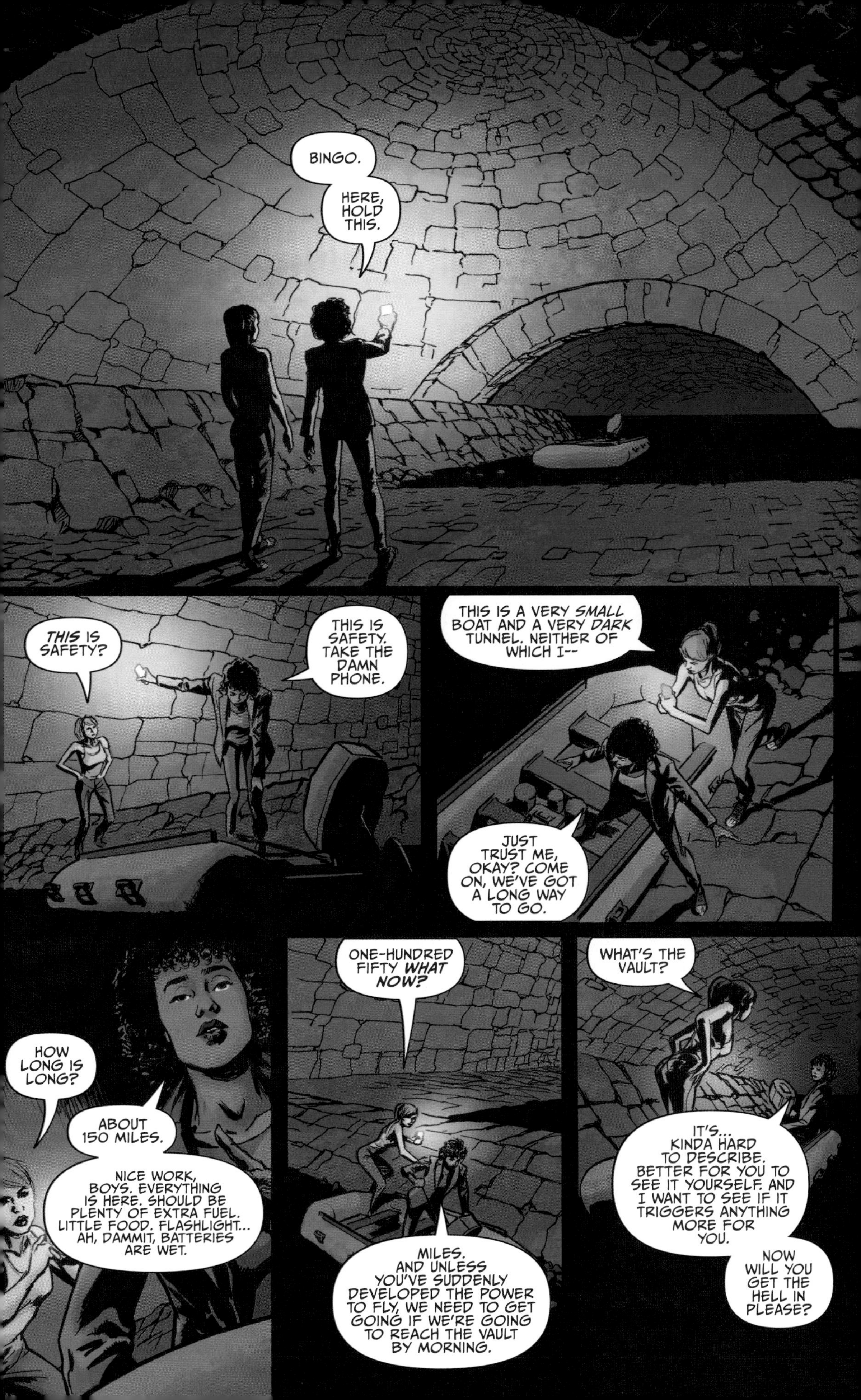
BINGO.
HERE, HOLD THIS.
THIS IS SAFETY?
THIS IS SAFETY. TAKE THE DAMN PHONE.
THIS IS A VERY SMALL BOAT AND A VERY DARK TUNNEL. NEITHER OF WHICH I--
JUST TRUST ME, OKAY? COME ON, WE'VE GOT A LONG WAY TO GO.
HOW LONG IS LONG?
ABOUT 150 MILES.
NICE WORK, BOYS. EVERYTHING IS HERE. SHOULD BE PLENTY OF EXTRA FUEL. LITTLE FOOD. FLASHLIGHT... AH, DAMMIT, BATTERIES ARE WET.
ONE-HUNDRED FIFTY WHAT NOW?
MILES. AND UNLESS YOU'VE SUDDENLY DEVELOPED THE POWER TO FLY, WE NEED TO GET GOING IF WE'RE GOING TO REACH THE VAULT BY MORNING.
WHAT'S THE VAULT?
IT'S... KINDA HARD TO DESCRIBE. BETTER FOR YOU TO SEE IT YOURSELF. AND I WANT TO SEE IF IT TRIGGERS ANYTHING MORE FOR YOU.
NOW WILL YOU GET THE HELL IN PLEASE?

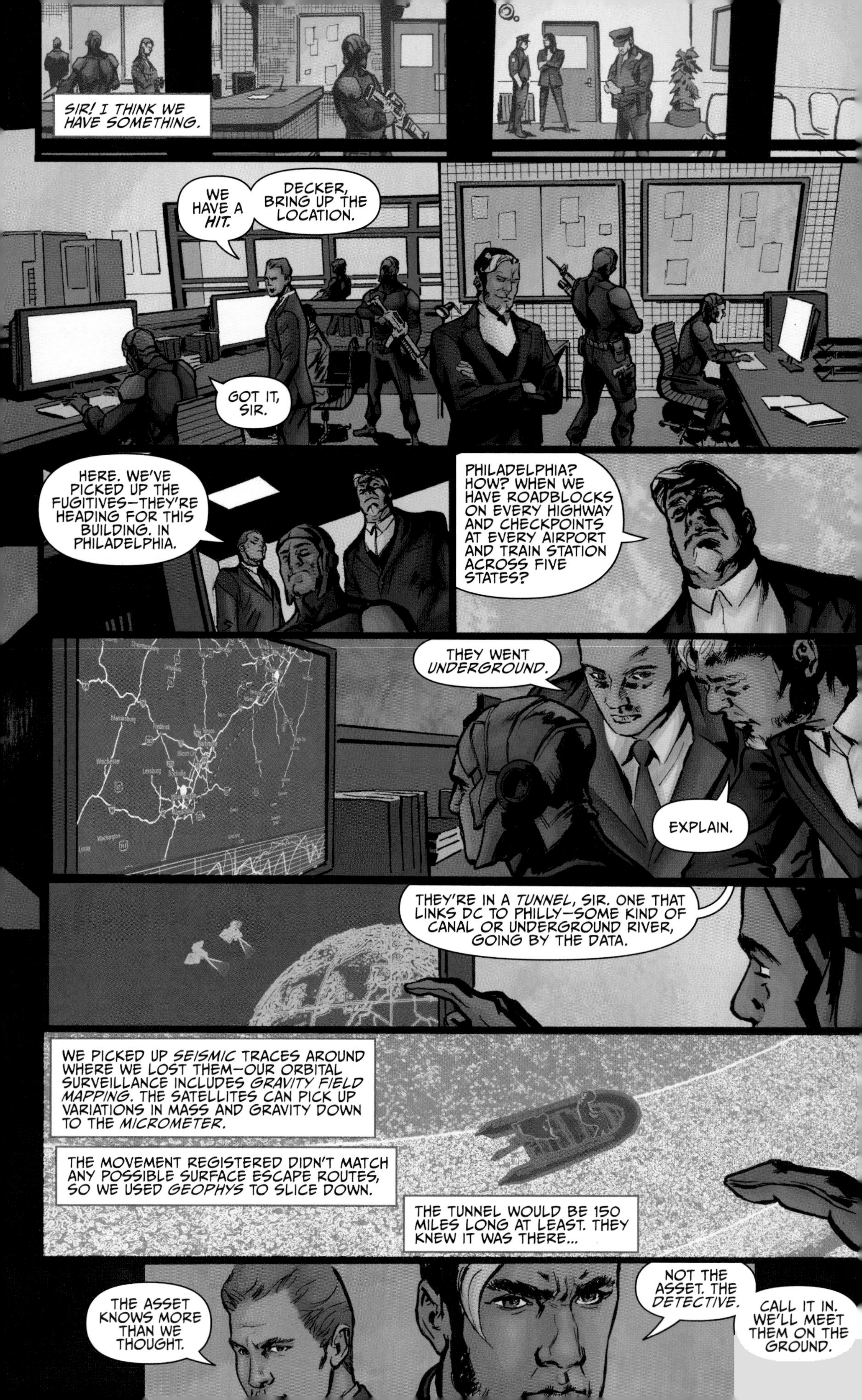
SIR! I THINK WE HAVE SOMETHING.
WE HAVE A HIT.
DECKER, BRING UP THE LOCATION.
GOT IT, SIR.
HERE. WE'VE PICKED UP THE FUGITIVES—THEY'RE HEADING FOR THIS BUILDING. IN PHILADELPHIA.
PHILADELPHIA? HOW? WHEN WE HAVE ROADBLOCKS ON EVERY HIGHWAY AND CHECKPOINTS AT EVERY AIRPORT AND TRAIN STATION ACROSS FIVE STATES?
THEY WENT UNDERGROUND.
EXPLAIN.
THEY'RE IN A TUNNEL, SIR. ONE THAT LINKS DC TO PHILLY—SOME KIND OF CANAL OR UNDERGROUND RIVER, GOING BY THE DATA.
WE PICKED UP SEISMIC TRACES AROUND WHERE WE LOST THEM—OUR ORBITAL SURVEILLANCE INCLUDES GRAVITY FIELD MAPPING. THE SATELLITES CAN PICK UP VARIATIONS IN MASS AND GRAVITY DOWN TO THE MICROMETER.
THE MOVEMENT REGISTERED DIDN'T MATCH ANY POSSIBLE SURFACE ESCAPE ROUTES, SO WE USED GEOPHYS TO SLICE DOWN.
THE TUNNEL WOULD BE 150 MILES LONG AT LEAST. THEY KNEW IT WAS THERE...
THE ASSET KNOWS MORE THAN WE THOUGHT.
NOT THE ASSET. THE DETECTIVE.
CALL IT IN. WE'LL MEET THEM ON THE GROUND.

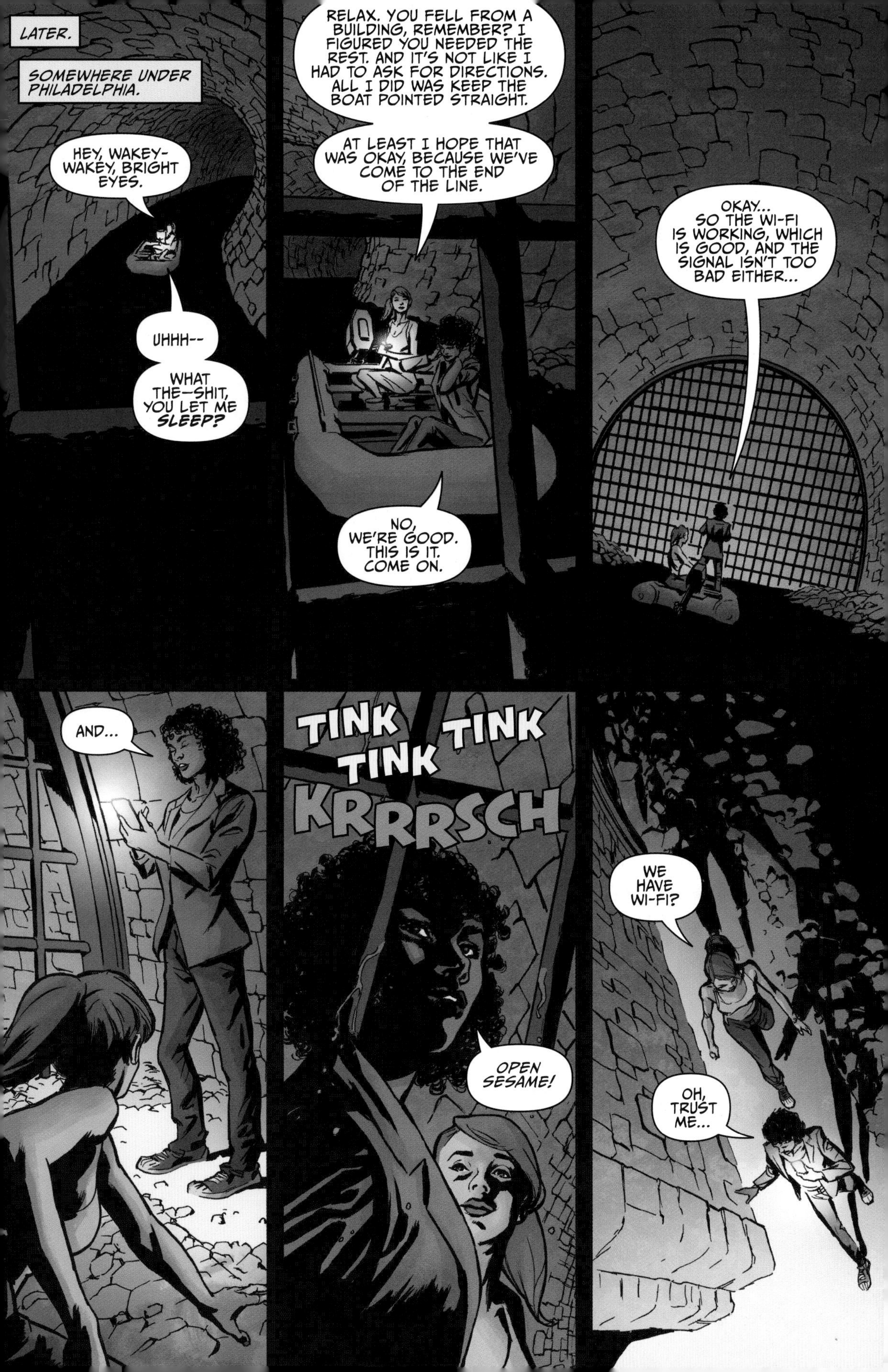
LATER.
SOMEWHERE UNDER PHILADELPHIA.
HEY, WAKEY-WAKEY, BRIGHT EYES.
UHHH--
WHAT THE—SHIT, YOU LET ME SLEEP?
RELAX. YOU FELL FROM A BUILDING, REMEMBER? I FIGURED YOU NEEDED THE REST. AND IT'S NOT LIKE I HAD TO ASK FOR DIRECTIONS. ALL I DID WAS KEEP THE BOAT POINTED STRAIGHT.
AT LEAST I HOPE THAT WAS OKAY, BECAUSE WE'VE COME TO THE END OF THE LINE.
NO, WE'RE GOOD. THIS IS IT. COME ON.
OKAY... SO THE WI-FI IS WORKING, WHICH IS GOOD, AND THE SIGNAL ISN'T TOO BAD EITHER...
AND...
TINK TINK TINK
KRRRSCH
OPEN SESAME!
WE HAVE WI-FI?
OH, TRUST ME...

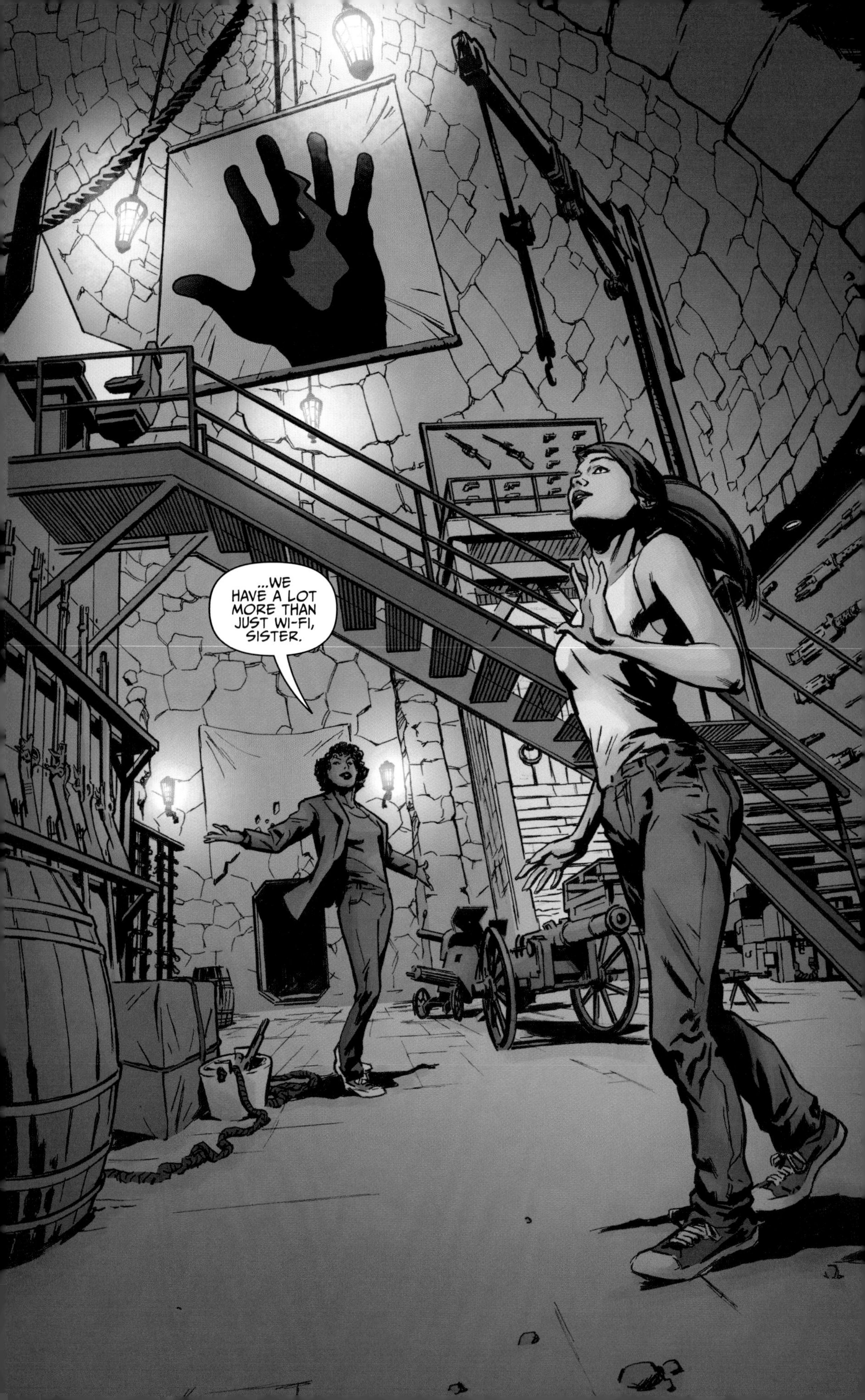
...WE HAVE A LOT MORE THAN JUST WI-FI, SISTER.

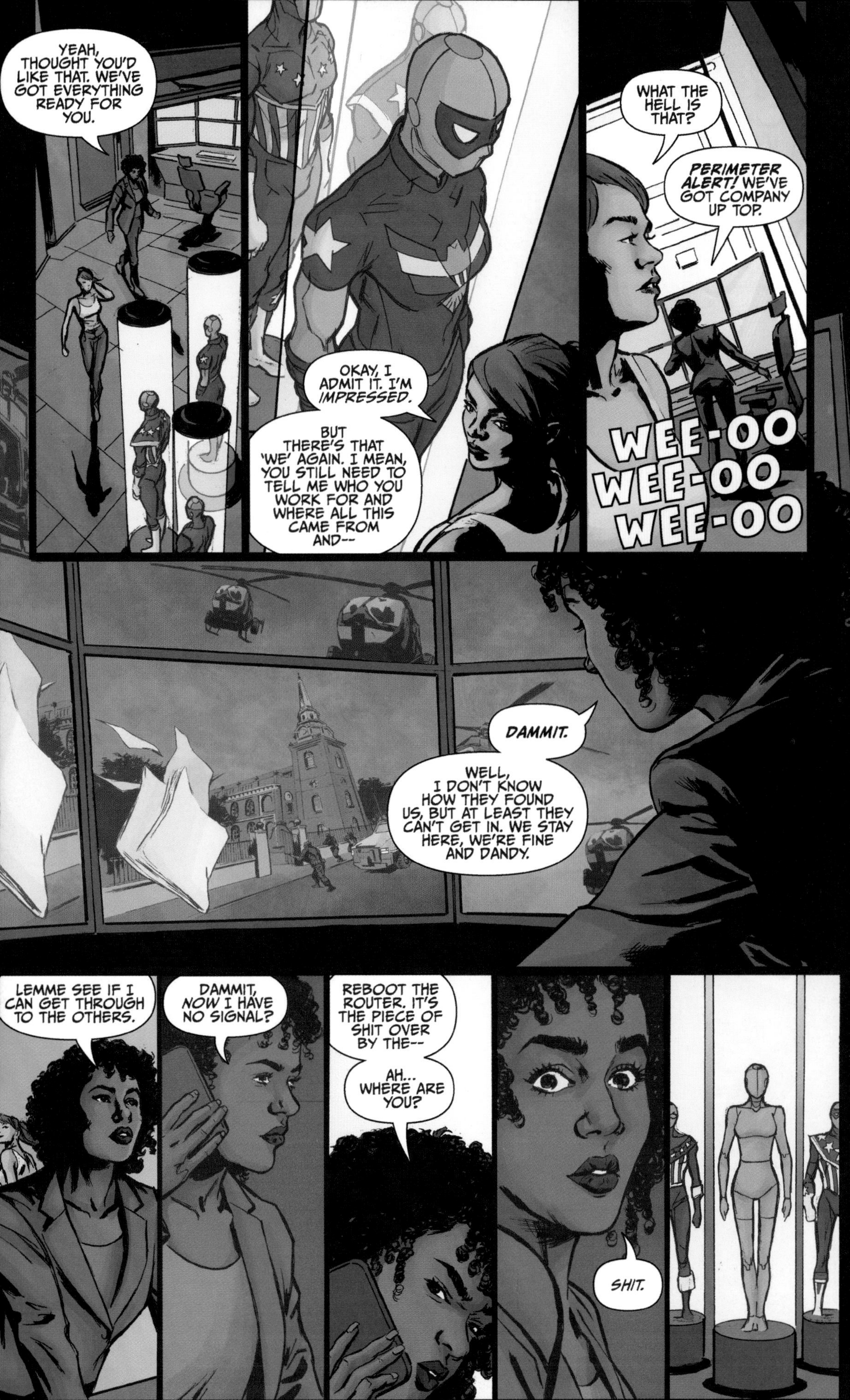
YEAH, THOUGHT YOU'D LIKE THAT. WE'VE GOT EVERYTHING READY FOR YOU.
OKAY, I ADMIT IT. I'M *IMPRESSED.*
BUT THERE'S THAT 'WE' AGAIN. I MEAN, YOU STILL NEED TO TELL ME WHO YOU WORK FOR AND WHERE ALL THIS CAME FROM AND--
WHAT THE HELL IS THAT?
PERIMETER ALERT! WE'VE GOT COMPANY UP TOP.
WEE-OO WEE-OO WEE-OO
DAMMIT.
WELL, I DON'T KNOW HOW THEY FOUND US, BUT AT LEAST THEY CAN'T GET IN. WE STAY HERE, WE'RE FINE AND DANDY.
LEMME SEE IF I CAN GET THROUGH TO THE OTHERS.
DAMMIT, *NOW* I HAVE NO SIGNAL?
REBOOT THE ROUTER. IT'S THE PIECE OF SHIT OVER BY THE--
AH... WHERE ARE YOU?
SHIT.

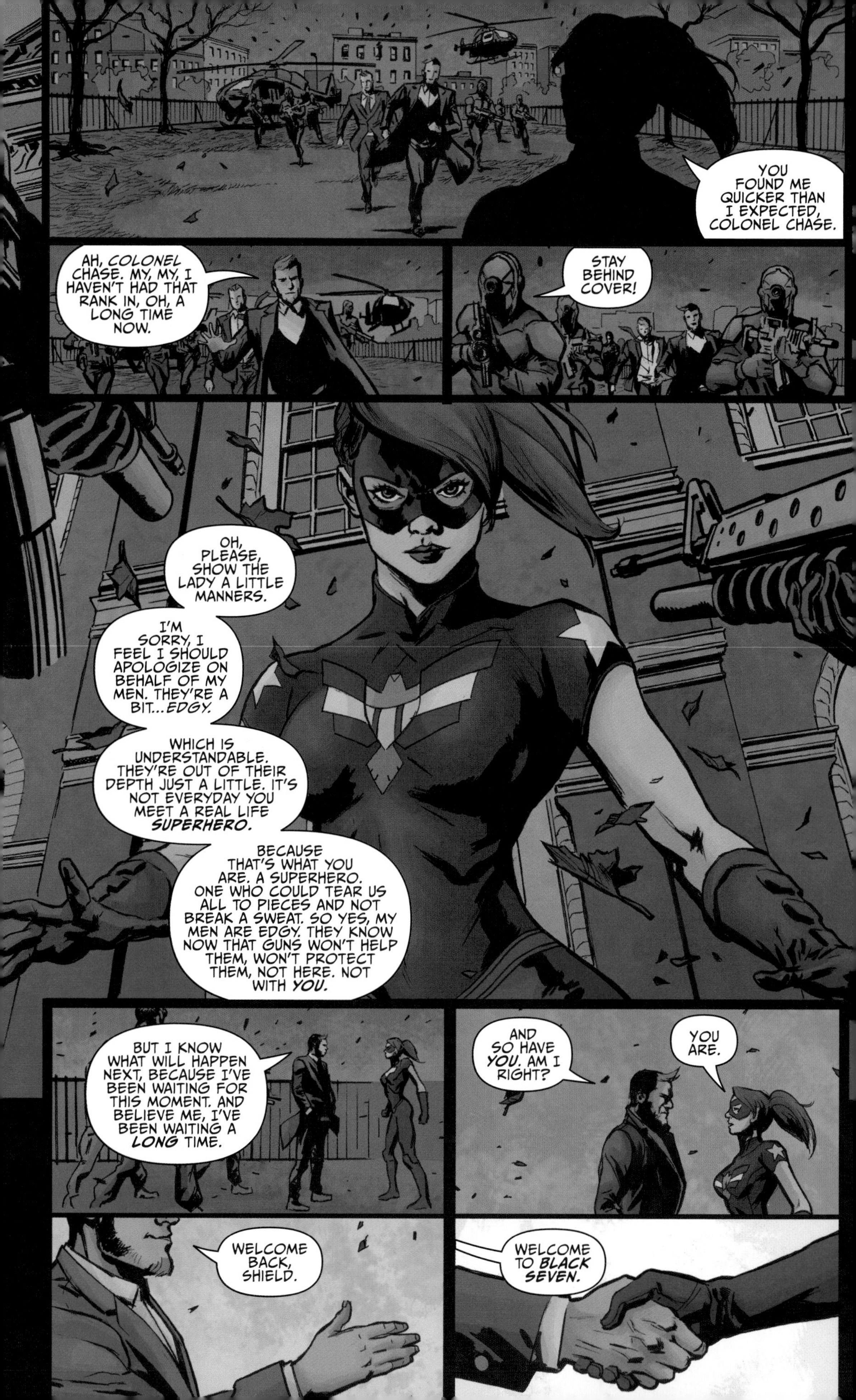
YOU FOUND ME QUICKER THAN I EXPECTED, COLONEL CHASE.
AH, COLONEL CHASE. MY, MY, I HAVEN'T HAD THAT RANK IN, OH, A LONG TIME NOW.
STAY BEHIND COVER!
OH, PLEASE, SHOW THE LADY A LITTLE MANNERS.
I'M SORRY, I FEEL I SHOULD APOLOGIZE ON BEHALF OF MY MEN. THEY'RE A BIT...EDGY.
WHICH IS UNDERSTANDABLE. THEY'RE OUT OF THEIR DEPTH JUST A LITTLE. IT'S NOT EVERYDAY YOU MEET A REAL LIFE SUPERHERO.
BECAUSE THAT'S WHAT YOU ARE. A SUPERHERO. ONE WHO COULD TEAR US ALL TO PIECES AND NOT BREAK A SWEAT. SO YES, MY MEN ARE EDGY. THEY KNOW NOW THAT GUNS WON'T HELP THEM, WON'T PROTECT THEM, NOT HERE. NOT WITH YOU.
BUT I KNOW WHAT WILL HAPPEN NEXT, BECAUSE I'VE BEEN WAITING FOR THIS MOMENT. AND BELIEVE ME, I'VE BEEN WAITING A LONG TIME.
AND SO HAVE YOU. AM I RIGHT?
YOU ARE.
WELCOME BACK, SHIELD.
WELCOME TO BLACK SEVEN.

ISSUE THREE

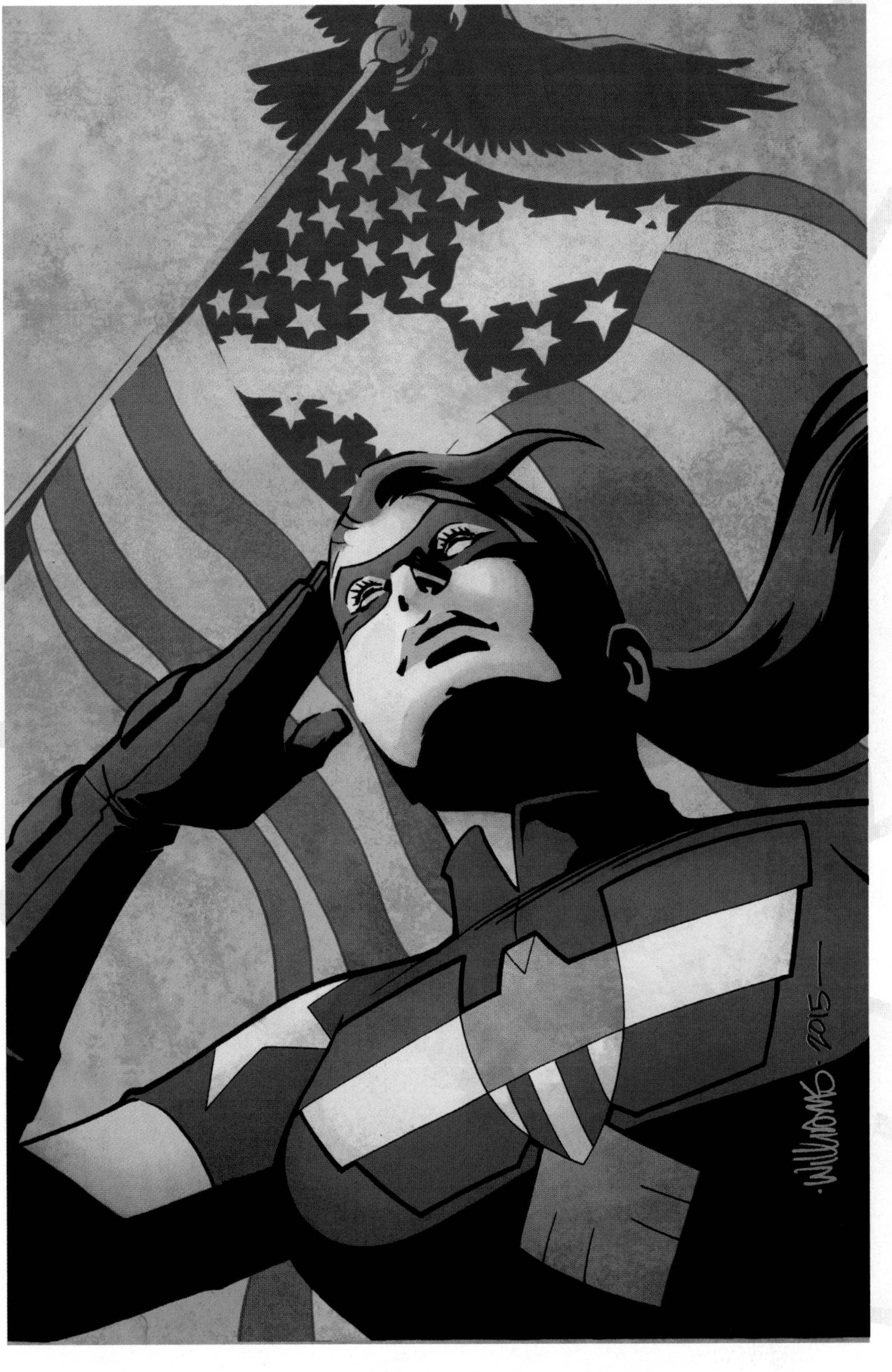

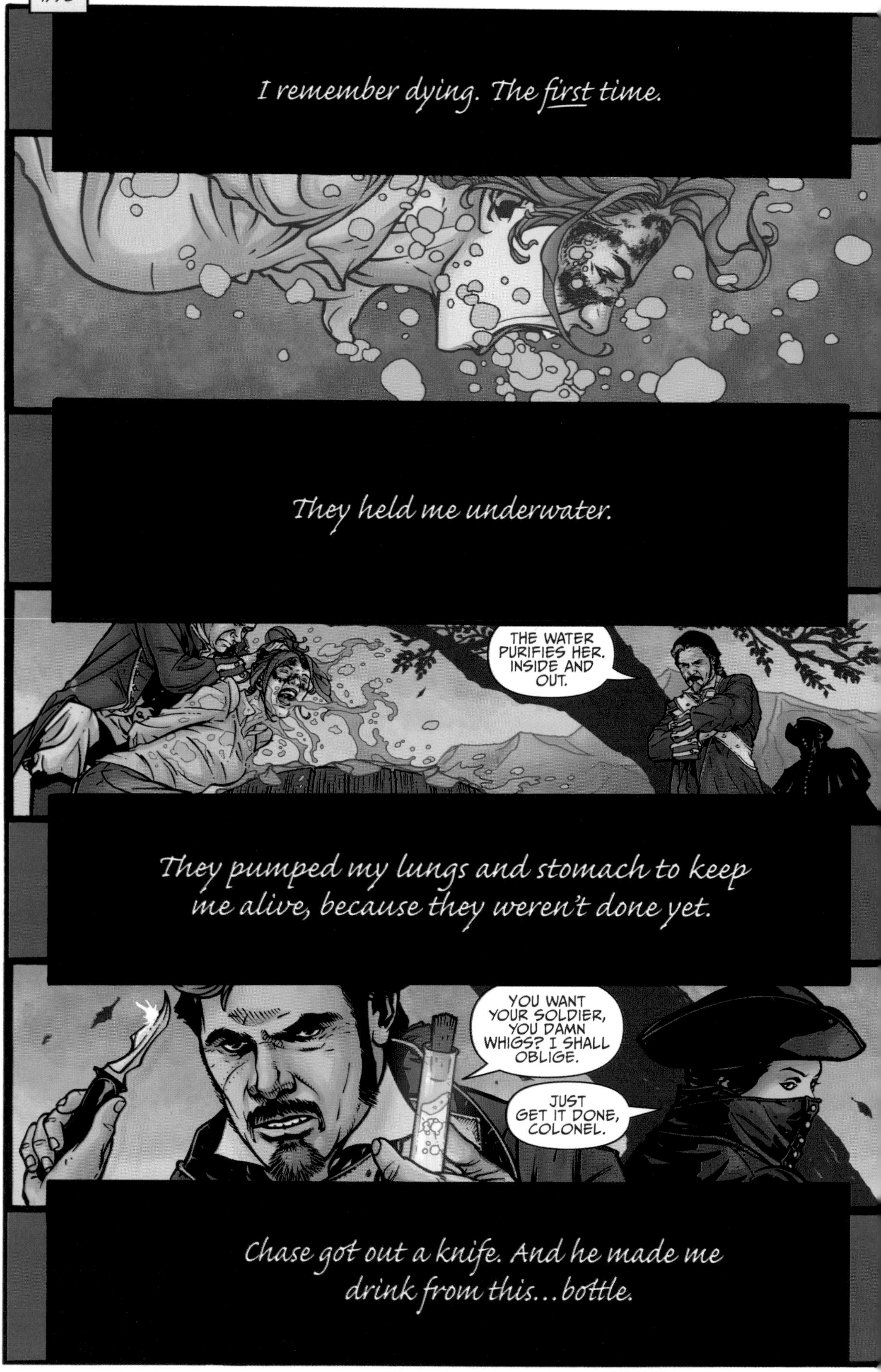
I remember dying. The first time.
They held me underwater.
THE WATER PURIFIES HER. INSIDE AND OUT.
They pumped my lungs and stomach to keep me alive, because they weren't done yet.
YOU WANT YOUR SOLDIER, YOU DAMN WHIGS? I SHALL OBLIGE.
JUST GET IT DONE, COLONEL.
Chase got out a knife. And he made me drink from this...bottle.

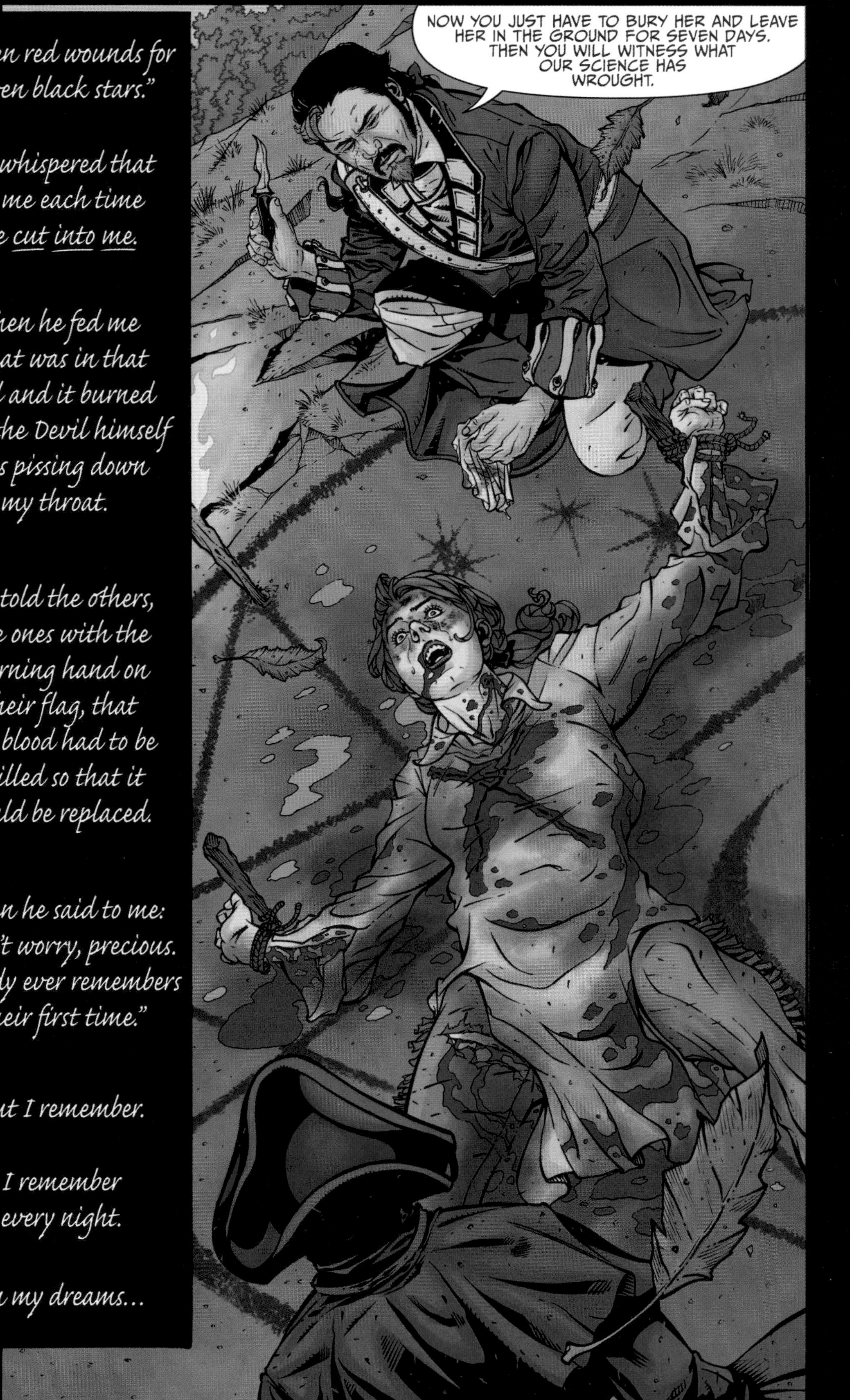
NOW YOU JUST HAVE TO BURY HER AND LEAVE HER IN THE GROUND FOR SEVEN DAYS. THEN YOU WILL WITNESS WHAT OUR SCIENCE HAS WROUGHT.
"Seven red wounds for Seven black stars."
He whispered that to me each time he cut into me.
Then he fed me what was in that vial and it burned like the Devil himself was pissing down my throat.
He told the others, the ones with the burning hand on their flag, that my blood had to be spilled so that it could be replaced.
Then he said to me: "Don't worry, precious. Nobody ever remembers their first time."
But I remember.
I remember every night.
In my dreams...

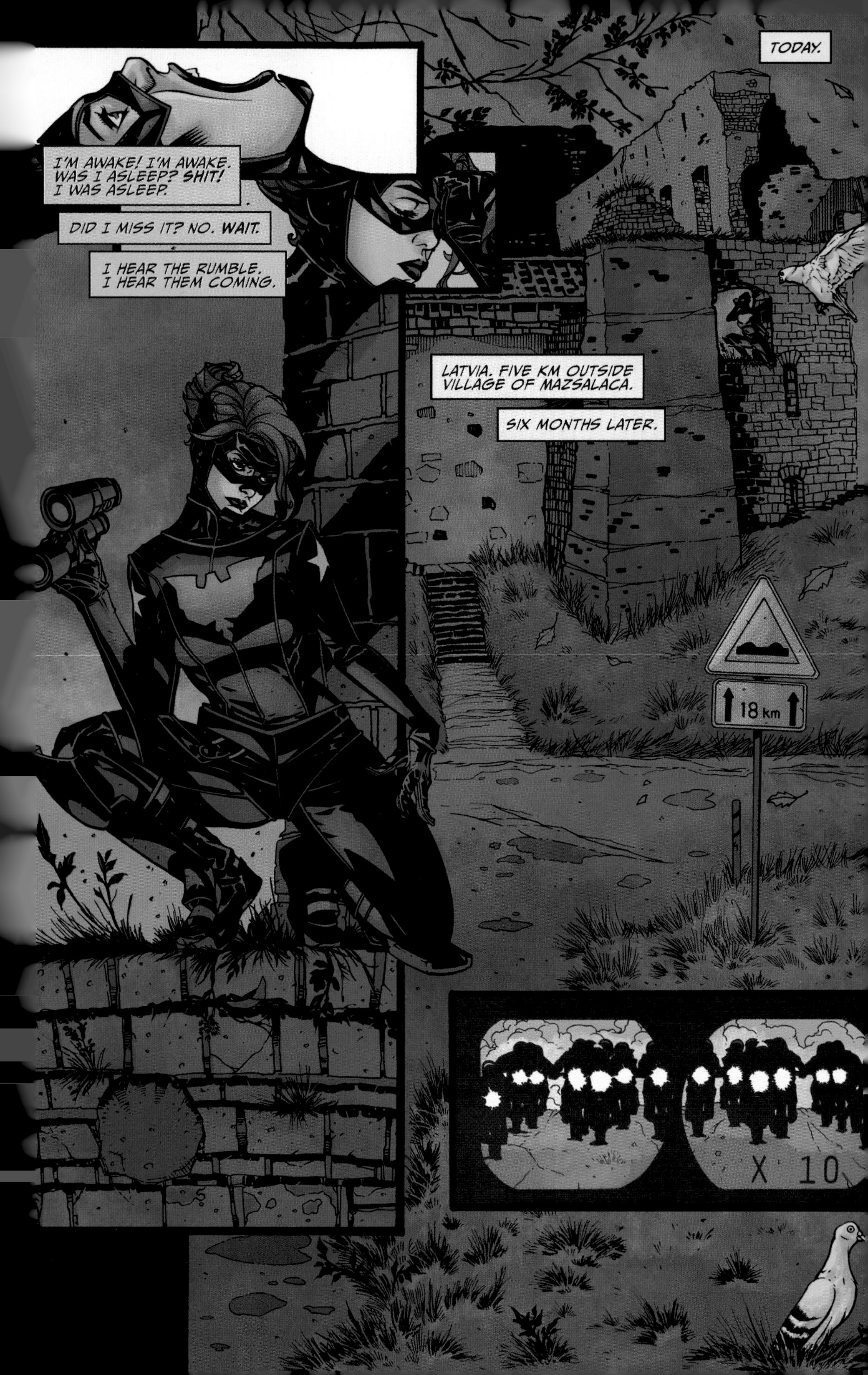
TODAY.
I'M AWAKE! I'M AWAKE. WAS I ASLEEP? SHIT! I WAS ASLEEP.
DID I MISS IT? NO. WAIT.
I HEAR THE RUMBLE. I HEAR THEM COMING.
LATVIA. FIVE KM OUTSIDE VILLAGE OF MAZSALACA.
SIX MONTHS LATER.
18 km
X 10

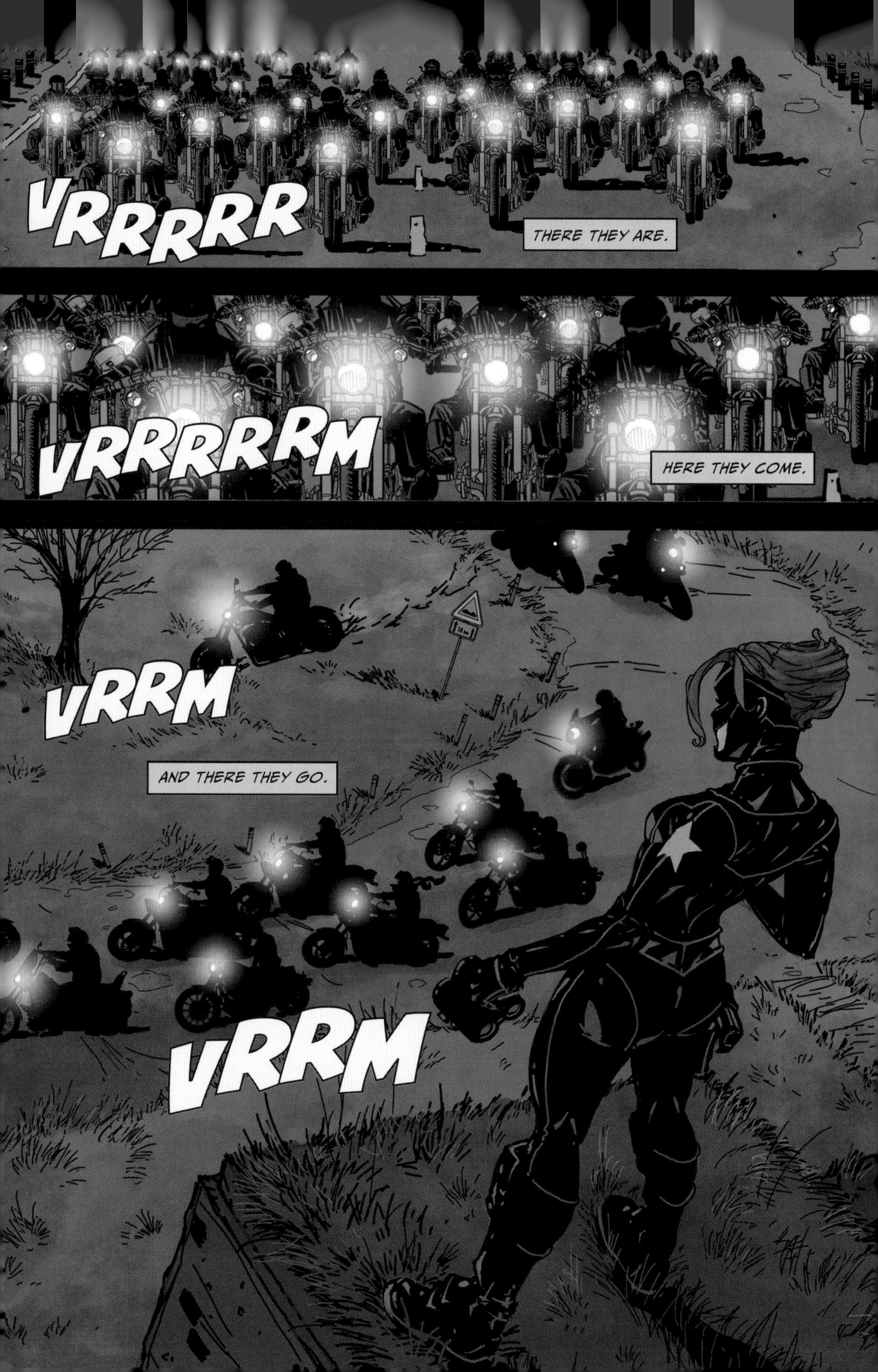
VRRRRRR
THERE THEY ARE.
VRRRRRRM
HERE THEY COME.
VRRM
AND THERE THEY GO.
VRRM

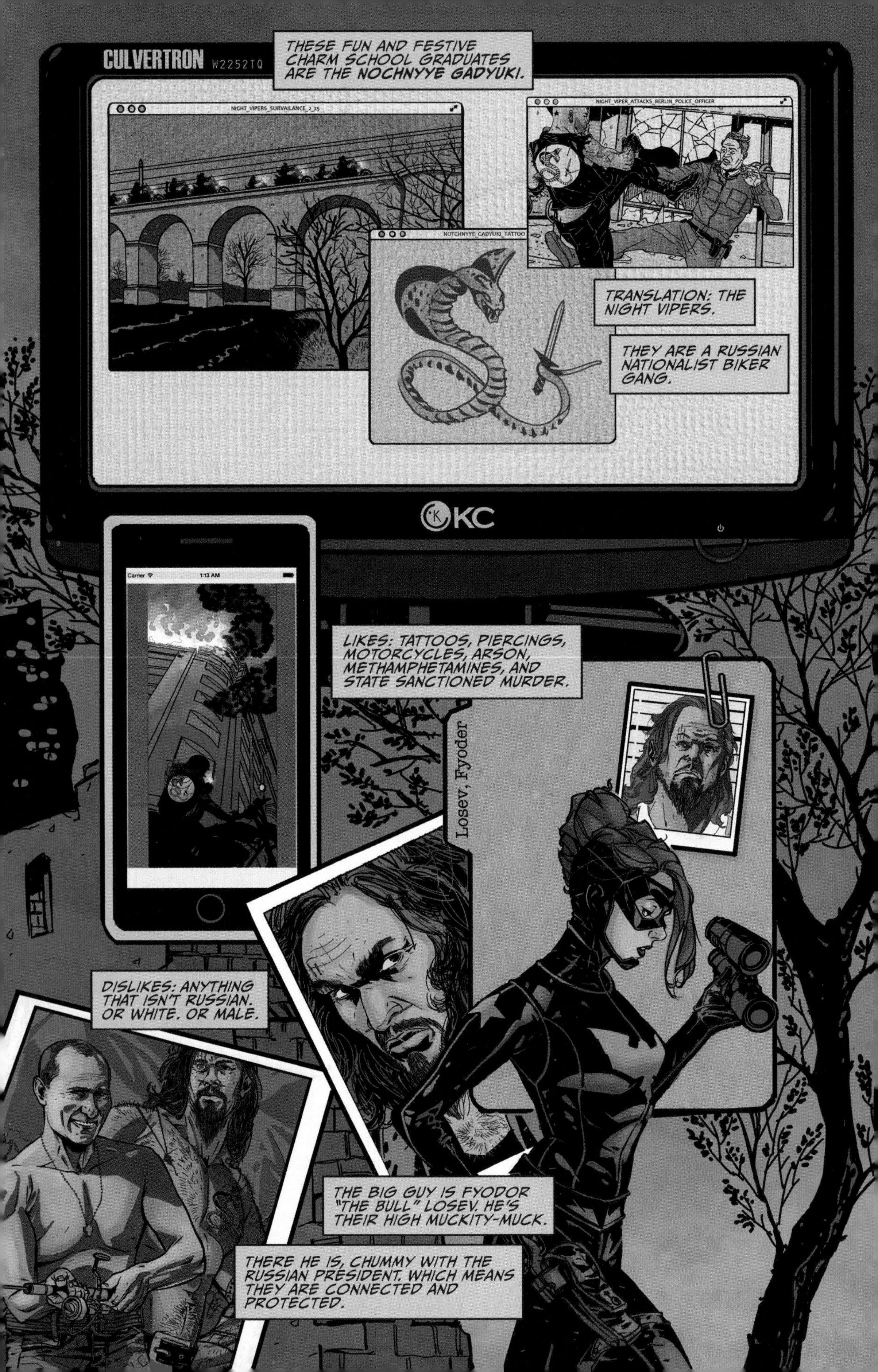
CULVERTRON W2252TQ
THESE FUN AND FESTIVE CHARM SCHOOL GRADUATES ARE THE NOCHNYYE GADYUKI.
NIGHT_VIPERS_SURVAILANCE_2_25
NIGHT_VIPER_ATTACKS_BERLIN_POLICE_OFFICER
NOTCHNYYE_GADYUKI_TATTOO
TRANSLATION: THE NIGHT VIPERS.
THEY ARE A RUSSIAN NATIONALIST BIKER GANG.
KC
Carrier
1:13 AM
LIKES: TATTOOS, PIERCINGS, MOTORCYCLES, ARSON, METHAMPHETAMINES, AND STATE SANCTIONED MURDER.
Losev, Fyoder
DISLIKES: ANYTHING THAT ISN'T RUSSIAN. OR WHITE. OR MALE.
THE BIG GUY IS FYODOR "THE BULL" LOSEV. HE'S THEIR HIGH MUCKITY-MUCK.
THERE HE IS, CHUMMY WITH THE RUSSIAN PRESIDENT. WHICH MEANS THEY ARE CONNECTED AND PROTECTED.

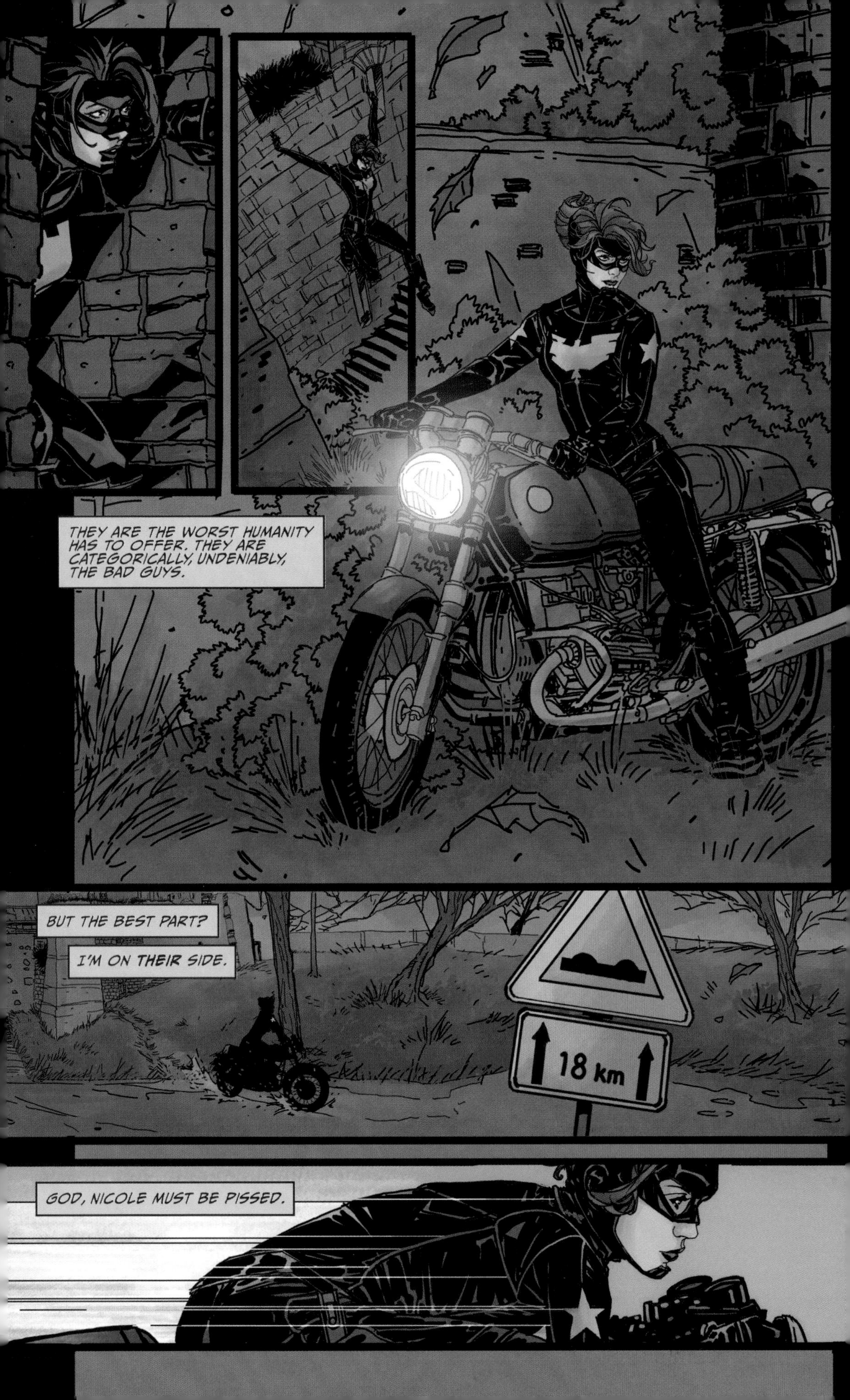
THEY ARE THE WORST HUMANITY HAS TO OFFER. THEY ARE CATEGORICALLY, UNDENIABLY, THE BAD GUYS.
BUT THE BEST PART?
I'M ON THEIR SIDE.
18 km
GOD, NICOLE MUST BE PISSED.

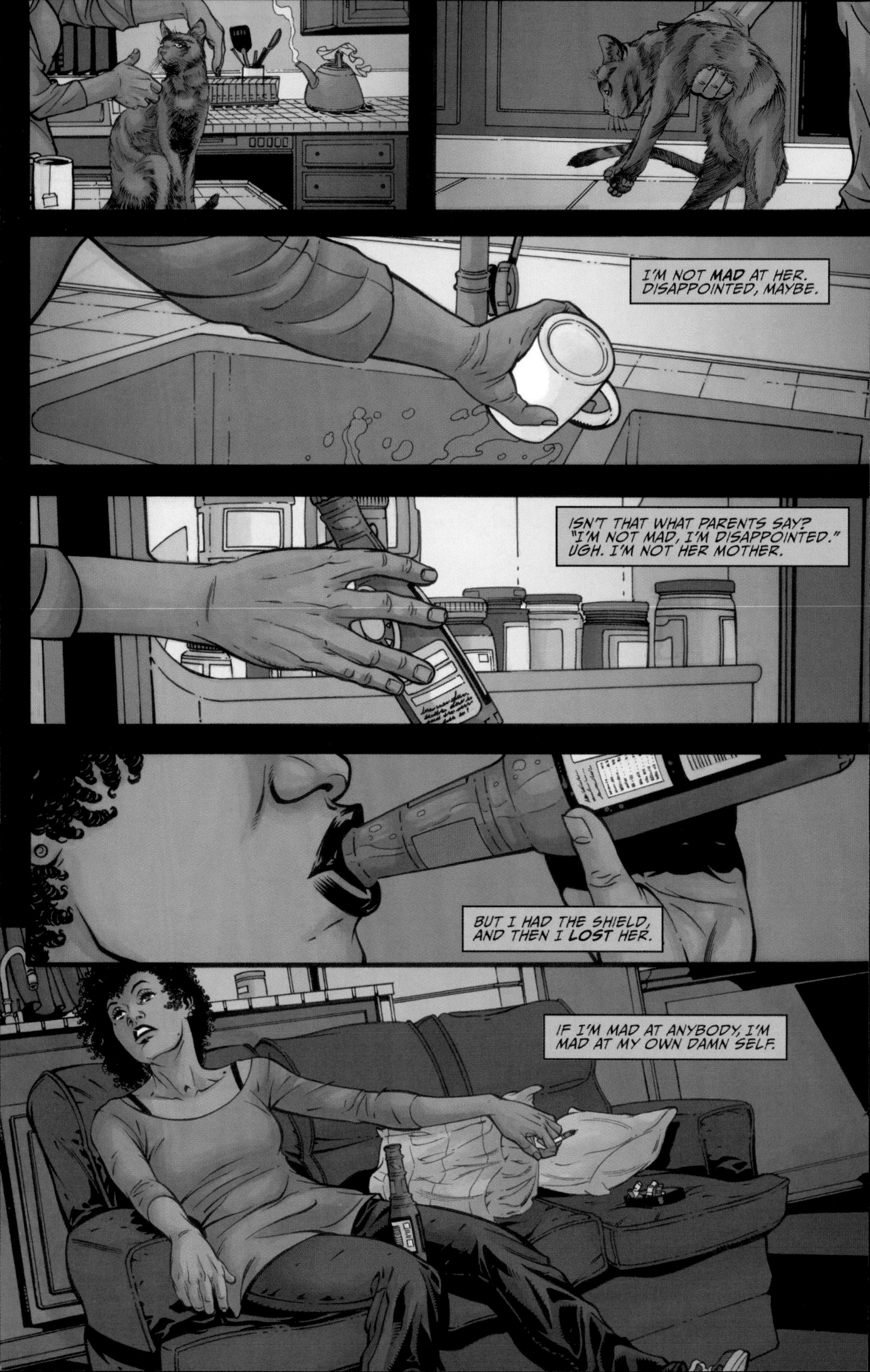
I'M NOT MAD AT HER. DISAPPOINTED, MAYBE.
ISN'T THAT WHAT PARENTS SAY? "I'M NOT MAD, I'M DISAPPOINTED." UGH. I'M NOT HER MOTHER.
BUT I HAD THE SHIELD, AND THEN I LOST HER.
IF I'M MAD AT ANYBODY, I'M MAD AT MY OWN DAMN SELF.

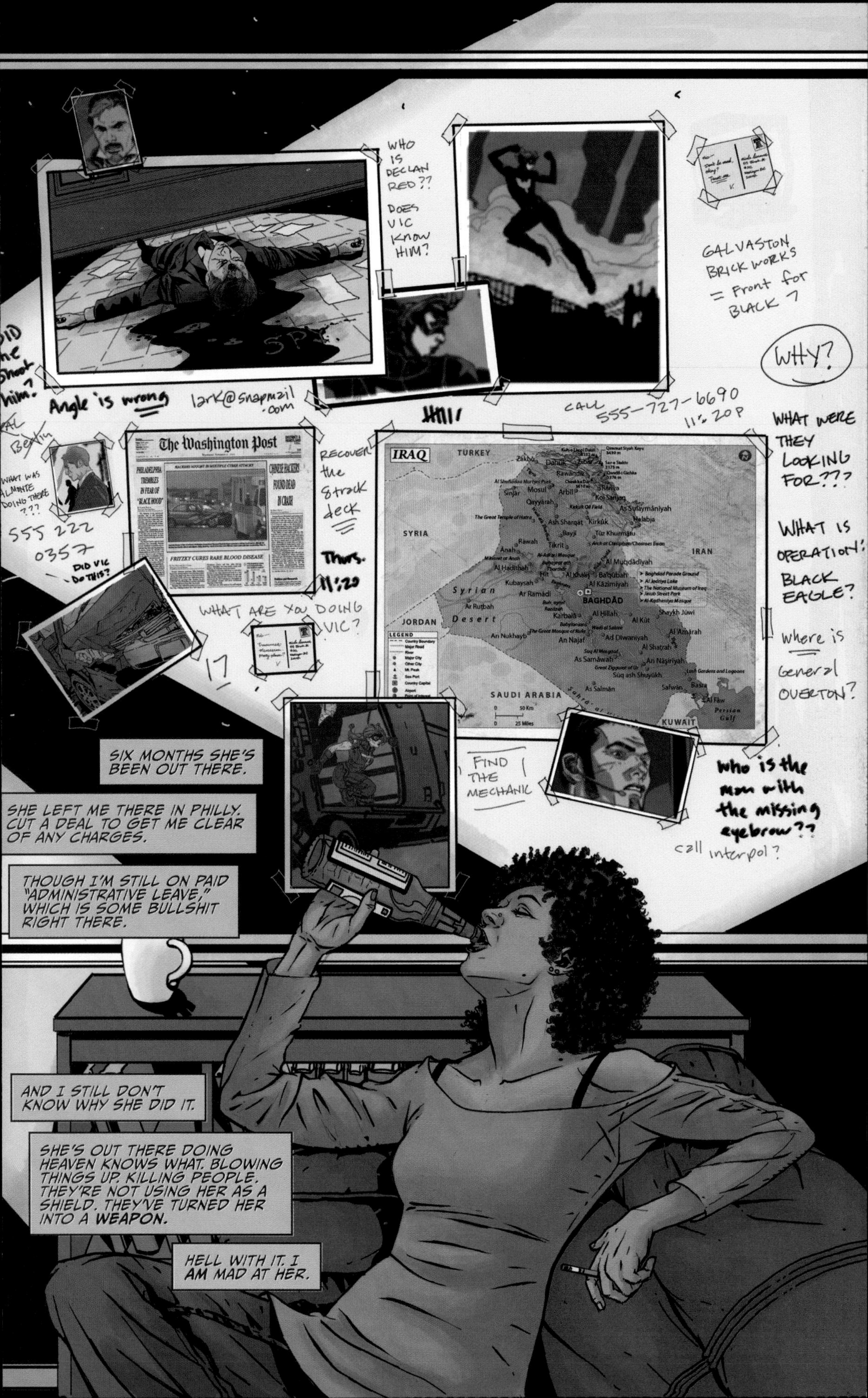

WHO IS DECLAN RED?? DOES VIC KNOW HIM?
GALVASTON BRICK WORKS = Front for BLACK 7
WHY?
DID he shoot him?
Angle is wrong
lark@snapmail.com
CALL 555-727-6690 11:20 P
WHAT WERE THEY LOOKING FOR???
The Washington Post
PHILADELPHIA TREMBLES IN FEAR OF "BLACK HOOD"
CHINESE HACKERS FOUND DEAD IN CRASH
FRITZKY CURES RARE BLOOD DISEASE
WHAT WAS ALMONTE DOING THERE???
555 222 0357
DID VIC DO THIS?
RECOVER the 8track deck
Thurs. 11:20
WHAT ARE YOU DOING VIC?
17
IRAQ
WHAT IS OPERATION: BLACK EAGLE?
where is General OVERTON?
FIND THE MECHANIC
Who is the man with the missing eyebrow??
call interpol?
SIX MONTHS SHE'S BEEN OUT THERE.
SHE LEFT ME THERE IN PHILLY. CUT A DEAL TO GET ME CLEAR OF ANY CHARGES.
THOUGH I'M STILL ON PAID "ADMINISTRATIVE LEAVE," WHICH IS SOME BULLSHIT RIGHT THERE.
AND I STILL DON'T KNOW WHY SHE DID IT.
SHE'S OUT THERE DOING HEAVEN KNOWS WHAT. BLOWING THINGS UP. KILLING PEOPLE. THEY'RE NOT USING HER AS A SHIELD. THEY'VE TURNED HER INTO A WEAPON.
HELL WITH IT. I AM MAD AT HER.

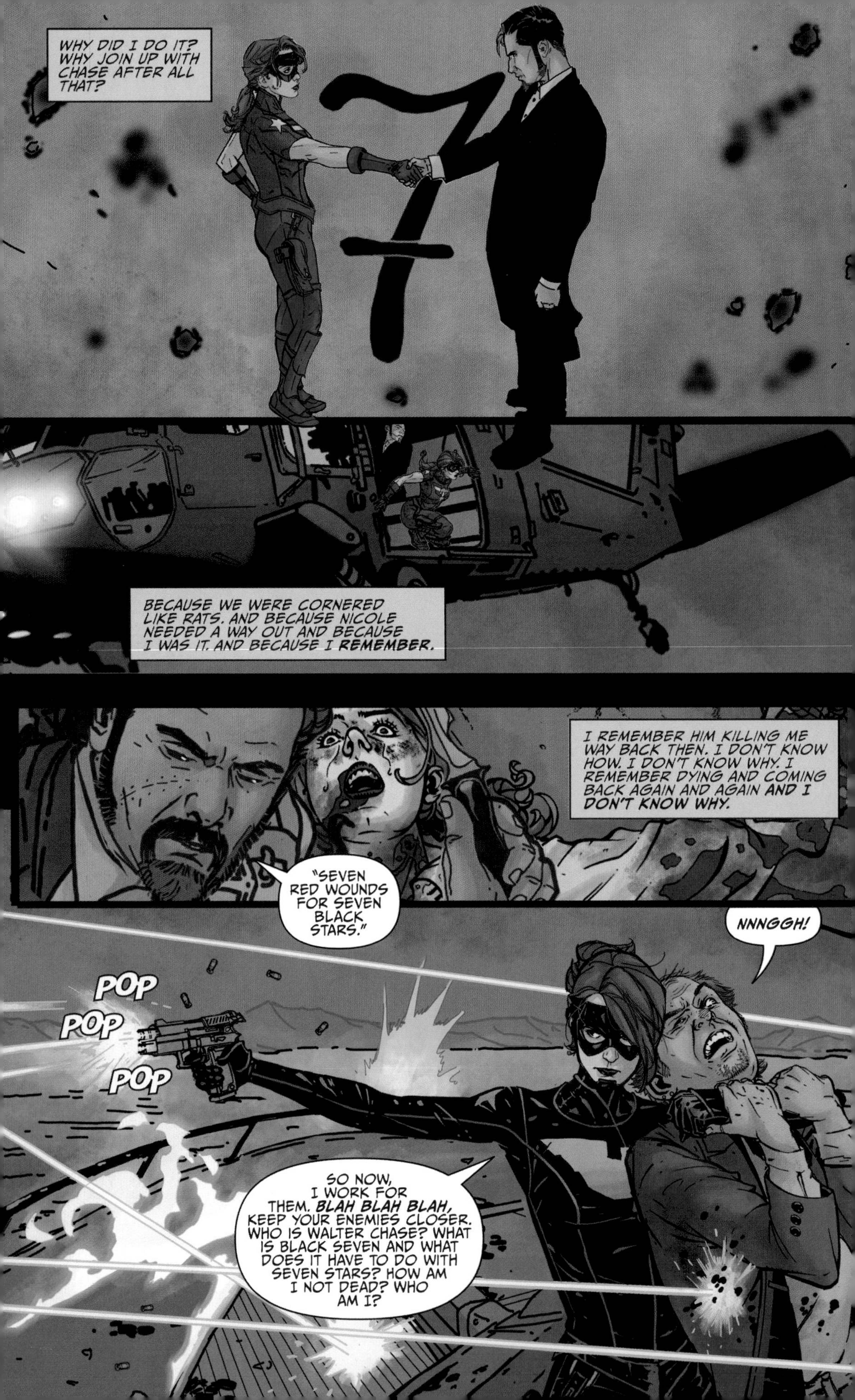
WHY DID I DO IT? WHY JOIN UP WITH CHASE AFTER ALL THAT?
BECAUSE WE WERE CORNERED LIKE RATS. AND BECAUSE NICOLE NEEDED A WAY OUT AND BECAUSE I WAS IT. AND BECAUSE I REMEMBER.
I REMEMBER HIM KILLING ME WAY BACK THEN. I DON'T KNOW HOW. I DON'T KNOW WHY. I REMEMBER DYING AND COMING BACK AGAIN AND AGAIN AND I DON'T KNOW WHY.
"SEVEN RED WOUNDS FOR SEVEN BLACK STARS."
NNNGGH!
POP
POP
POP
SO NOW, I WORK FOR THEM. BLAH BLAH BLAH, KEEP YOUR ENEMIES CLOSER. WHO IS WALTER CHASE? WHAT IS BLACK SEVEN AND WHAT DOES IT HAVE TO DO WITH SEVEN STARS? HOW AM I NOT DEAD? WHO AM I?

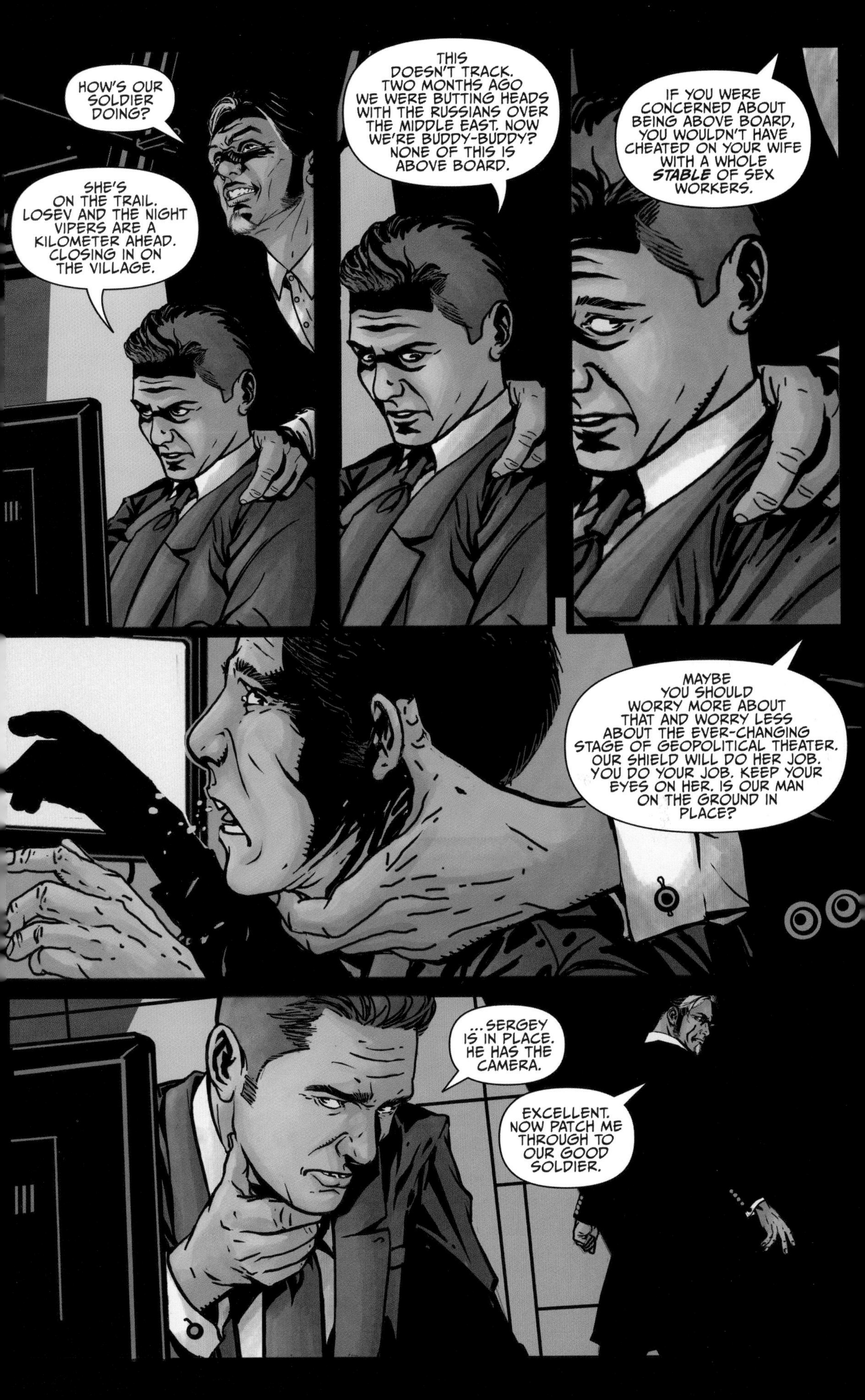
HOW'S OUR SOLDIER DOING?
SHE'S ON THE TRAIL. LOSEV AND THE NIGHT VIPERS ARE A KILOMETER AHEAD. CLOSING IN ON THE VILLAGE.
THIS DOESN'T TRACK. TWO MONTHS AGO WE WERE BUTTING HEADS WITH THE RUSSIANS OVER THE MIDDLE EAST. NOW WE'RE BUDDY-BUDDY? NONE OF THIS IS ABOVE BOARD.
IF YOU WERE CONCERNED ABOUT BEING ABOVE BOARD, YOU WOULDN'T HAVE CHEATED ON YOUR WIFE WITH A WHOLE *STABLE* OF SEX WORKERS.
MAYBE YOU SHOULD WORRY MORE ABOUT THAT AND WORRY LESS ABOUT THE EVER-CHANGING STAGE OF GEOPOLITICAL THEATER. OUR SHIELD WILL DO HER JOB. YOU DO YOUR JOB. KEEP YOUR EYES ON HER. IS OUR MAN ON THE GROUND IN PLACE?
...SERGEY IS IN PLACE. HE HAS THE CAMERA.
EXCELLENT. NOW PATCH ME THROUGH TO OUR GOOD SOLDIER.

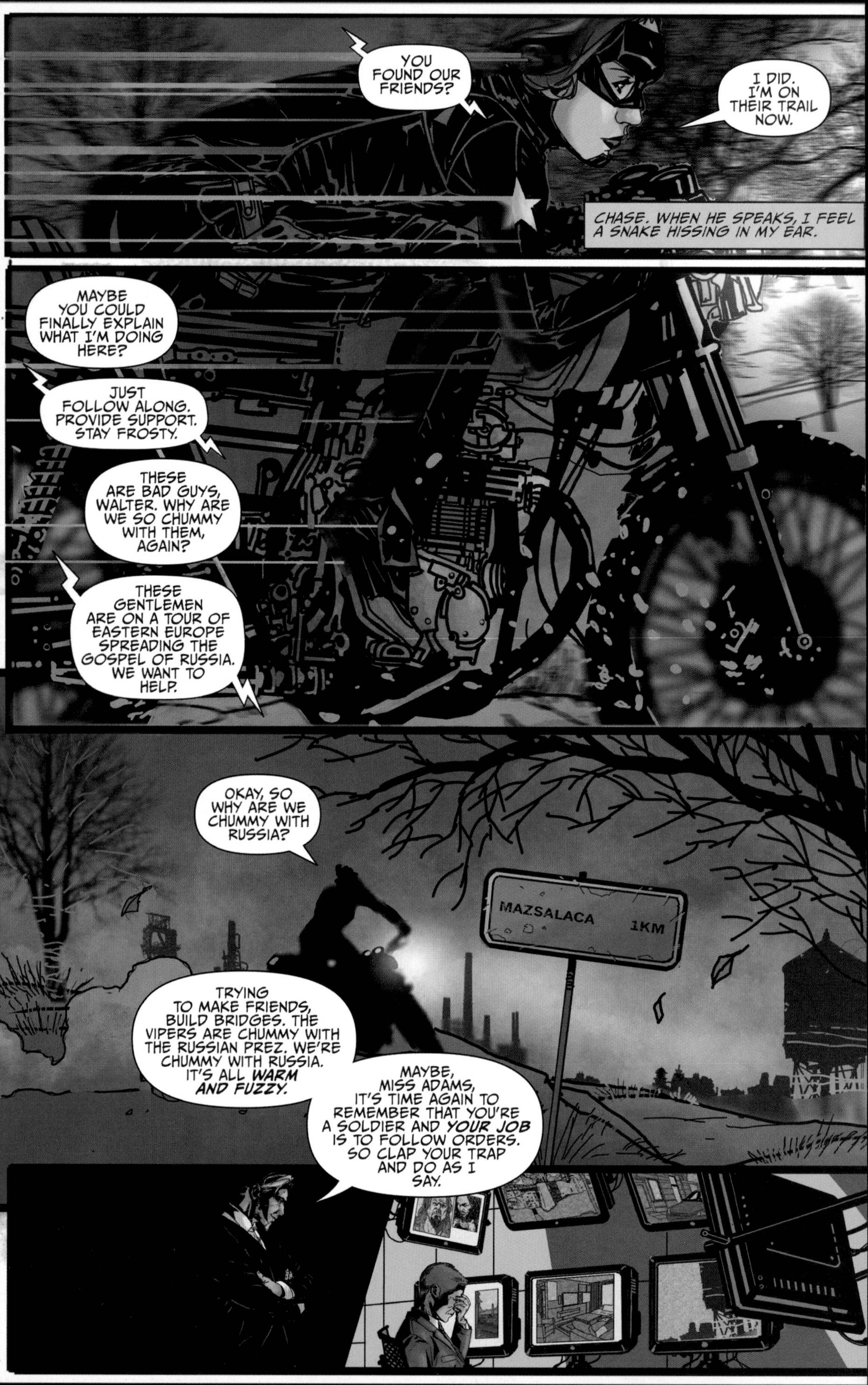
YOU FOUND OUR FRIENDS?
I DID. I'M ON THEIR TRAIL NOW.
CHASE. WHEN HE SPEAKS, I FEEL A SNAKE HISSING IN MY EAR.
MAYBE YOU COULD FINALLY EXPLAIN WHAT I'M DOING HERE?
JUST FOLLOW ALONG. PROVIDE SUPPORT. STAY FROSTY.
THESE ARE BAD GUYS, WALTER. WHY ARE WE SO CHUMMY WITH THEM, AGAIN?
THESE GENTLEMEN ARE ON A TOUR OF EASTERN EUROPE SPREADING THE GOSPEL OF RUSSIA. WE WANT TO HELP.
OKAY, SO WHY ARE WE CHUMMY WITH RUSSIA?
MAZSALACA 1KM
TRYING TO MAKE FRIENDS, BUILD BRIDGES. THE VIPERS ARE CHUMMY WITH THE RUSSIAN PREZ. WE'RE CHUMMY WITH RUSSIA. IT'S ALL *WARM AND FUZZY.*
MAYBE, MISS ADAMS, IT'S TIME AGAIN TO REMEMBER THAT YOU'RE A SOLDIER AND *YOUR JOB* IS TO FOLLOW ORDERS. SO CLAP YOUR TRAP AND DO AS I SAY.

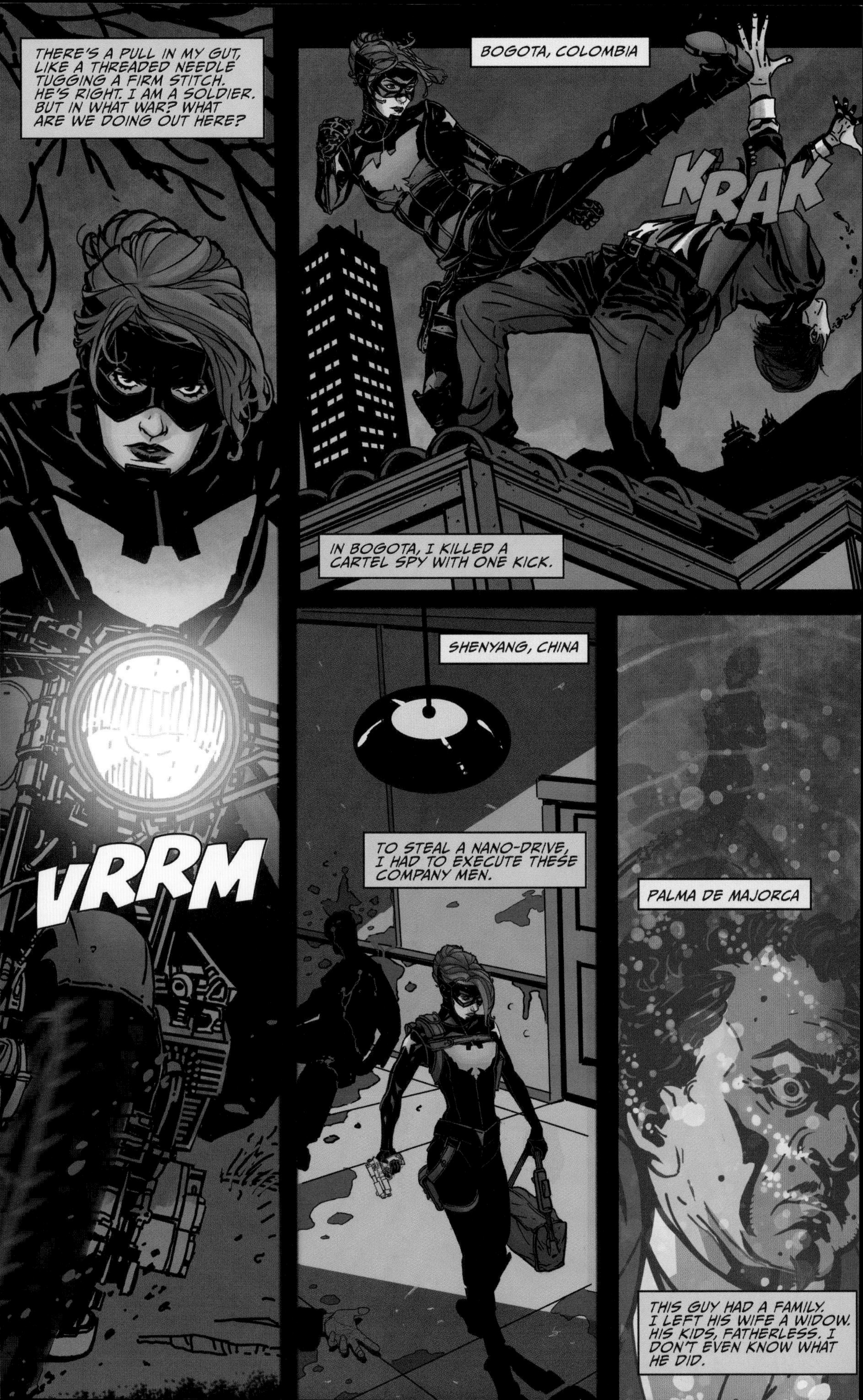
THERE'S A PULL IN MY GUT, LIKE A THREADED NEEDLE TUGGING A FIRM STITCH. HE'S RIGHT. I AM A SOLDIER. BUT IN WHAT WAR? WHAT ARE WE DOING OUT HERE?
VRRM
BOGOTA, COLOMBIA
KRAK
IN BOGOTA, I KILLED A CARTEL SPY WITH ONE KICK.
SHENYANG, CHINA
TO STEAL A NANO-DRIVE, I HAD TO EXECUTE THESE COMPANY MEN.
PALMA DE MAJORCA
THIS GUY HAD A FAMILY. I LEFT HIS WIFE A WIDOW. HIS KIDS, FATHERLESS. I DON'T EVEN KNOW WHAT HE DID.

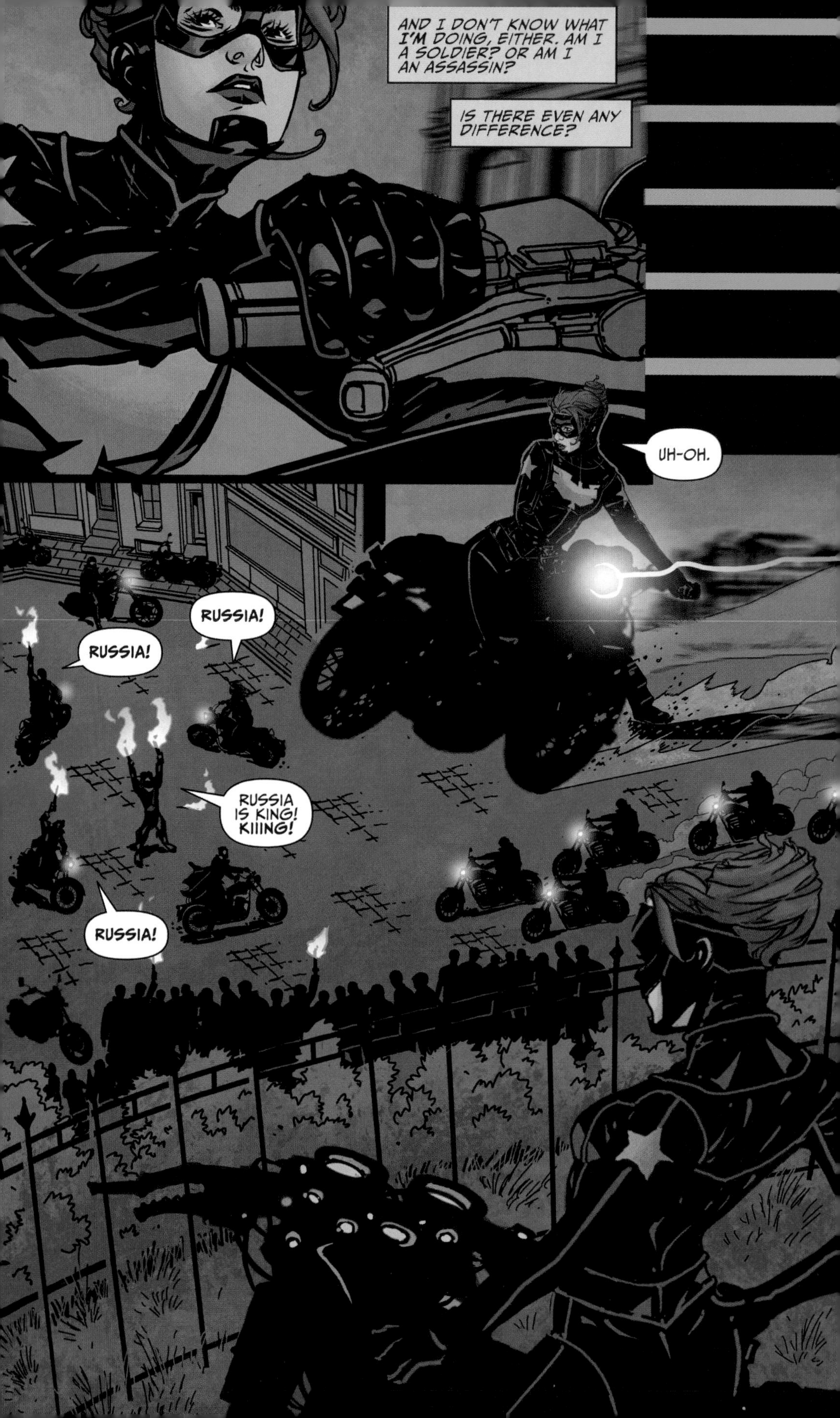
AND I DON'T KNOW WHAT I'M DOING, EITHER. AM I A SOLDIER? OR AM I AN ASSASSIN?
IS THERE EVEN ANY DIFFERENCE?
UH-OH.
RUSSIA!
RUSSIA!
RUSSIA IS KING! KIIING!
RUSSIA!

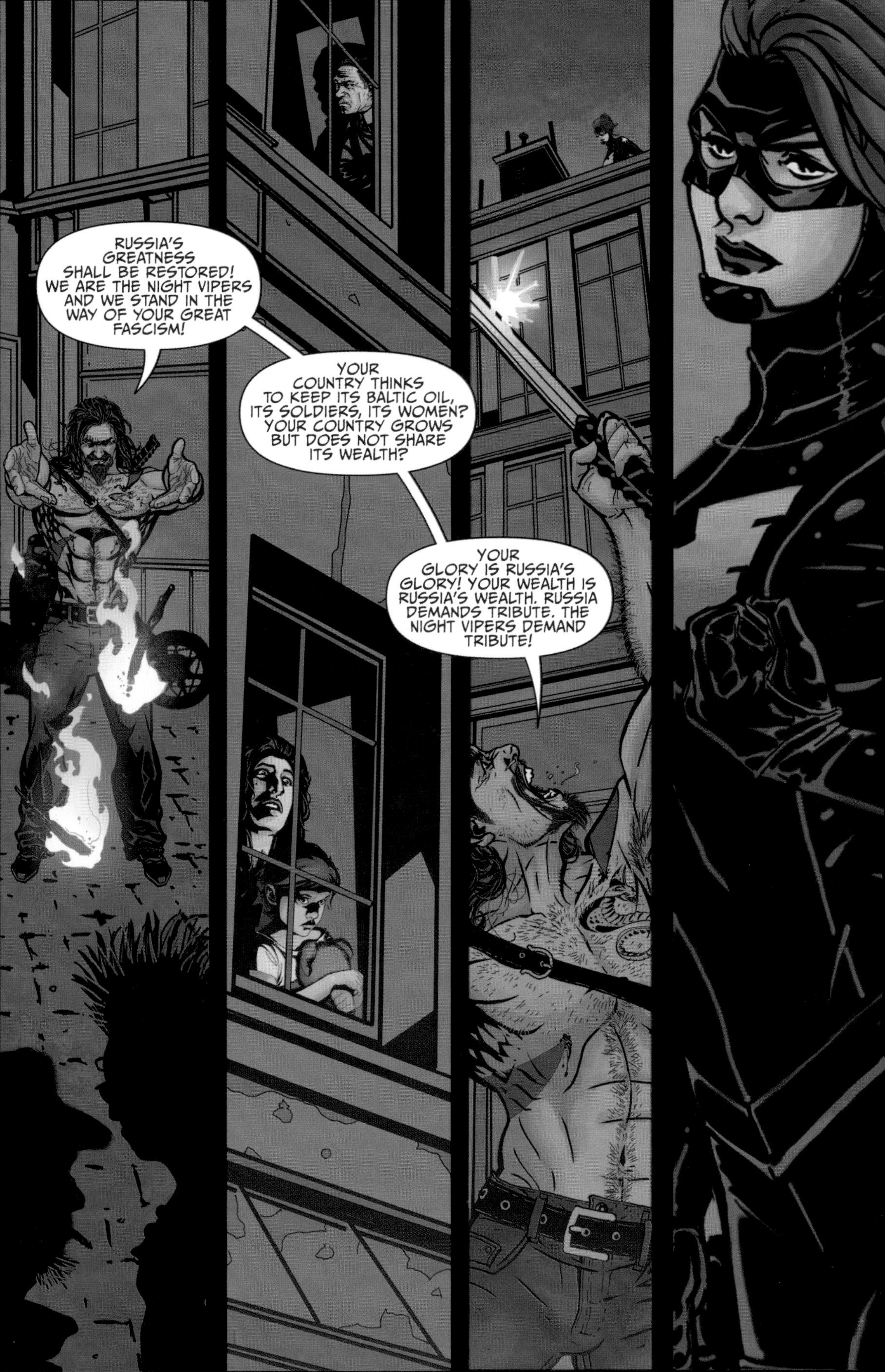
RUSSIA'S GREATNESS SHALL BE RESTORED! WE ARE THE NIGHT VIPERS AND WE STAND IN THE WAY OF YOUR GREAT FASCISM!
YOUR COUNTRY THINKS TO KEEP ITS BALTIC OIL, ITS SOLDIERS, ITS WOMEN? YOUR COUNTRY GROWS BUT DOES NOT SHARE ITS WEALTH?
YOUR GLORY IS RUSSIA'S GLORY! YOUR WEALTH IS RUSSIA'S WEALTH. RUSSIA DEMANDS TRIBUTE. THE NIGHT VIPERS DEMAND TRIBUTE!

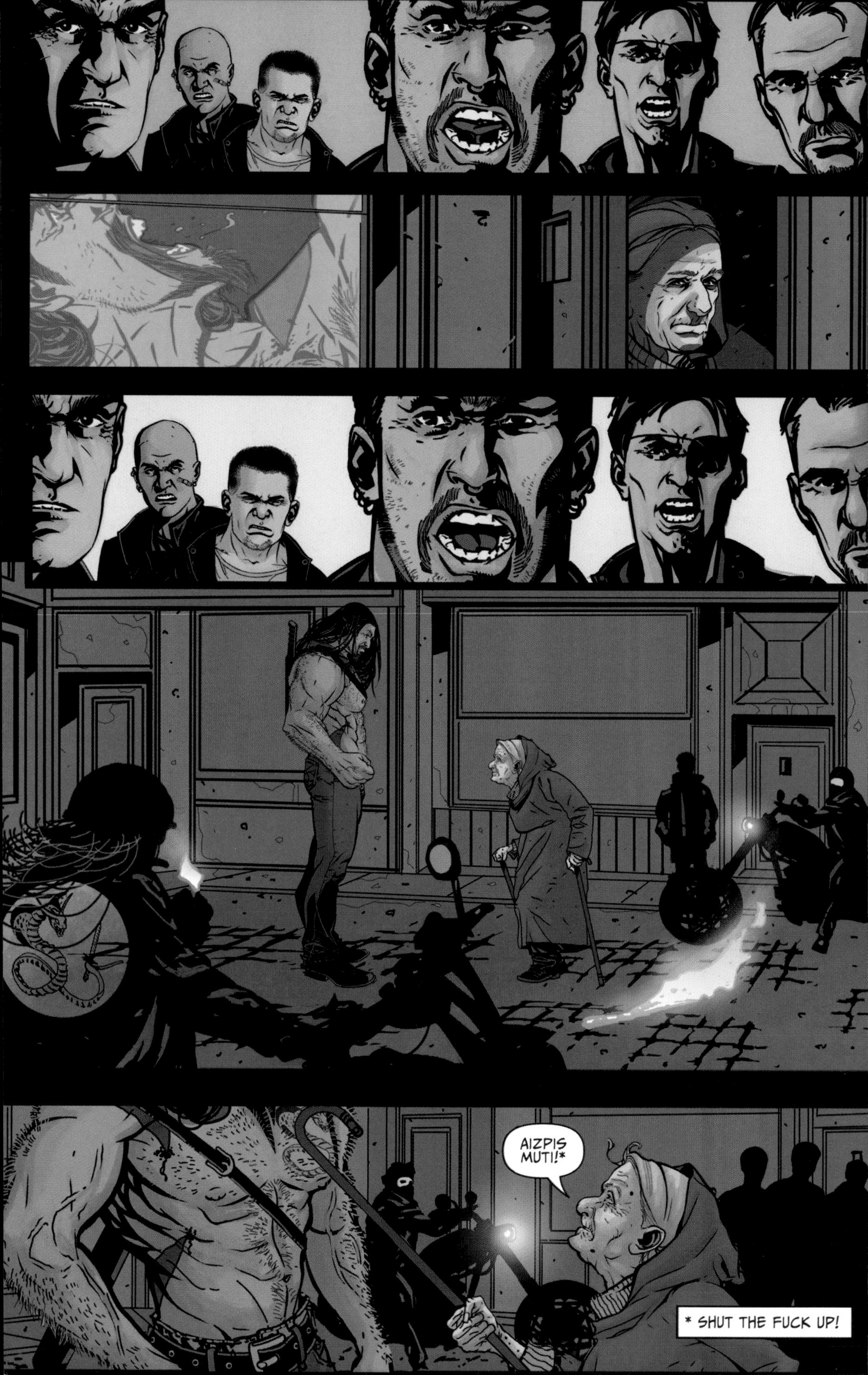
AIZPIS MUTI!*
* SHUT THE FUCK UP!

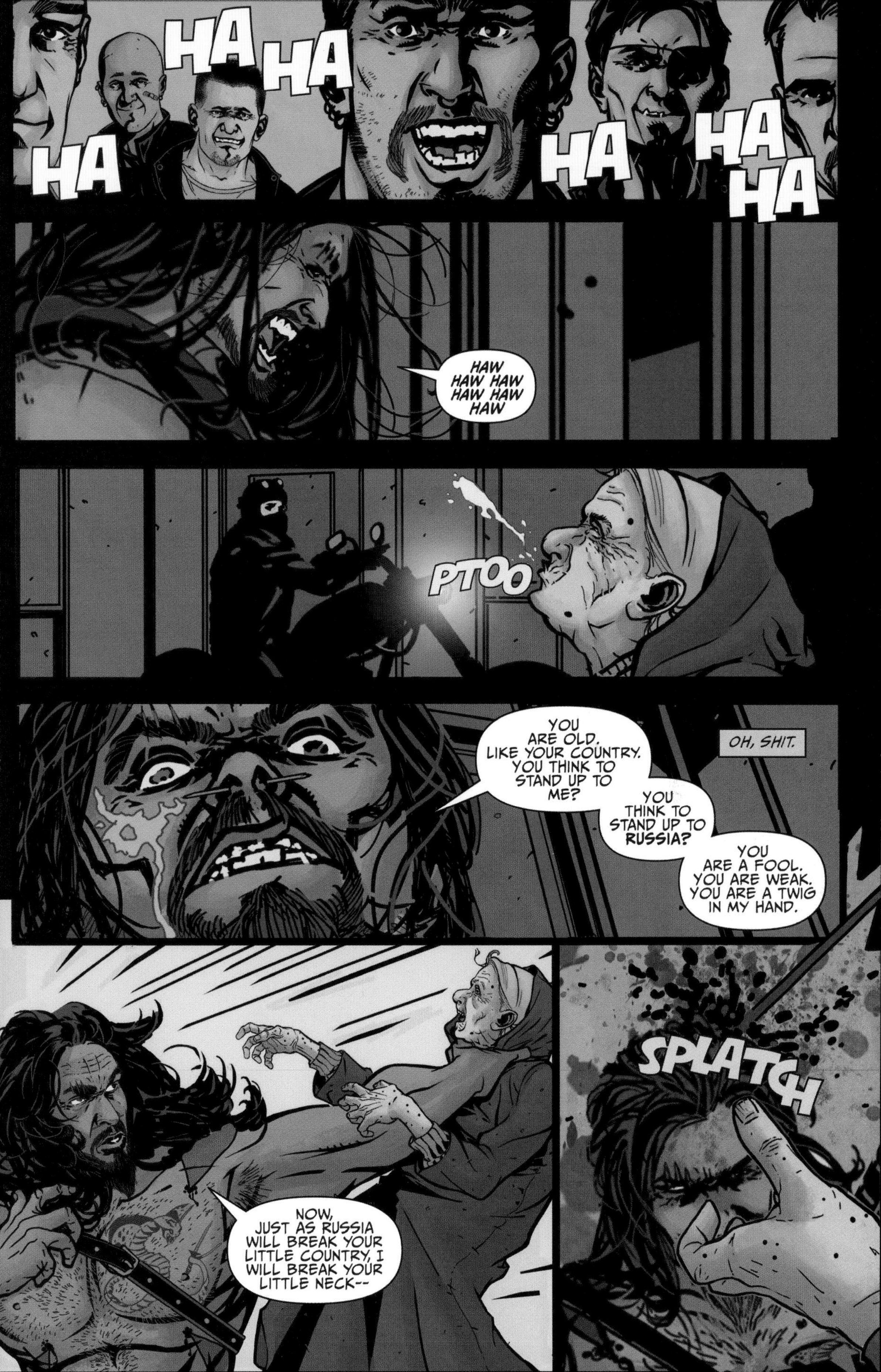
HA
HA
HA
HA
HA
HA
HAW HAW HAW HAW HAW HAW
PTOO
YOU ARE OLD. LIKE YOUR COUNTRY. YOU THINK TO STAND UP TO ME?
YOU THINK TO STAND UP TO RUSSIA?
YOU ARE A FOOL. YOU ARE WEAK. YOU ARE A TWIG IN MY HAND.
OH, SHIT.
NOW, JUST AS RUSSIA WILL BREAK YOUR LITTLE COUNTRY, I WILL BREAK YOUR LITTLE NECK--
SPLATCH

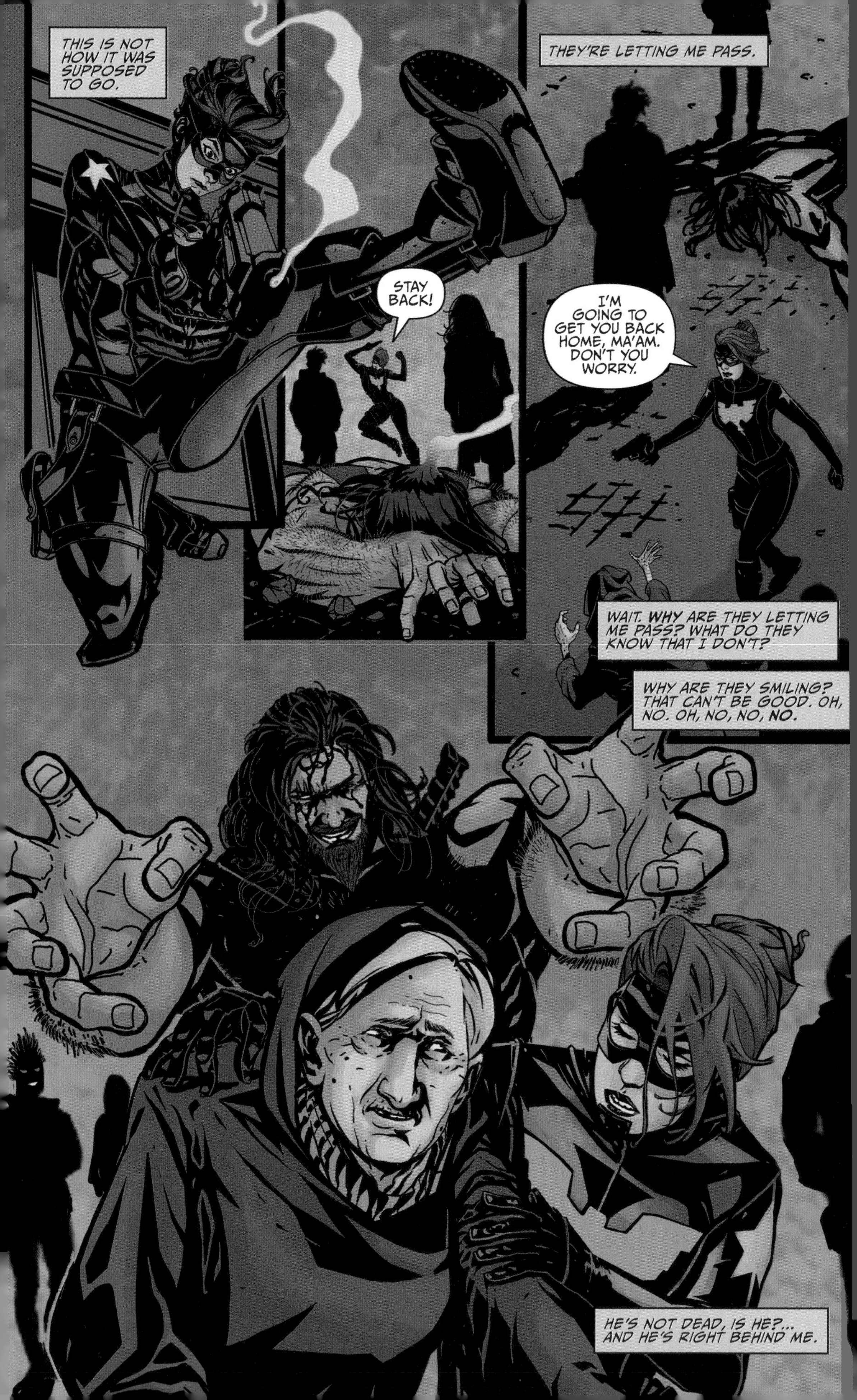
THIS IS NOT HOW IT WAS SUPPOSED TO GO.
STAY BACK!
THEY'RE LETTING ME PASS.
I'M GOING TO GET YOU BACK HOME, MA'AM. DON'T YOU WORRY.
WAIT. WHY ARE THEY LETTING ME PASS? WHAT DO THEY KNOW THAT I DON'T?
WHY ARE THEY SMILING? THAT CAN'T BE GOOD. OH, NO. OH, NO, NO, NO.
HE'S NOT DEAD, IS HE?... AND HE'S RIGHT BEHIND ME.

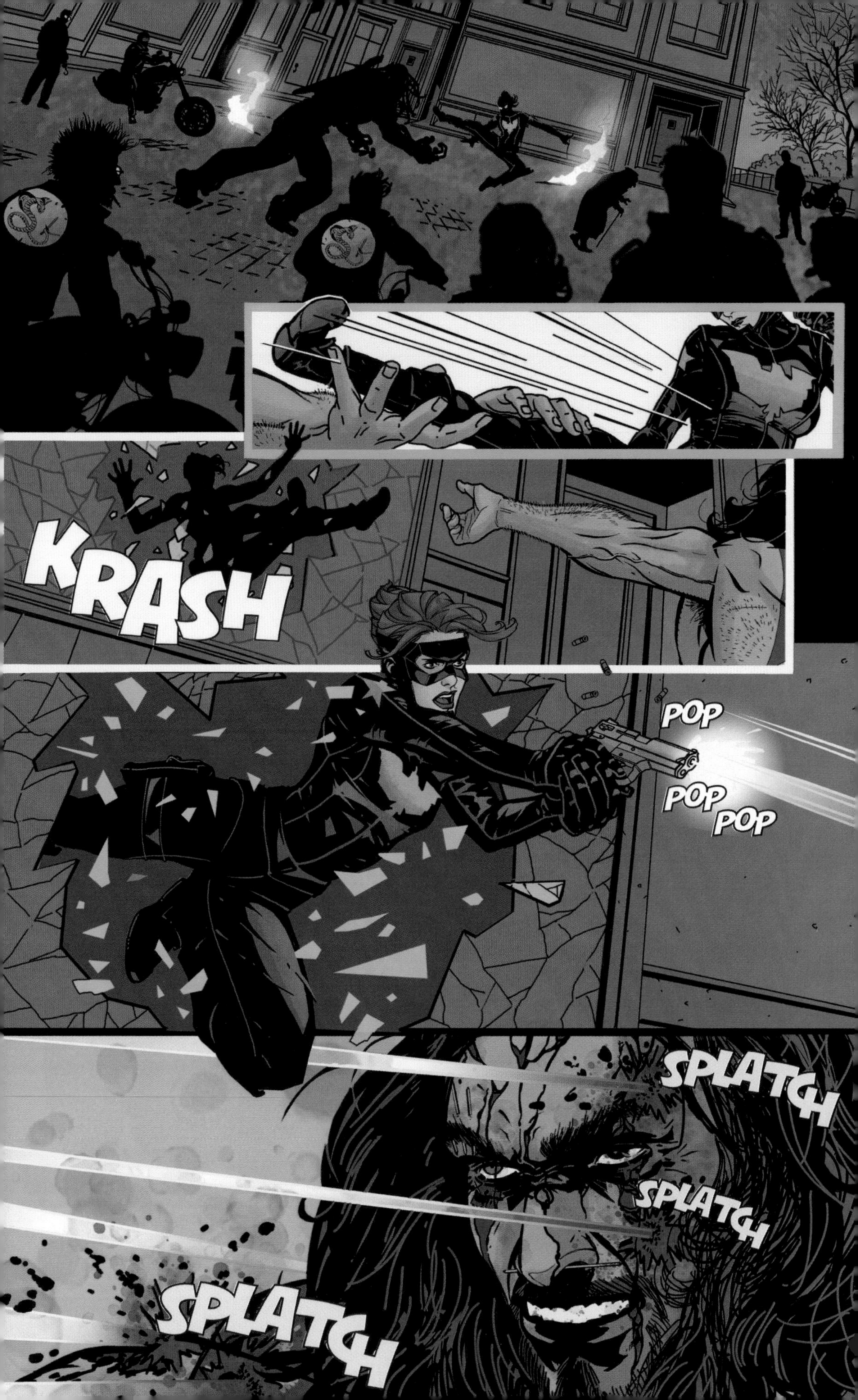
KRASH
POP
POP
POP
SPLATCH
SPLATCH
SPLATCH

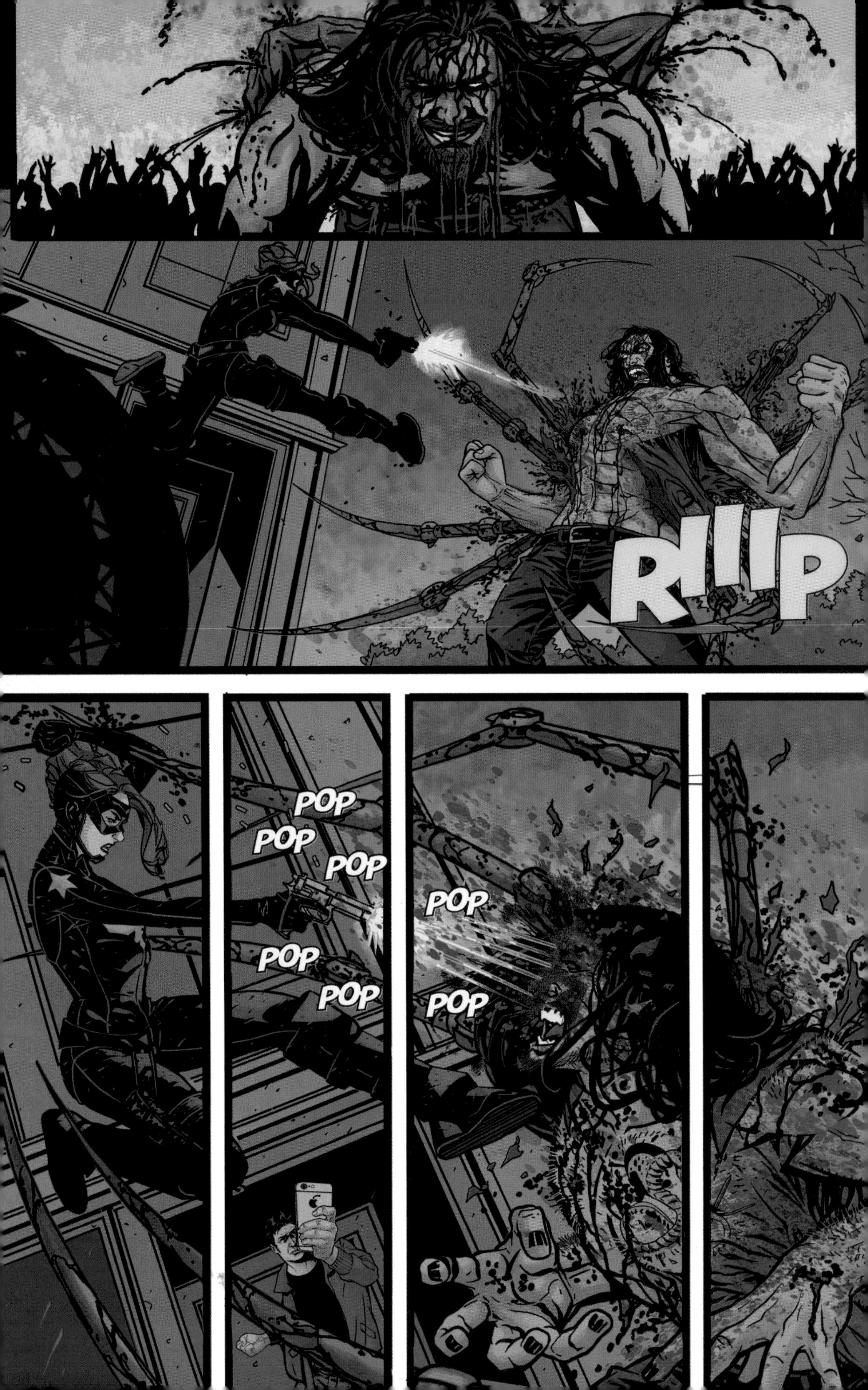
RIIIP
POP
POP
POP
POP
POP
POP
POP

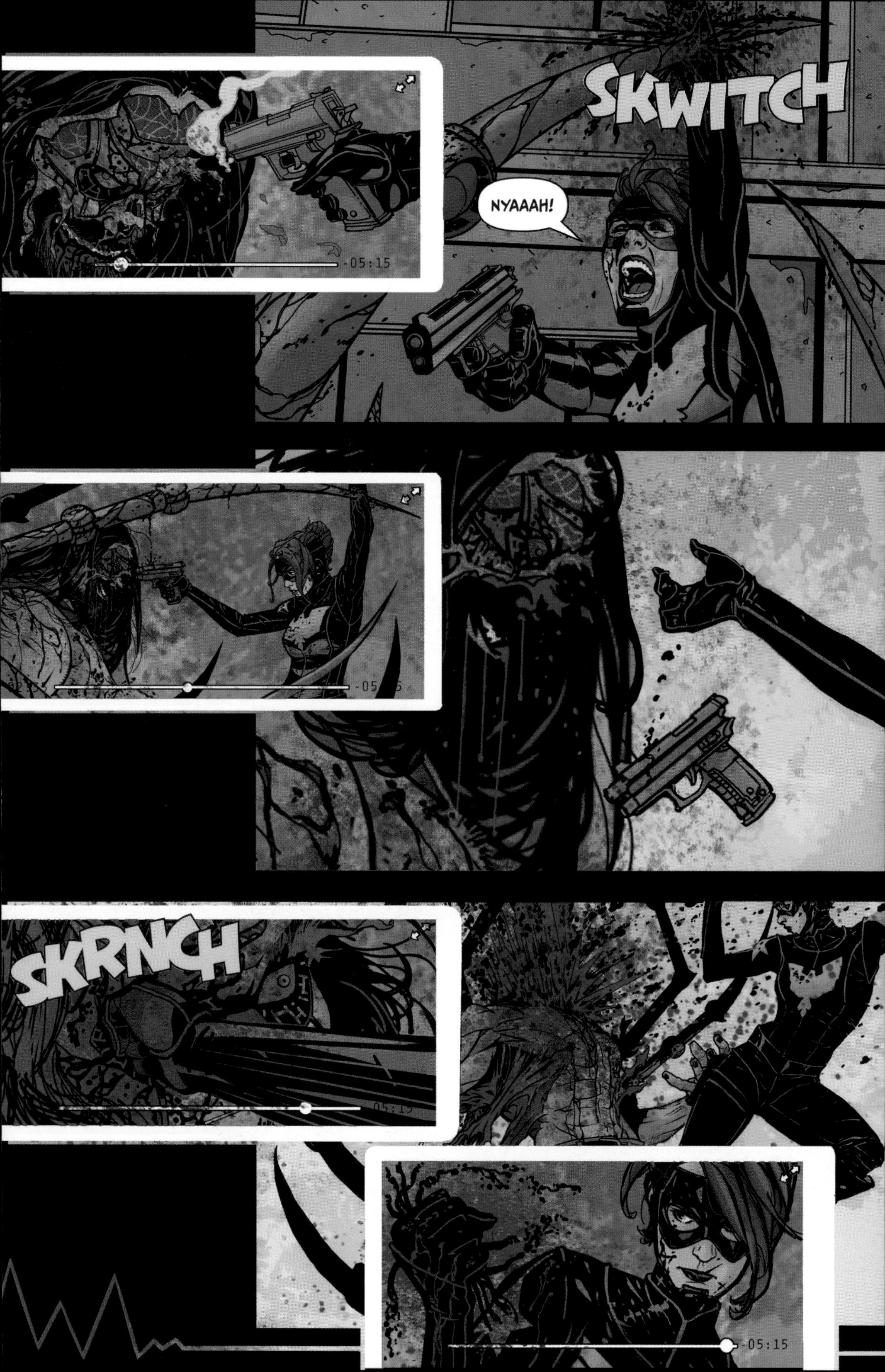

-05:15
SKWITCH
NYAAAH!
-05:15
SKRNCH
-05:15
-05:15

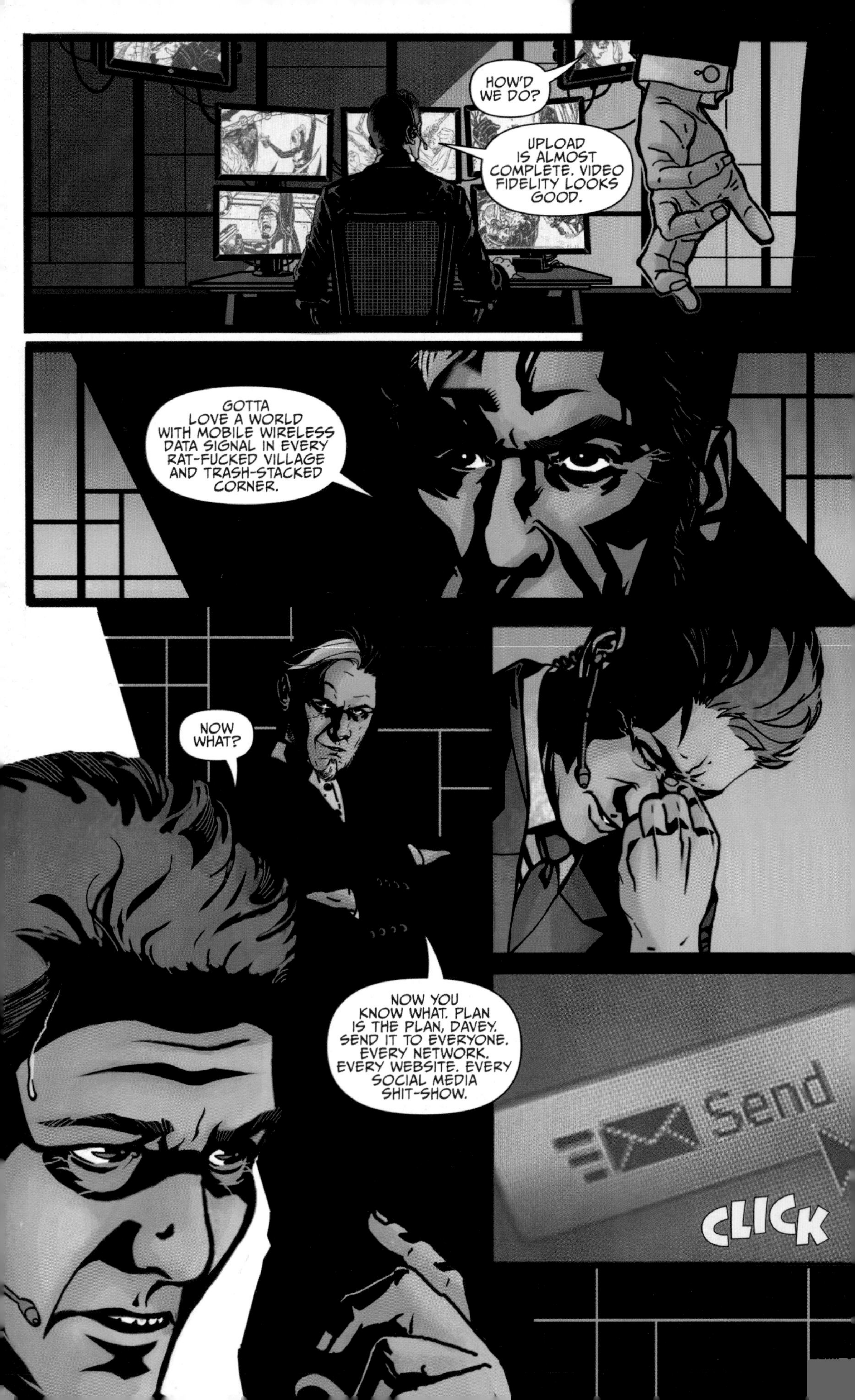
HOW'D WE DO?
UPLOAD IS ALMOST COMPLETE. VIDEO FIDELITY LOOKS GOOD.
GOTTA LOVE A WORLD WITH MOBILE WIRELESS DATA SIGNAL IN EVERY RAT-FUCKED VILLAGE AND TRASH-STACKED CORNER.
NOW WHAT?
NOW YOU KNOW WHAT. PLAN IS THE PLAN, DAVEY. SEND IT TO EVERYONE. EVERY NETWORK. EVERY WEBSITE. EVERY SOCIAL MEDIA SHIT-SHOW.
Send
CLICK

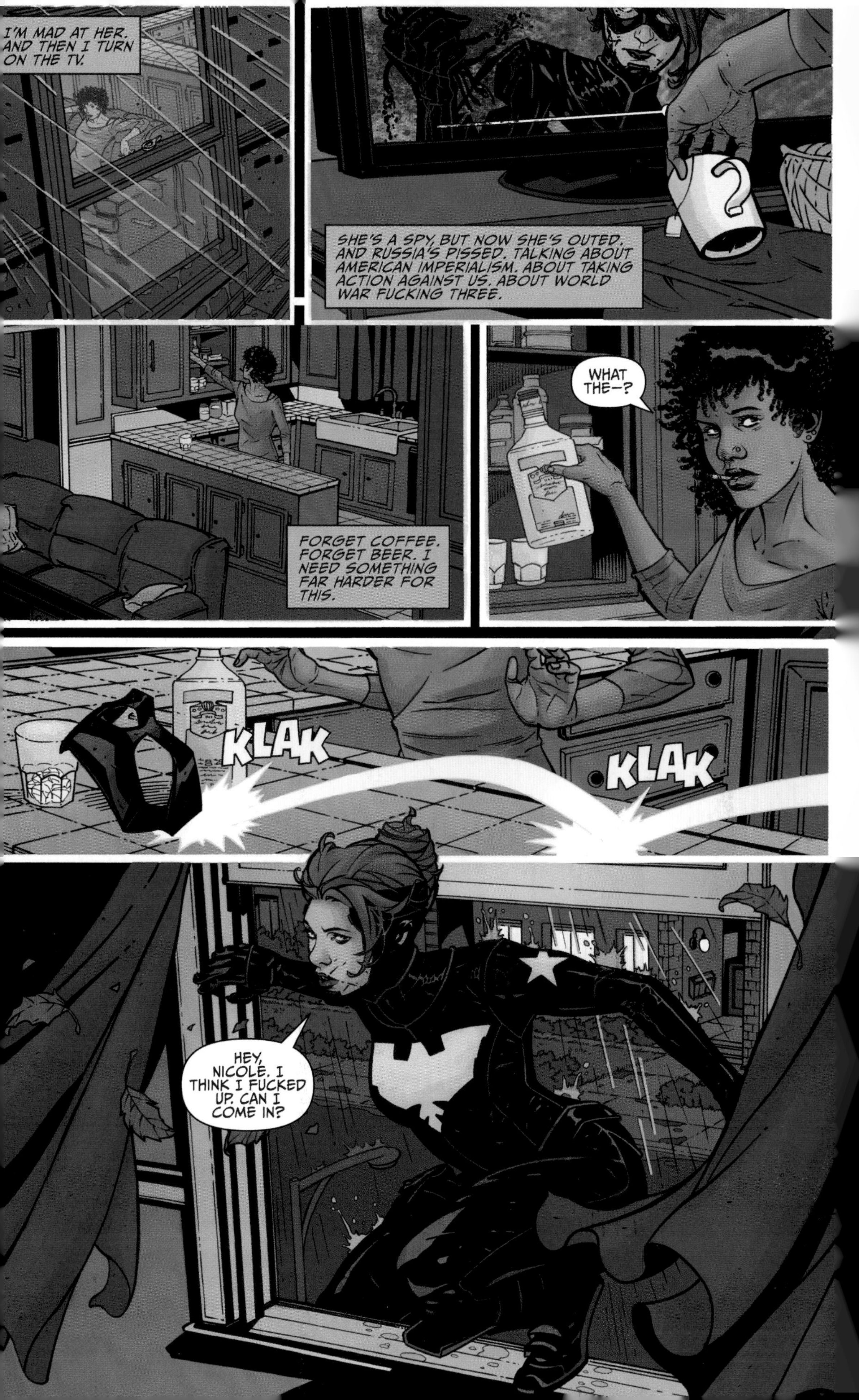
I'M MAD AT HER. AND THEN I TURN ON THE TV.
SHE'S A SPY, BUT NOW SHE'S OUTED. AND RUSSIA'S PISSED. TALKING ABOUT AMERICAN IMPERIALISM. ABOUT TAKING ACTION AGAINST US. ABOUT WORLD WAR FUCKING THREE.
FORGET COFFEE. FORGET BEER. I NEED SOMETHING FAR HARDER FOR THIS.
WHAT THE—?
KLAK
KLAK
HEY, NICOLE. I THINK I FUCKED UP. CAN I COME IN?

ISSUE FOUR

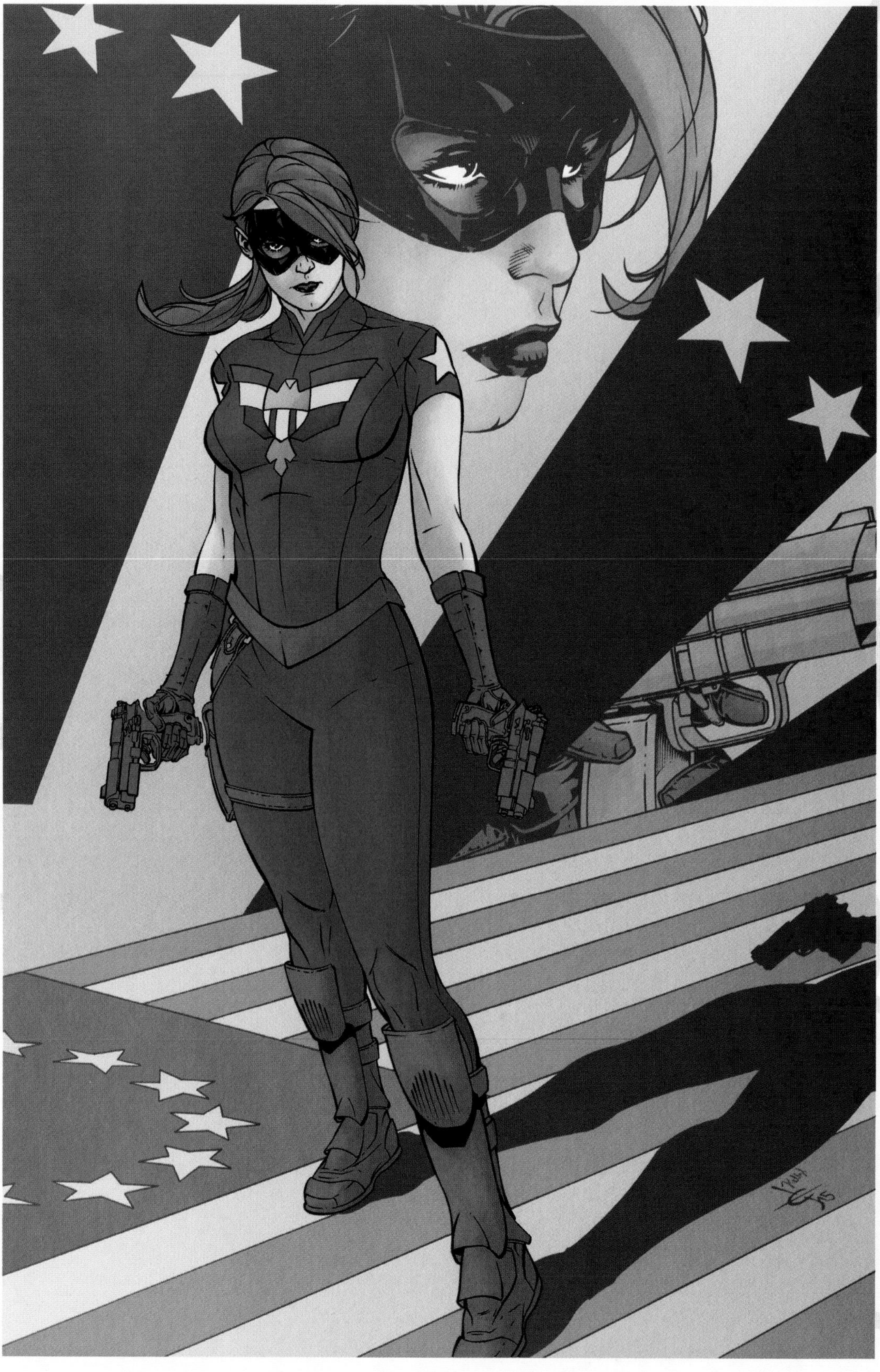

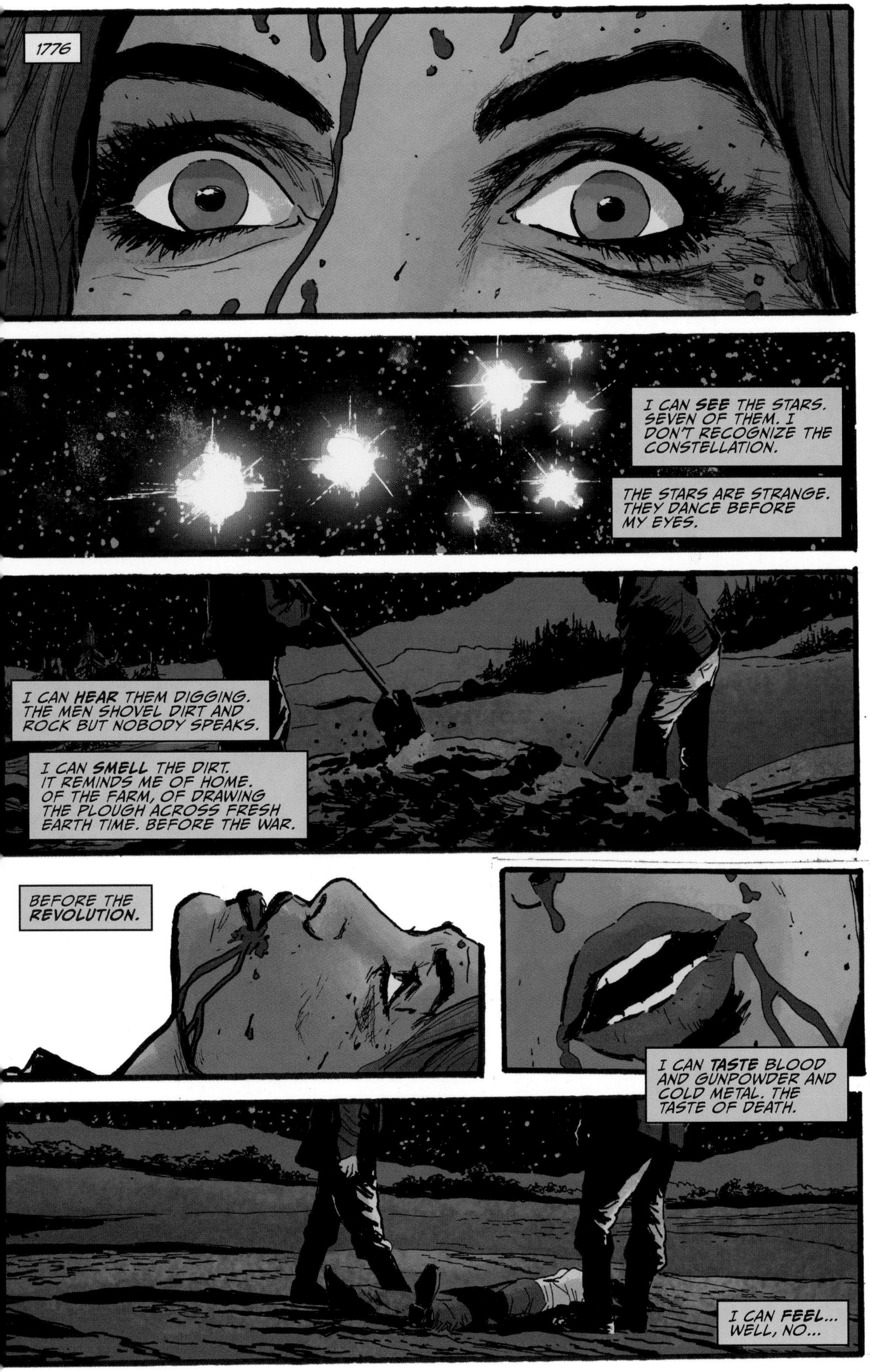
1776
I CAN SEE THE STARS. SEVEN OF THEM. I DON'T RECOGNIZE THE CONSTELLATION.
THE STARS ARE STRANGE. THEY DANCE BEFORE MY EYES.
I CAN HEAR THEM DIGGING. THE MEN SHOVEL DIRT AND ROCK BUT NOBODY SPEAKS.
I CAN SMELL THE DIRT. IT REMINDS ME OF HOME. OF THE FARM, OF DRAWING THE PLOUGH ACROSS FRESH EARTH TIME. BEFORE THE WAR.
BEFORE THE REVOLUTION.
I CAN TASTE BLOOD AND GUNPOWDER AND COLD METAL. THE TASTE OF DEATH.
I CAN FEEL... WELL, NO...

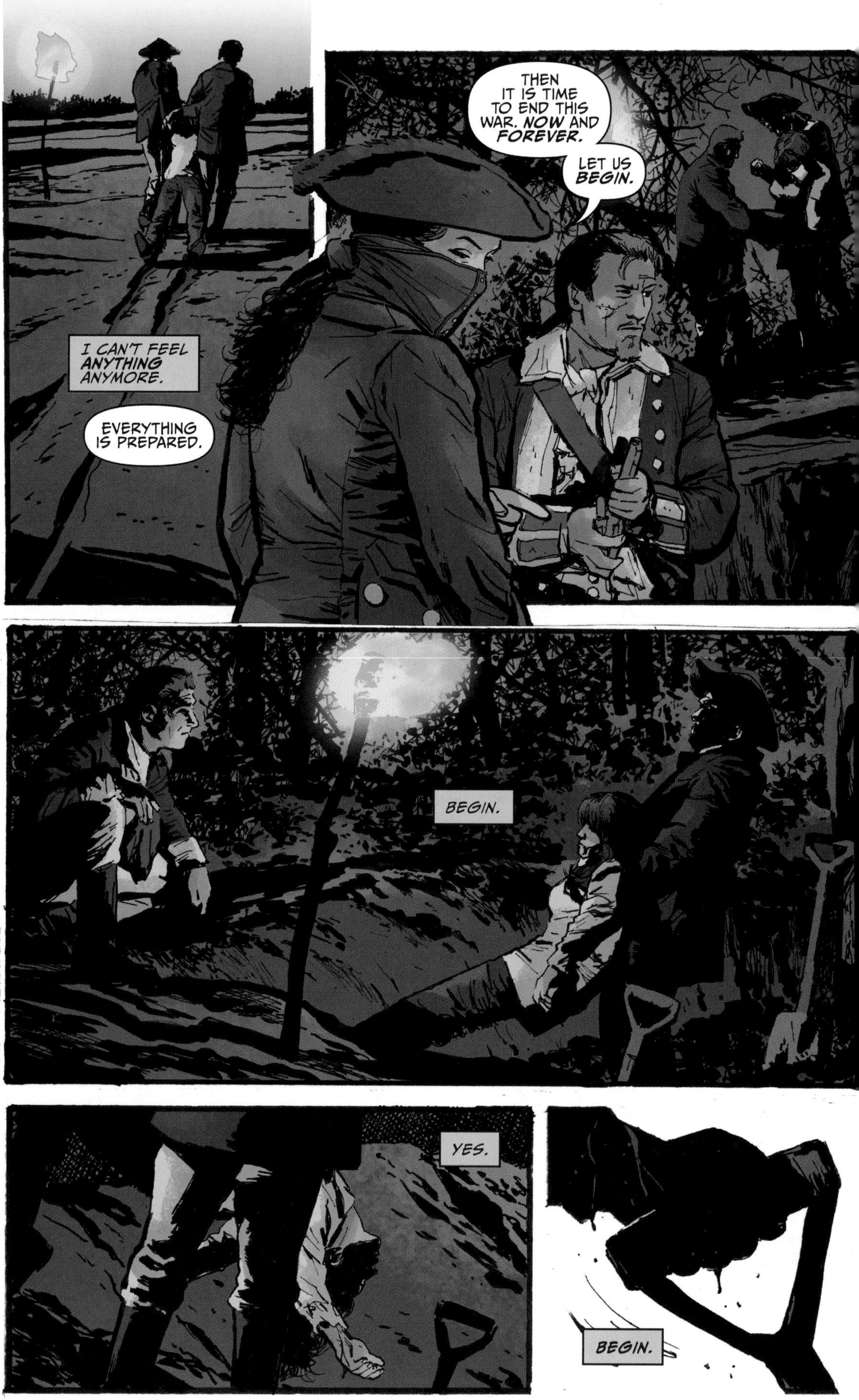
I CAN'T FEEL ANYTHING ANYMORE.
EVERYTHING IS PREPARED.
THEN IT IS TIME TO END THIS WAR. NOW AND FOREVER.
LET US BEGIN.
BEGIN.
YES.
BEGIN.

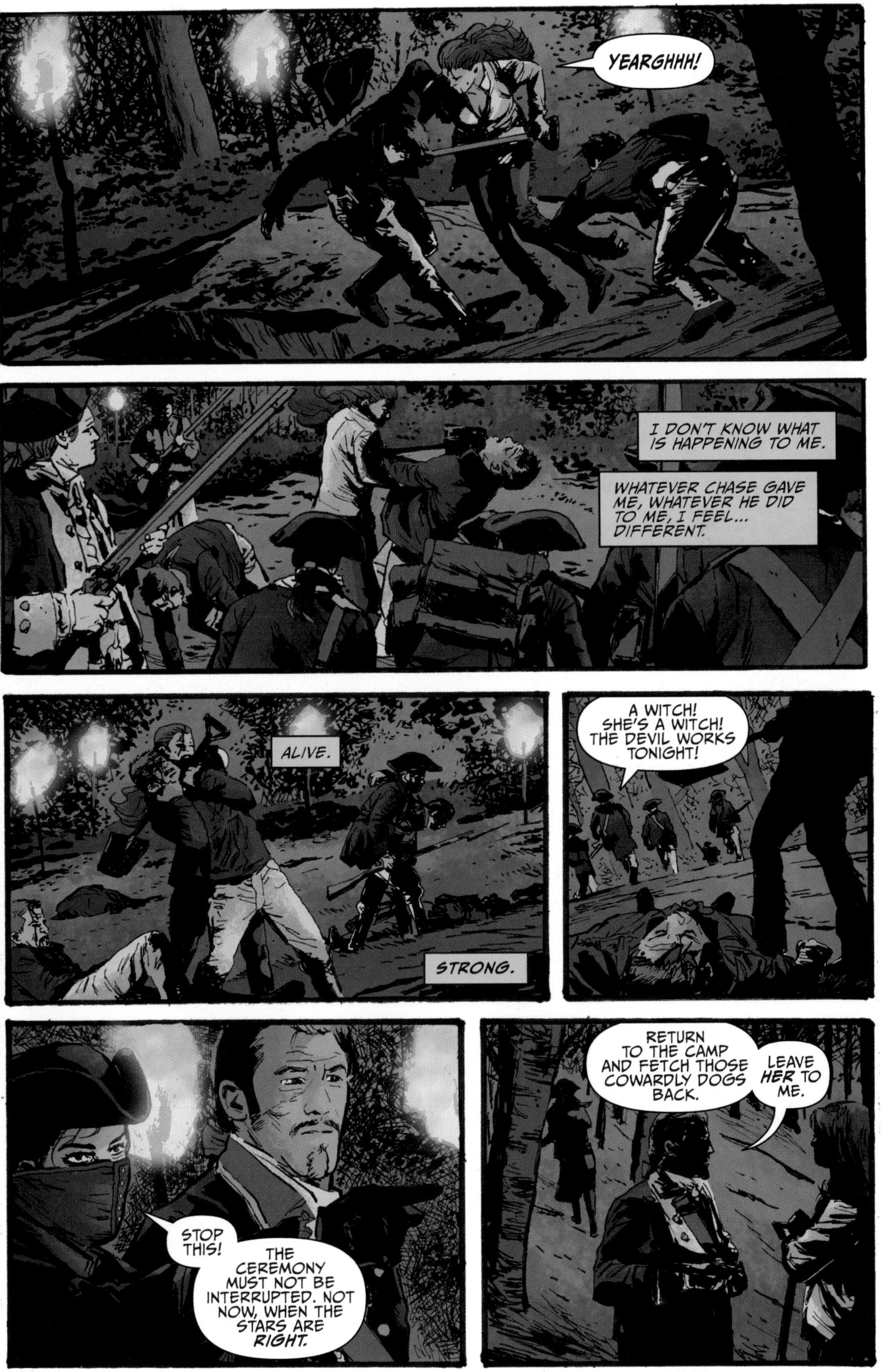
YEARGHHH!
I DON'T KNOW WHAT IS HAPPENING TO ME.
WHATEVER CHASE GAVE ME, WHATEVER HE DID TO ME, I FEEL... DIFFERENT.
ALIVE.
STRONG.
A WITCH! SHE'S A WITCH! THE DEVIL WORKS TONIGHT!
STOP THIS!
THE CEREMONY MUST NOT BE INTERRUPTED. NOT NOW, WHEN THE STARS ARE *RIGHT.*
RETURN TO THE CAMP AND FETCH THOSE COWARDLY DOGS BACK.
LEAVE *HER* TO ME.

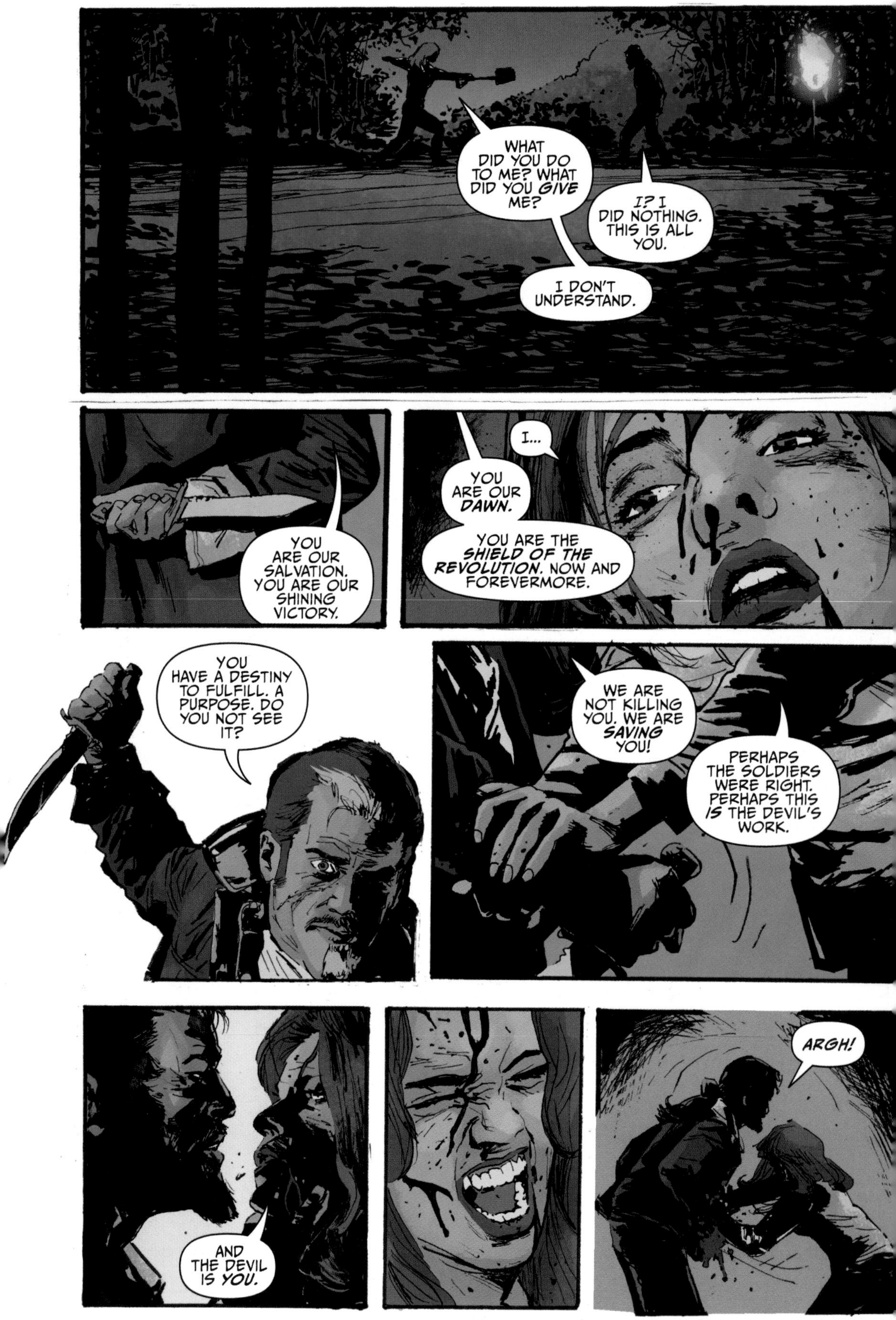
WHAT DID YOU DO TO ME? WHAT DID YOU *GIVE* ME?
I? I DID NOTHING. THIS IS ALL YOU.
I DON'T UNDERSTAND.
YOU ARE OUR SALVATION. YOU ARE OUR SHINING VICTORY.
I...
YOU ARE OUR *DAWN.*
YOU ARE THE *SHIELD OF THE REVOLUTION.* NOW AND FOREVERMORE.
YOU HAVE A DESTINY TO FULFILL. A PURPOSE. DO YOU NOT SEE IT?
WE ARE NOT KILLING YOU. WE ARE *SAVING* YOU!
PERHAPS THE SOLDIERS WERE RIGHT. PERHAPS THIS *IS* THE DEVIL'S WORK.
AND THE DEVIL IS *YOU.*
ARGH!

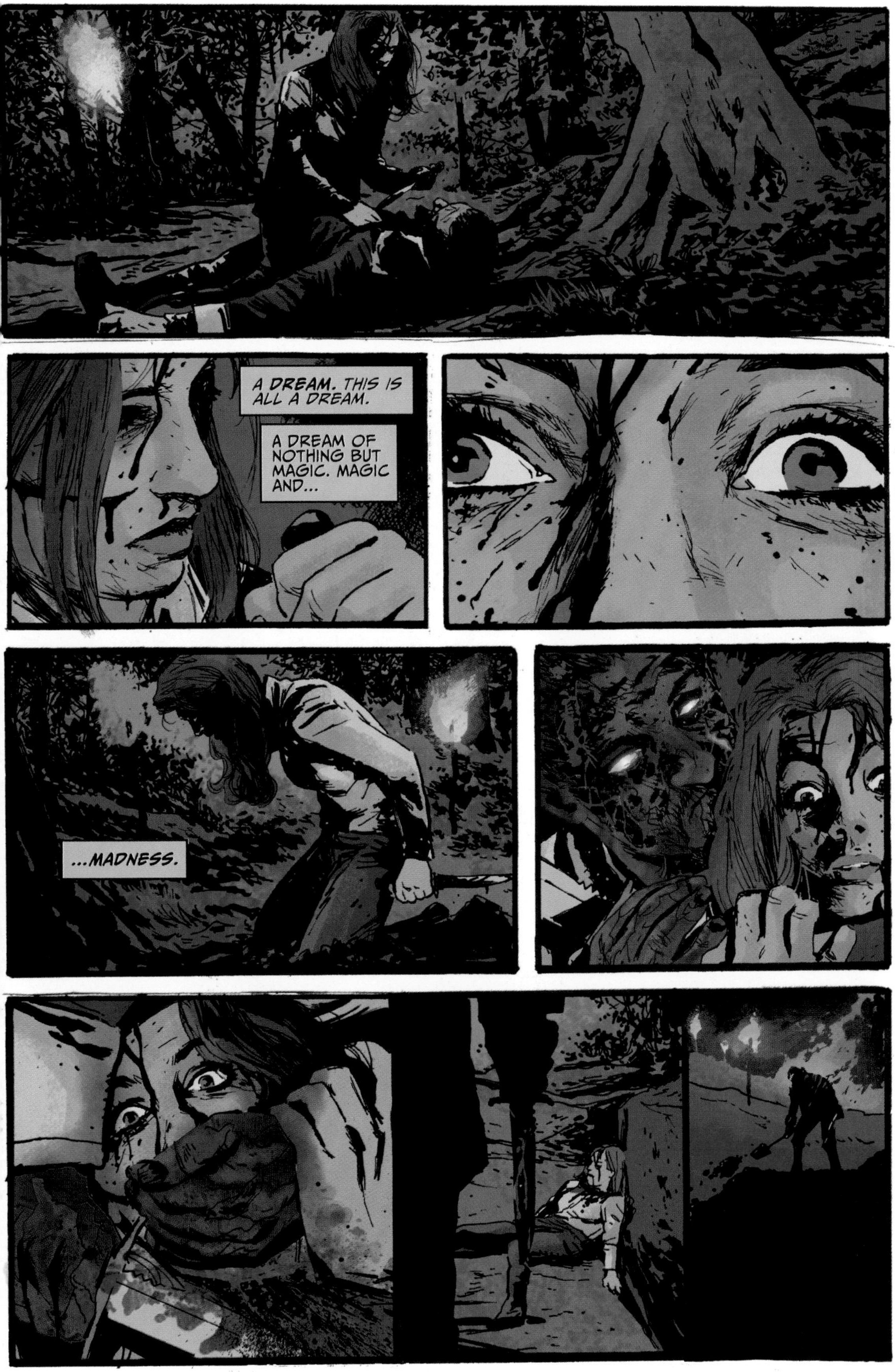
A DREAM. THIS IS ALL A DREAM.
A DREAM OF NOTHING BUT MAGIC. MAGIC AND...
...MADNESS.

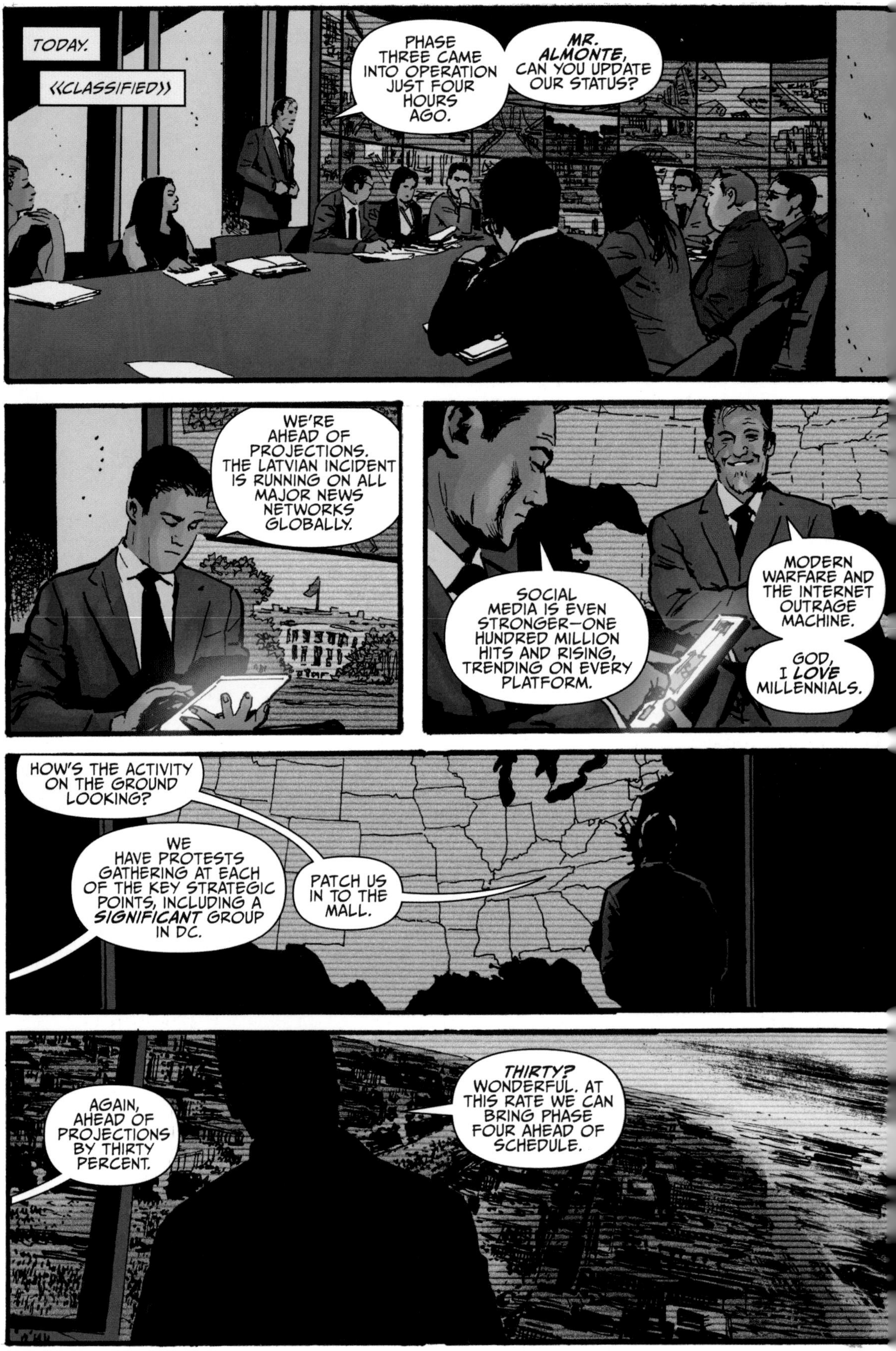
TODAY.
<<CLASSIFIED>>
MR. ALMONTE, CAN YOU UPDATE OUR STATUS?
PHASE THREE CAME INTO OPERATION JUST FOUR HOURS AGO.
WE'RE AHEAD OF PROJECTIONS. THE LATVIAN INCIDENT IS RUNNING ON ALL MAJOR NEWS NETWORKS GLOBALLY.
SOCIAL MEDIA IS EVEN STRONGER—ONE HUNDRED MILLION HITS AND RISING, TRENDING ON EVERY PLATFORM.
MODERN WARFARE AND THE INTERNET OUTRAGE MACHINE.
GOD, I LOVE MILLENNIALS.
HOW'S THE ACTIVITY ON THE GROUND LOOKING?
WE HAVE PROTESTS GATHERING AT EACH OF THE KEY STRATEGIC POINTS, INCLUDING A SIGNIFICANT GROUP IN DC.
PATCH US IN TO THE MALL.
AGAIN, AHEAD OF PROJECTIONS BY THIRTY PERCENT.
THIRTY? WONDERFUL. AT THIS RATE WE CAN BRING PHASE FOUR AHEAD OF SCHEDULE.

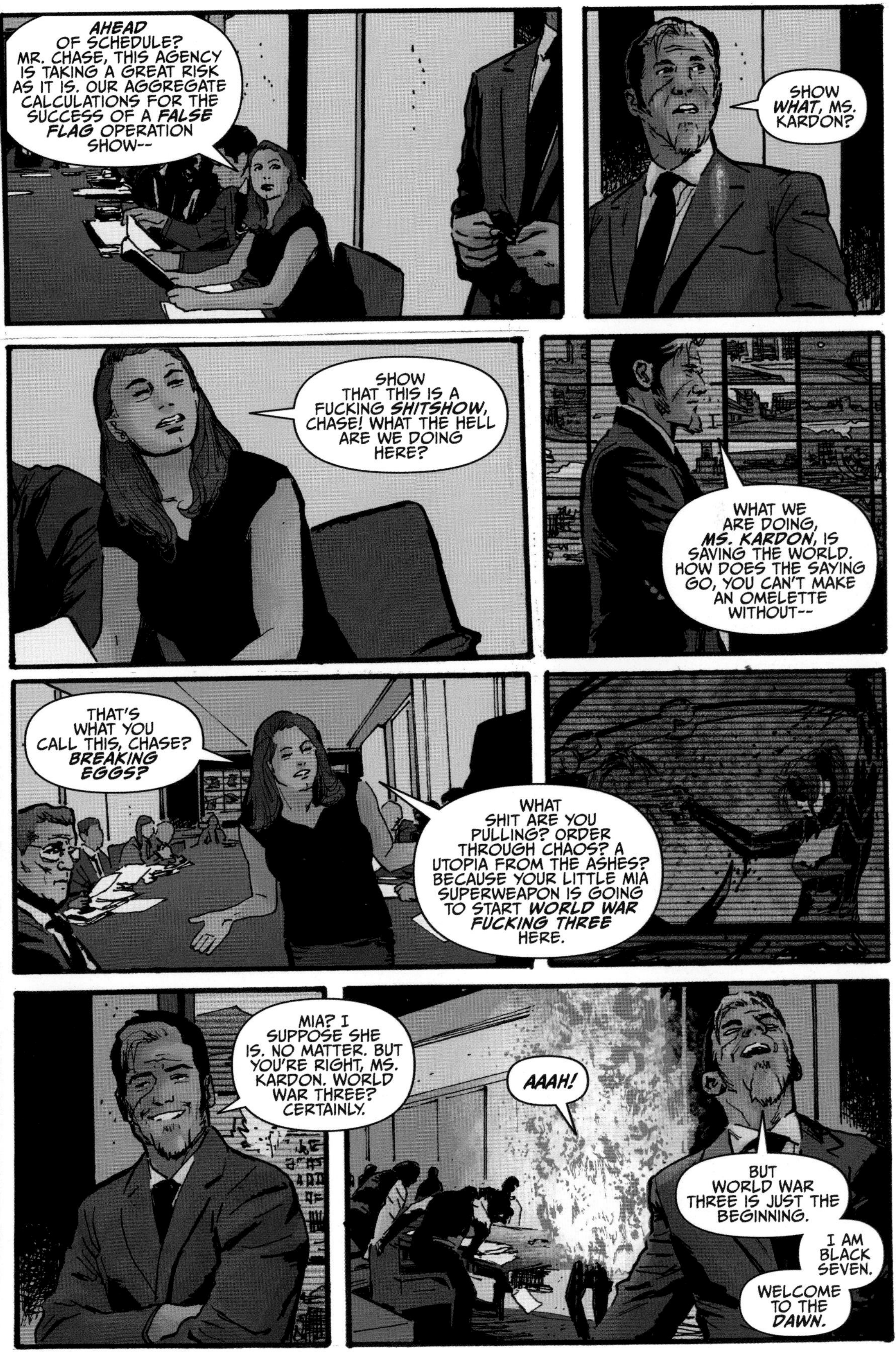

AHEAD OF SCHEDULE? MR. CHASE, THIS AGENCY IS TAKING A GREAT RISK AS IT IS. OUR AGGREGATE CALCULATIONS FOR THE SUCCESS OF A FALSE FLAG OPERATION SHOW--
SHOW WHAT, MS. KARDON?
SHOW THAT THIS IS A FUCKING SHITSHOW, CHASE! WHAT THE HELL ARE WE DOING HERE?
WHAT WE ARE DOING, MS. KARDON, IS SAVING THE WORLD. HOW DOES THE SAYING GO, YOU CAN'T MAKE AN OMELETTE WITHOUT--
THAT'S WHAT YOU CALL THIS, CHASE? BREAKING EGGS?
WHAT SHIT ARE YOU PULLING? ORDER THROUGH CHAOS? A UTOPIA FROM THE ASHES? BECAUSE YOUR LITTLE MIA SUPERWEAPON IS GOING TO START WORLD WAR FUCKING THREE HERE.
MIA? I SUPPOSE SHE IS. NO MATTER. BUT YOU'RE RIGHT, MS. KARDON. WORLD WAR THREE? CERTAINLY.
AAAH!
BUT WORLD WAR THREE IS JUST THE BEGINNING.
I AM BLACK SEVEN.
WELCOME TO THE DAWN.

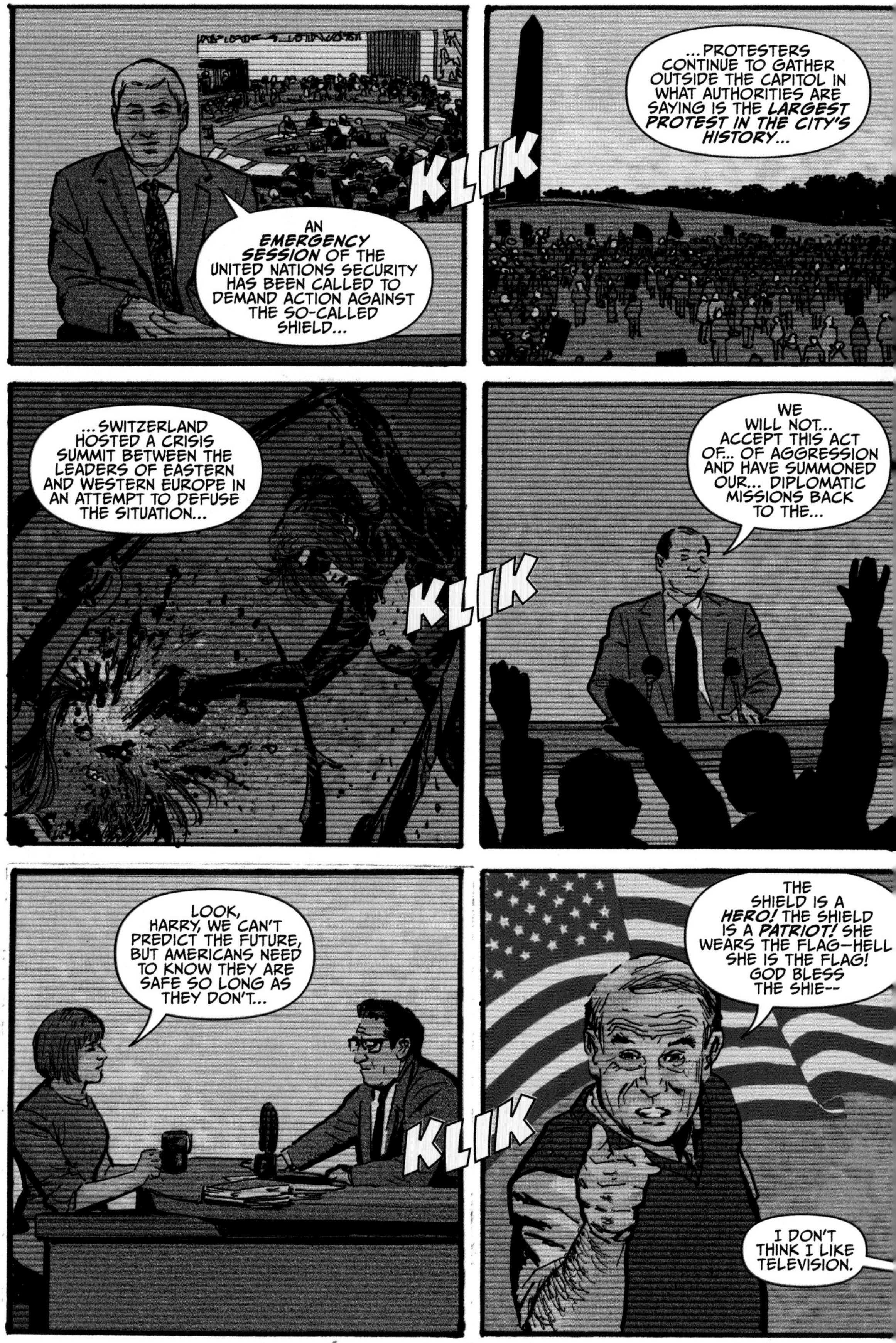

AN EMERGENCY SESSION OF THE UNITED NATIONS SECURITY HAS BEEN CALLED TO DEMAND ACTION AGAINST THE SO-CALLED SHIELD...
KLIK
...PROTESTERS CONTINUE TO GATHER OUTSIDE THE CAPITOL IN WHAT AUTHORITIES ARE SAYING IS THE LARGEST PROTEST IN THE CITY'S HISTORY...
...SWITZERLAND HOSTED A CRISIS SUMMIT BETWEEN THE LEADERS OF EASTERN AND WESTERN EUROPE IN AN ATTEMPT TO DEFUSE THE SITUATION...
KLIK
WE WILL NOT... ACCEPT THIS ACT OF... OF AGGRESSION AND HAVE SUMMONED OUR... DIPLOMATIC MISSIONS BACK TO THE...
LOOK, HARRY, WE CAN'T PREDICT THE FUTURE, BUT AMERICANS NEED TO KNOW THEY ARE SAFE SO LONG AS THEY DON'T...
KLIK
THE SHIELD IS A HERO! THE SHIELD IS A PATRIOT! SHE WEARS THE FLAG—HELL SHE IS THE FLAG! GOD BLESS THE SHIE--
I DON'T THINK I LIKE TELEVISION.

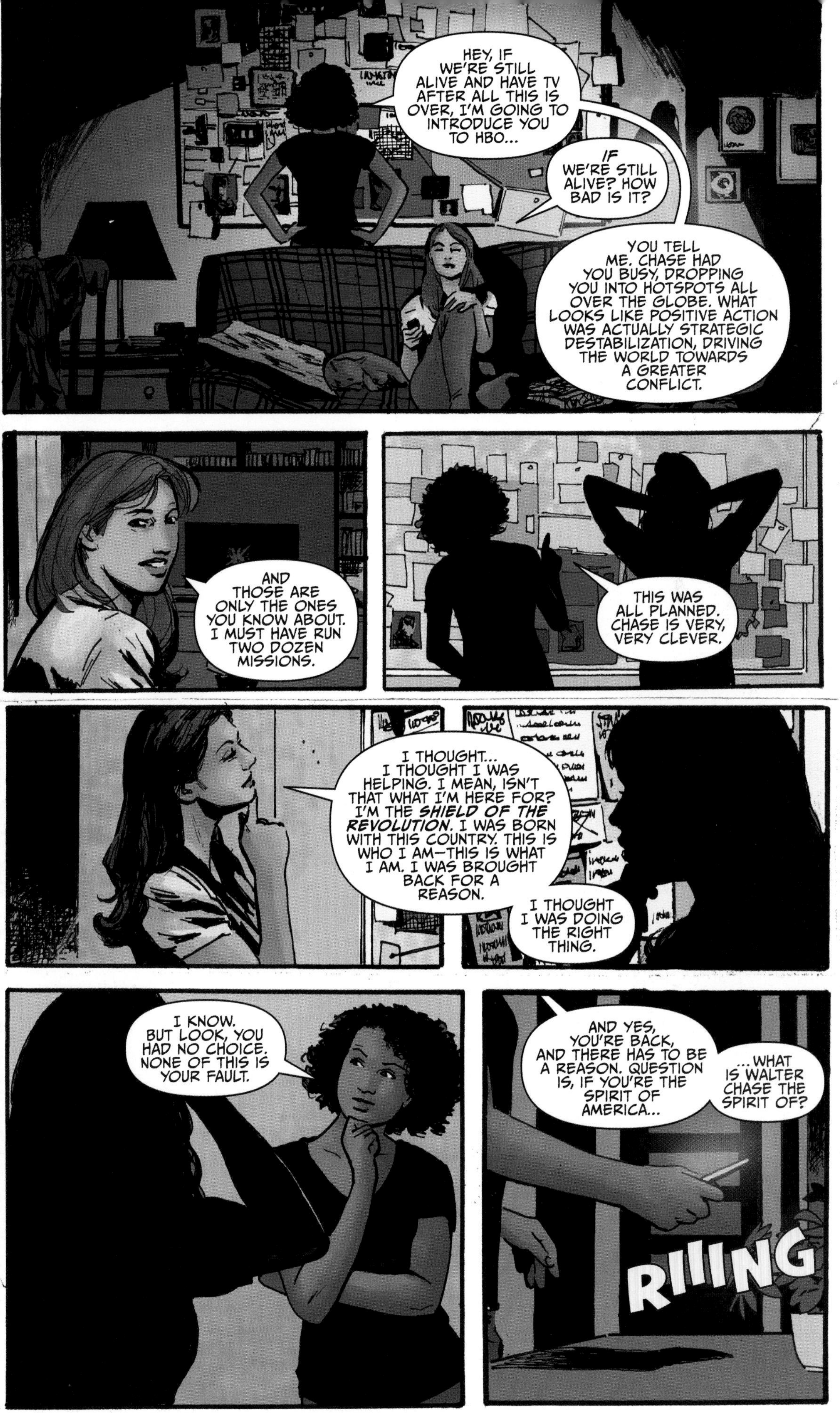
HEY, IF WE'RE STILL ALIVE AND HAVE TV AFTER ALL THIS IS OVER, I'M GOING TO INTRODUCE YOU TO HBO...
IF WE'RE STILL ALIVE? HOW BAD IS IT?
YOU TELL ME. CHASE HAD YOU BUSY, DROPPING YOU INTO HOTSPOTS ALL OVER THE GLOBE. WHAT LOOKS LIKE POSITIVE ACTION WAS ACTUALLY STRATEGIC DESTABILIZATION, DRIVING THE WORLD TOWARDS A GREATER CONFLICT.
AND THOSE ARE ONLY THE ONES YOU KNOW ABOUT. I MUST HAVE RUN TWO DOZEN MISSIONS.
THIS WAS ALL PLANNED. CHASE IS VERY, VERY CLEVER.
I THOUGHT... I THOUGHT I WAS HELPING. I MEAN, ISN'T THAT WHAT I'M HERE FOR? I'M THE SHIELD OF THE REVOLUTION. I WAS BORN WITH THIS COUNTRY. THIS IS WHO I AM—THIS IS WHAT I AM. I WAS BROUGHT BACK FOR A REASON.
I THOUGHT I WAS DOING THE RIGHT THING.
I KNOW. BUT LOOK, YOU HAD NO CHOICE. NONE OF THIS IS YOUR FAULT.
AND YES, YOU'RE BACK, AND THERE HAS TO BE A REASON. QUESTION IS, IF YOU'RE THE SPIRIT OF AMERICA...
...WHAT IS WALTER CHASE THE SPIRIT OF?
RIIING

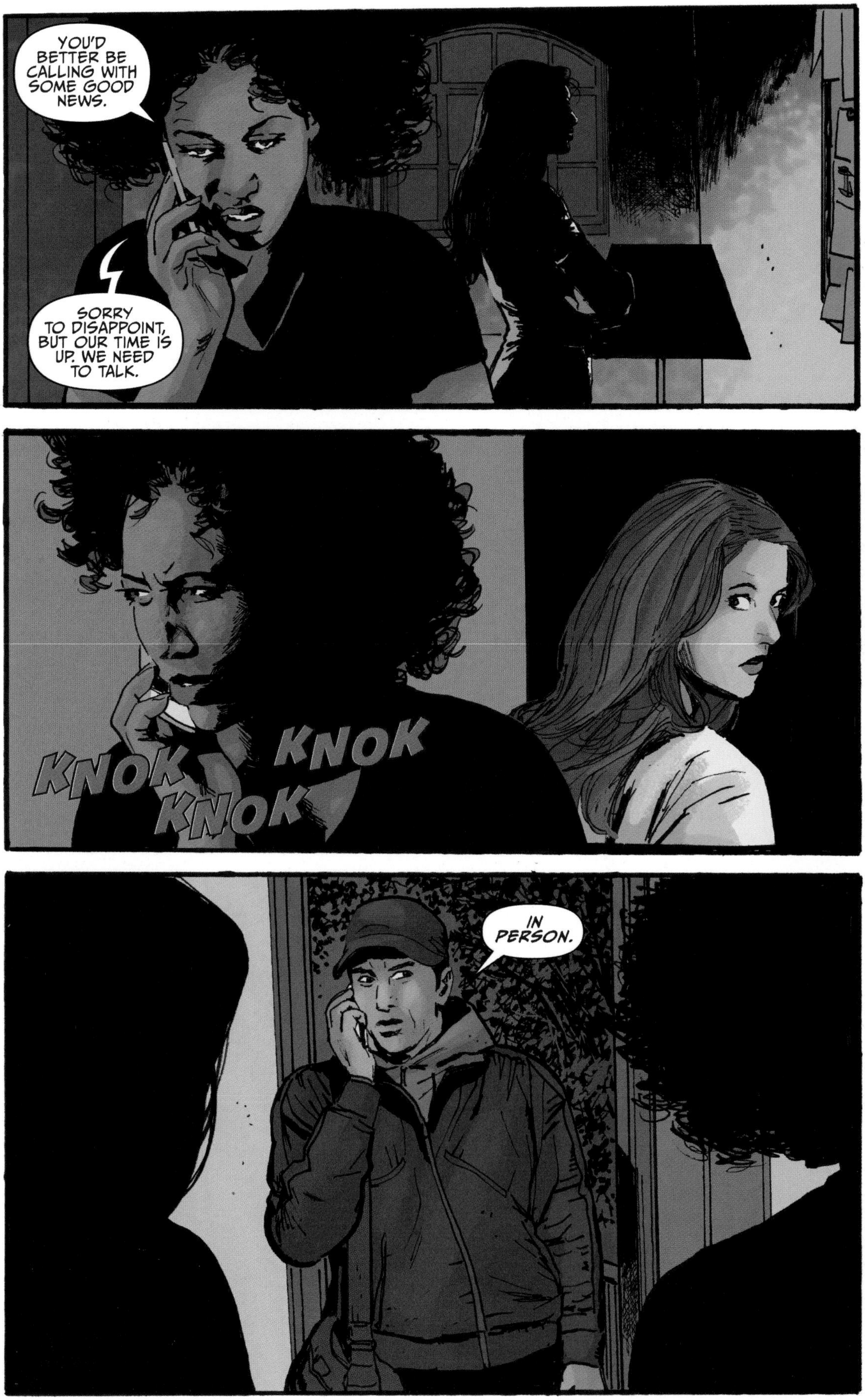
YOU'D BETTER BE CALLING WITH SOME GOOD NEWS.
SORRY TO DISAPPOINT, BUT OUR TIME IS UP. WE NEED TO TALK.
KNOK KNOK KNOK
IN PERSON.

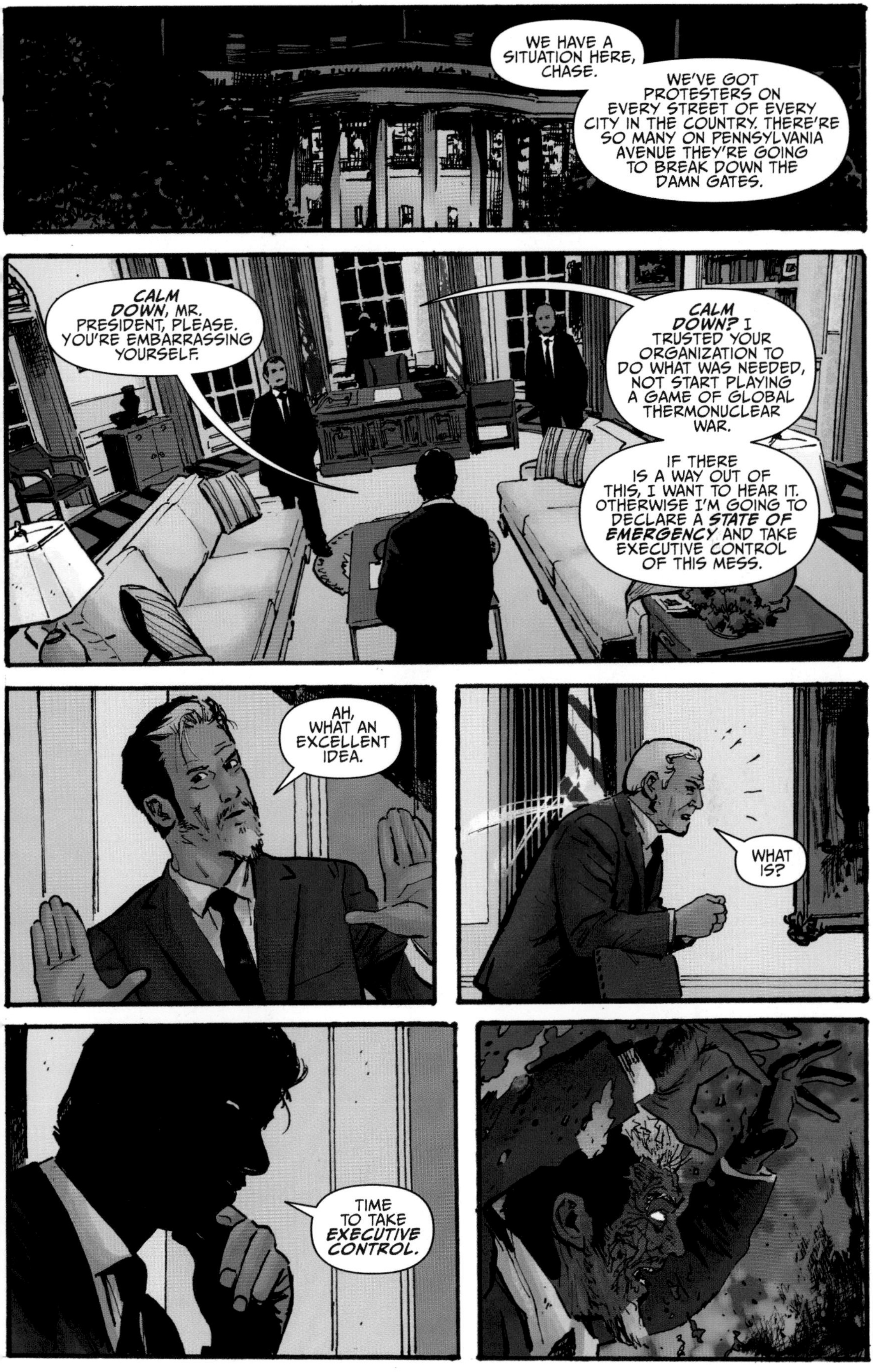
WE HAVE A SITUATION HERE, CHASE.
WE'VE GOT PROTESTERS ON EVERY STREET OF EVERY CITY IN THE COUNTRY. THERE'RE SO MANY ON PENNSYLVANIA AVENUE THEY'RE GOING TO BREAK DOWN THE DAMN GATES.
CALM DOWN, MR. PRESIDENT, PLEASE. YOU'RE EMBARRASSING YOURSELF.
CALM DOWN? I TRUSTED YOUR ORGANIZATION TO DO WHAT WAS NEEDED, NOT START PLAYING A GAME OF GLOBAL THERMONUCLEAR WAR.
IF THERE IS A WAY OUT OF THIS, I WANT TO HEAR IT. OTHERWISE I'M GOING TO DECLARE A STATE OF EMERGENCY AND TAKE EXECUTIVE CONTROL OF THIS MESS.
AH, WHAT AN EXCELLENT IDEA.
WHAT IS?
TIME TO TAKE EXECUTIVE CONTROL.

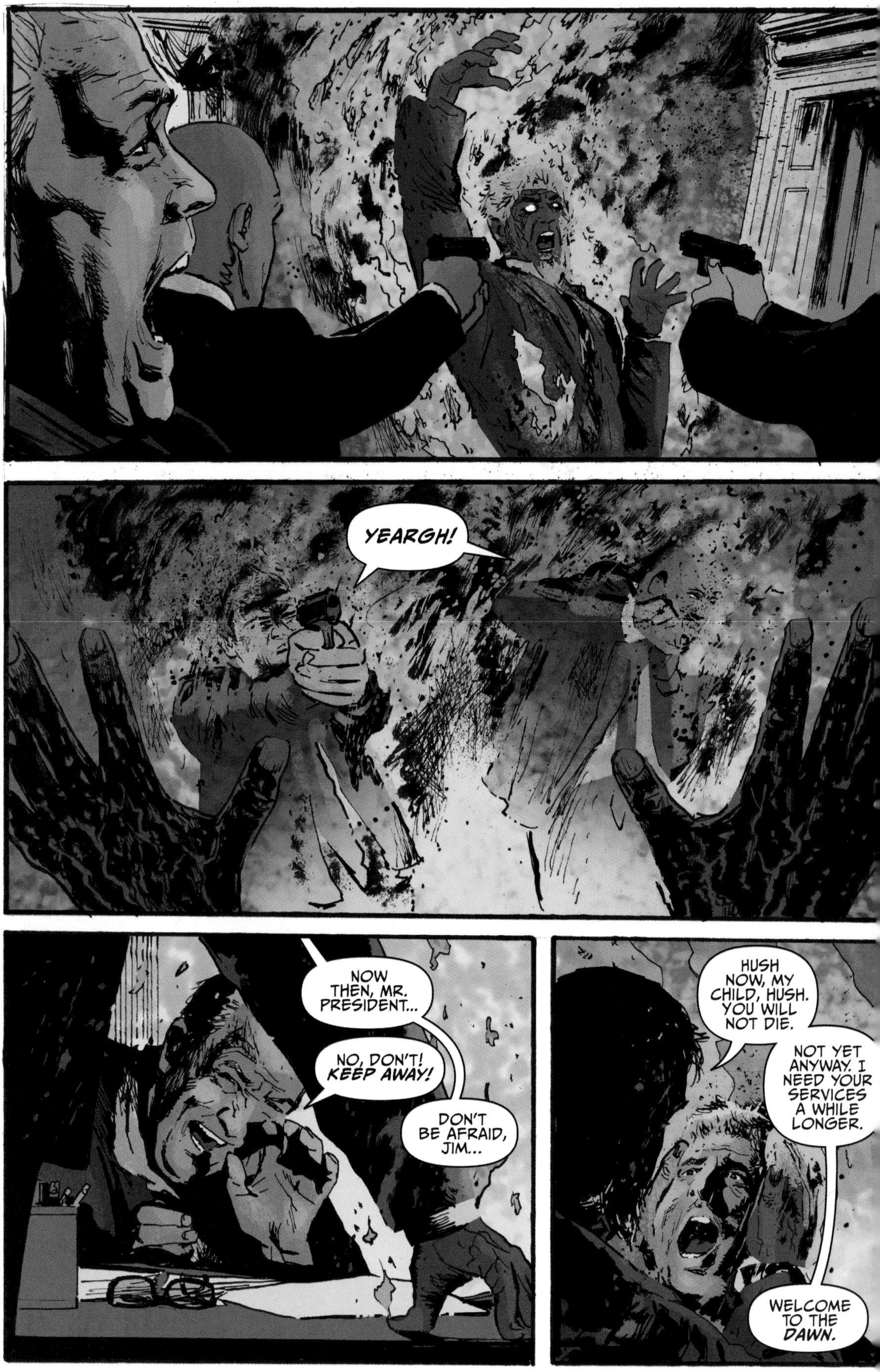
YEARGH!
NOW THEN, MR. PRESIDENT...
NO, DON'T! KEEP AWAY!
DON'T BE AFRAID, JIM...
HUSH NOW, MY CHILD, HUSH. YOU WILL NOT DIE.
NOT YET ANYWAY. I NEED YOUR SERVICES A WHILE LONGER.
WELCOME TO THE DAWN.

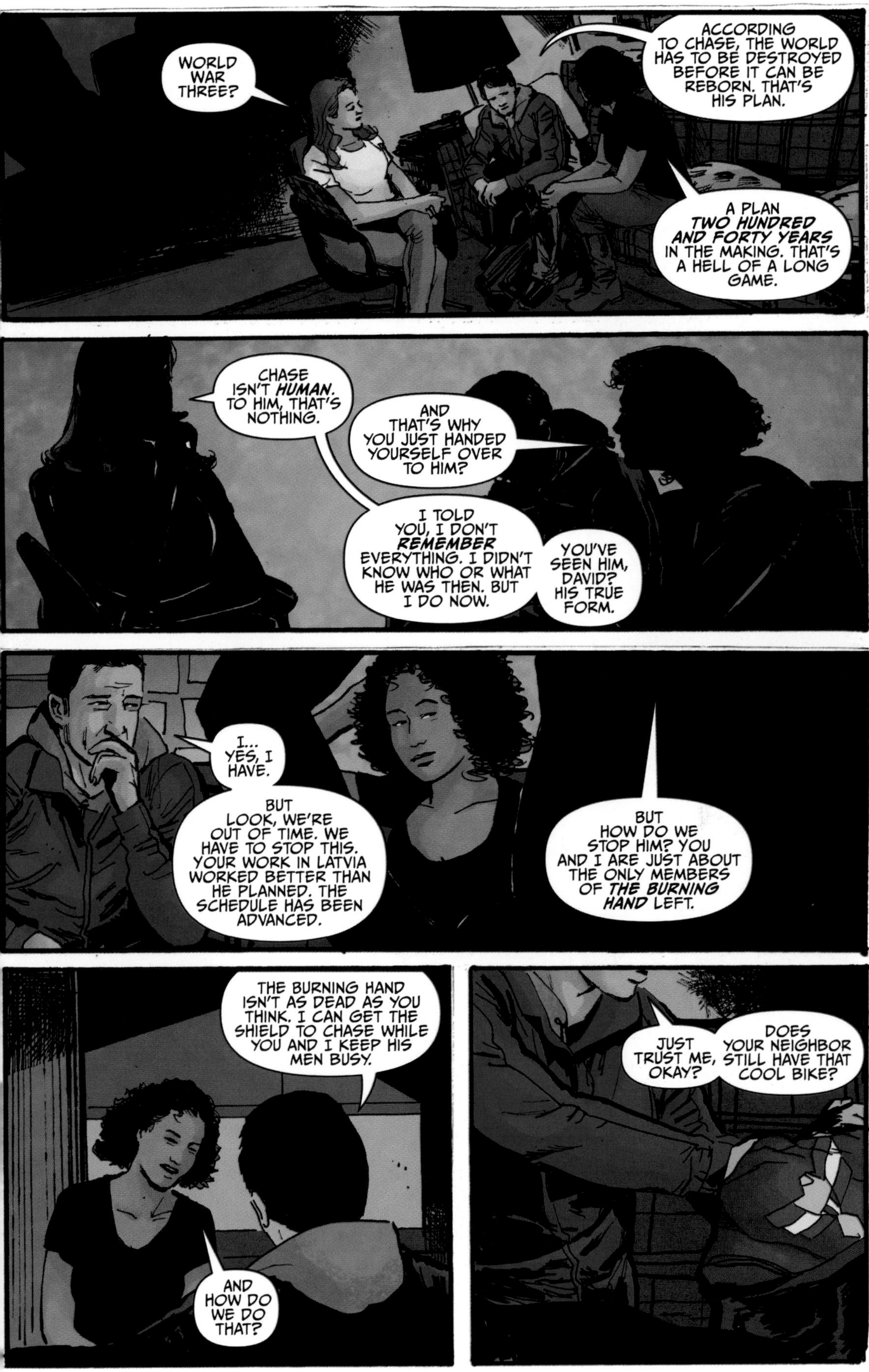

WORLD WAR THREE?
ACCORDING TO CHASE, THE WORLD HAS TO BE DESTROYED BEFORE IT CAN BE REBORN. THAT'S HIS PLAN.
A PLAN ***TWO HUNDRED AND FORTY YEARS*** IN THE MAKING. THAT'S A HELL OF A LONG GAME.
CHASE ISN'T ***HUMAN.*** TO HIM, THAT'S NOTHING.
AND THAT'S WHY YOU JUST HANDED YOURSELF OVER TO HIM?
I TOLD YOU, I DON'T ***REMEMBER*** EVERYTHING. I DIDN'T KNOW WHO OR WHAT HE WAS THEN. BUT I DO NOW.
YOU'VE SEEN HIM, DAVID? HIS TRUE FORM.
I... YES, I HAVE.
BUT LOOK, WE'RE OUT OF TIME. WE HAVE TO STOP THIS. YOUR WORK IN LATVIA WORKED BETTER THAN HE PLANNED. THE SCHEDULE HAS BEEN ADVANCED.
BUT HOW DO WE STOP HIM? YOU AND I ARE JUST ABOUT THE ONLY MEMBERS OF ***THE BURNING HAND*** LEFT.
THE BURNING HAND ISN'T AS DEAD AS YOU THINK. I CAN GET THE SHIELD TO CHASE WHILE YOU AND I KEEP HIS MEN BUSY.
AND HOW DO WE DO THAT?
DOES YOUR NEIGHBOR STILL HAVE THAT COOL BIKE?
JUST TRUST ME, OKAY?

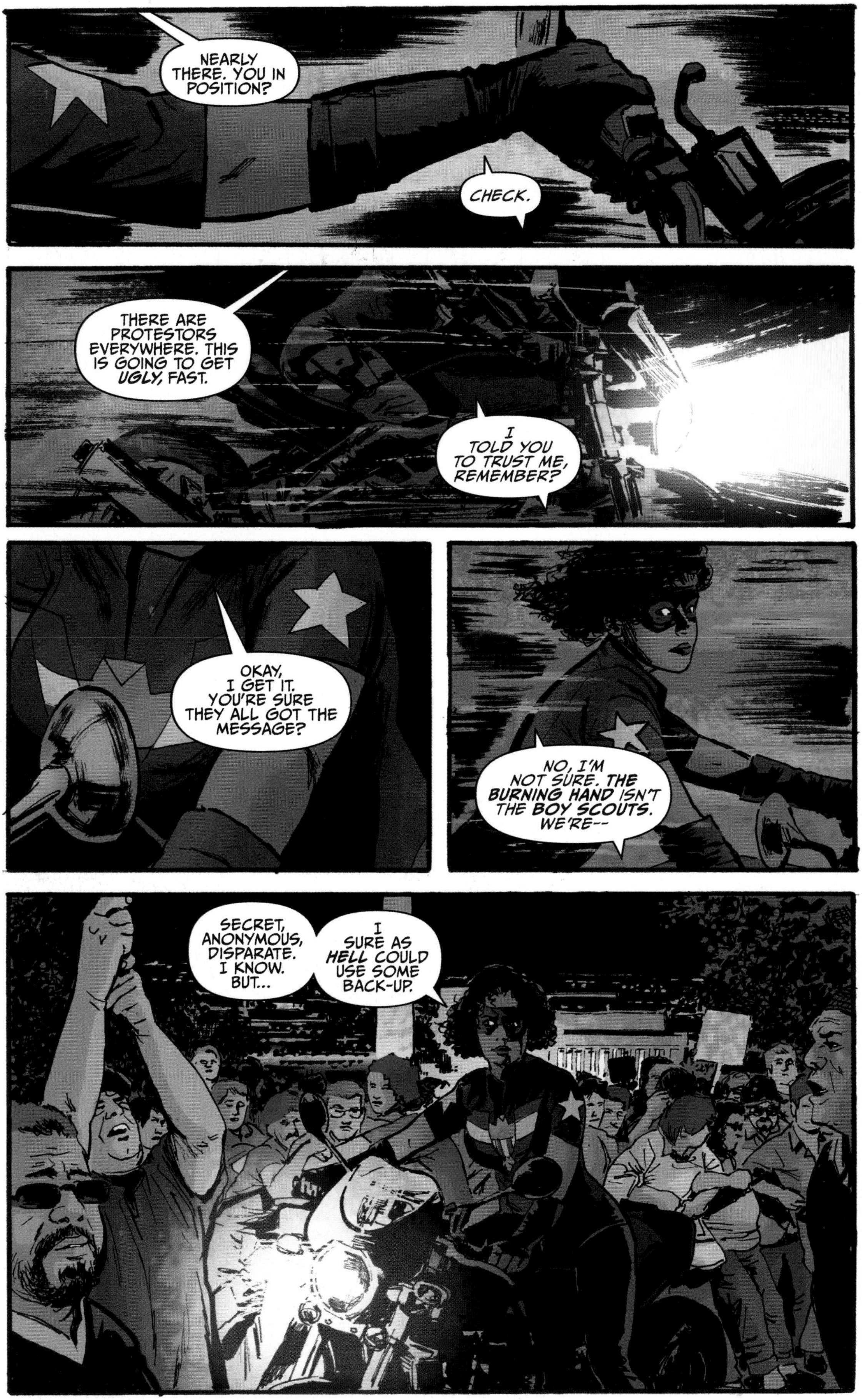
NEARLY THERE. YOU IN POSITION?
CHECK.
THERE ARE PROTESTORS EVERYWHERE. THIS IS GOING TO GET UGLY, FAST.
I TOLD YOU TO TRUST ME, REMEMBER?
OKAY, I GET IT. YOU'RE SURE THEY ALL GOT THE MESSAGE?
NO, I'M NOT SURE. THE BURNING HAND ISN'T THE BOY SCOUTS. WE'RE--
SECRET, ANONYMOUS, DISPARATE. I KNOW. BUT...
I SURE AS HELL COULD USE SOME BACK-UP.

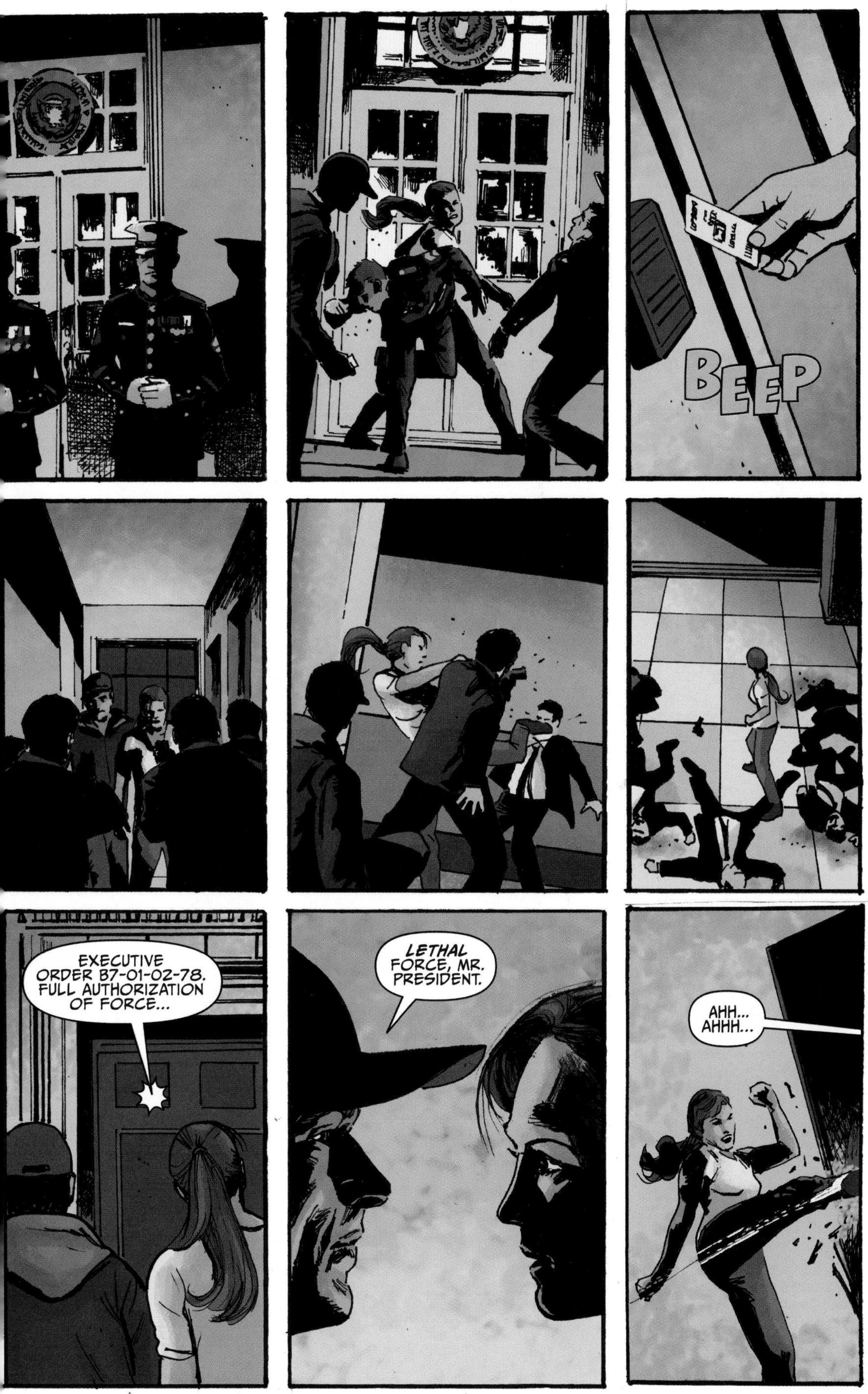
BEEP
EXECUTIVE ORDER B7-01-02-78. FULL AUTHORIZATION OF FORCE...
LETHAL FORCE, MR. PRESIDENT.
AHH... AHHH...

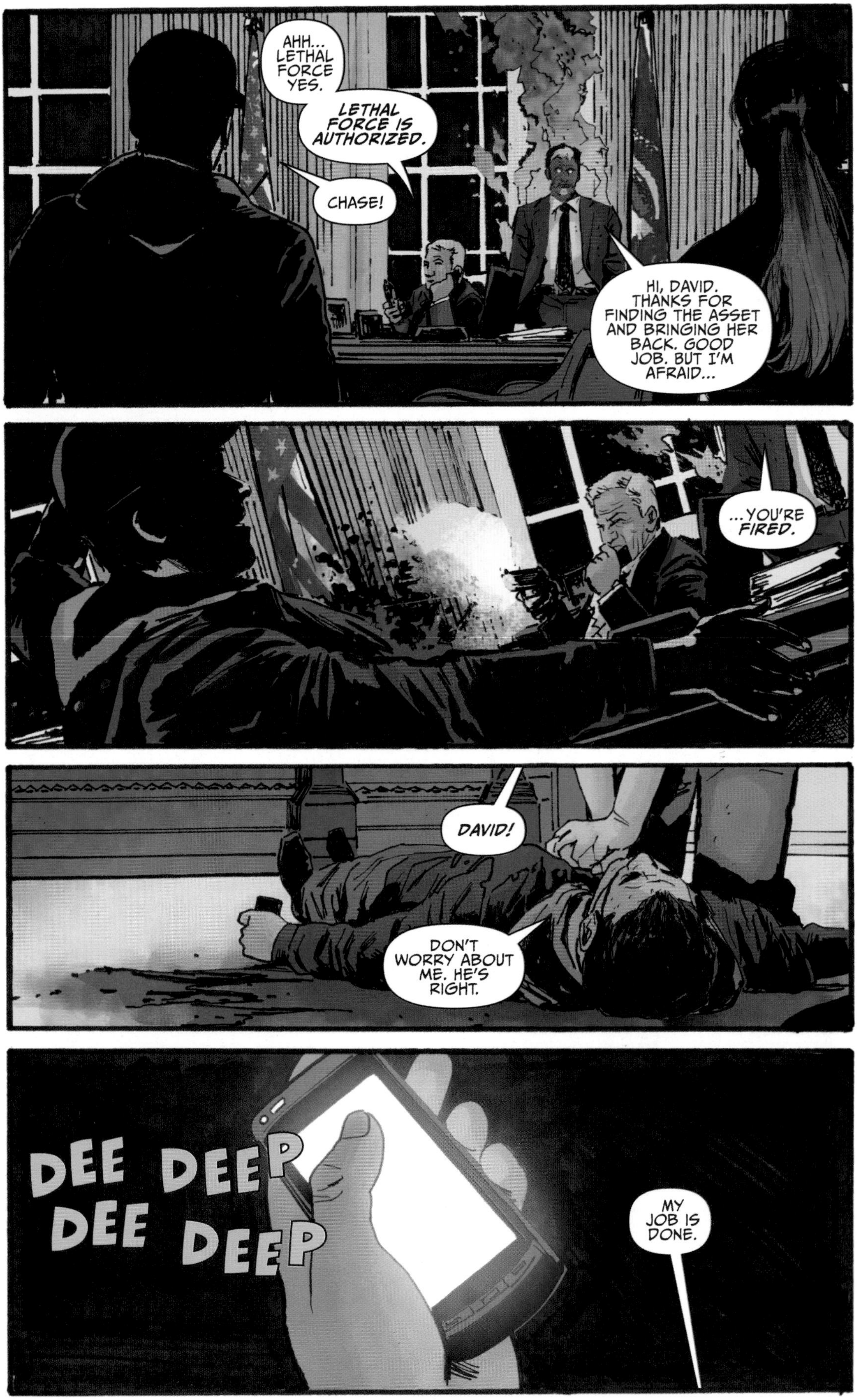
AHH... LETHAL FORCE YES.
LETHAL FORCE IS AUTHORIZED.
CHASE!
HI, DAVID. THANKS FOR FINDING THE ASSET AND BRINGING HER BACK. GOOD JOB. BUT I'M AFRAID...
...YOU'RE FIRED.
DAVID!
DON'T WORRY ABOUT ME. HE'S RIGHT.
DEE DEEP DEE DEEP
MY JOB IS DONE.

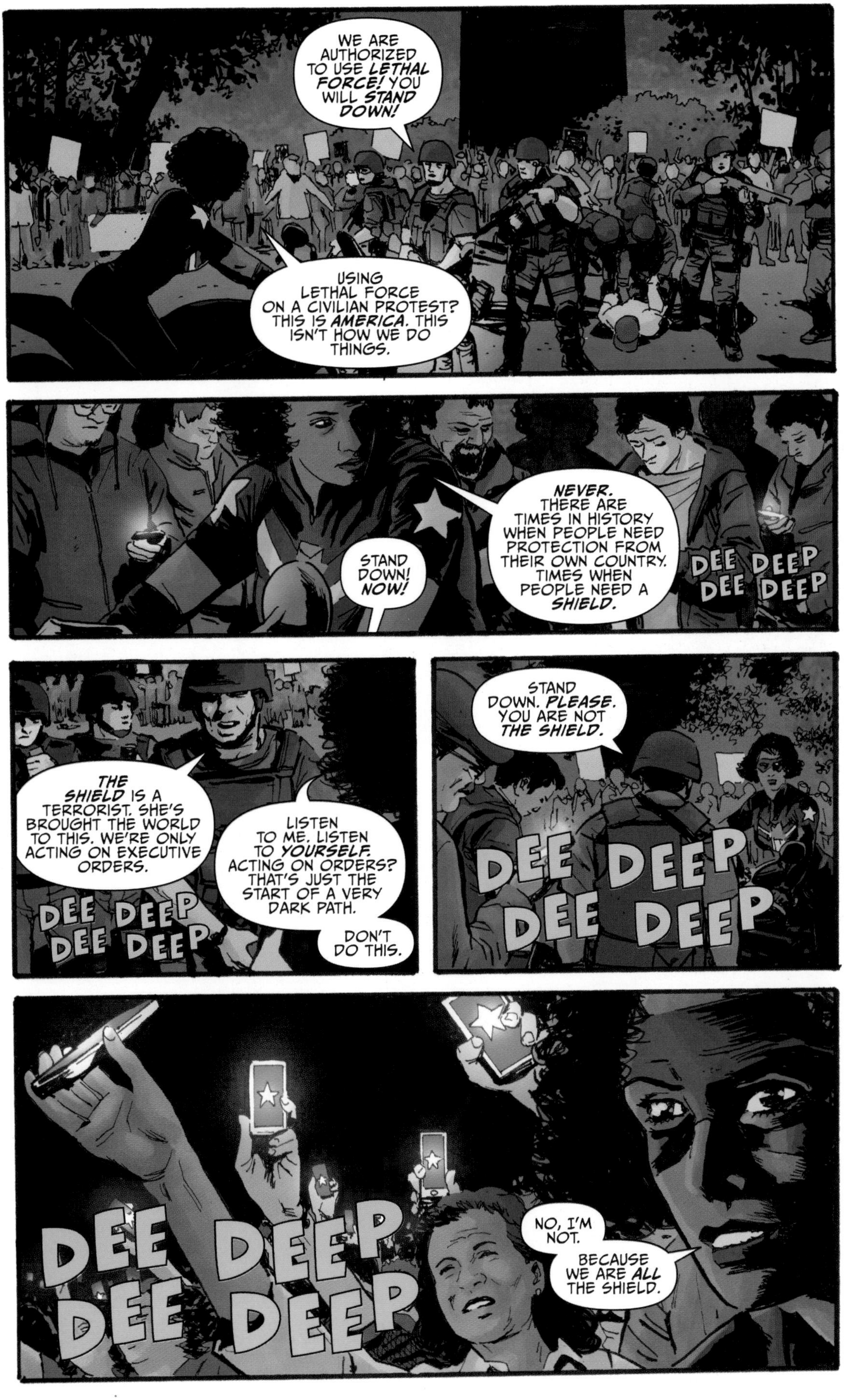

WE ARE AUTHORIZED TO USE LETHAL FORCE! YOU WILL STAND DOWN!
USING LETHAL FORCE ON A CIVILIAN PROTEST? THIS IS AMERICA. THIS ISN'T HOW WE DO THINGS.
STAND DOWN! NOW!
NEVER. THERE ARE TIMES IN HISTORY WHEN PEOPLE NEED PROTECTION FROM THEIR OWN COUNTRY. TIMES WHEN PEOPLE NEED A SHIELD.
DEE DEEP DEE DEEP
THE SHIELD IS A TERRORIST. SHE'S BROUGHT THE WORLD TO THIS. WE'RE ONLY ACTING ON EXECUTIVE ORDERS.
LISTEN TO ME. LISTEN TO YOURSELF. ACTING ON ORDERS? THAT'S JUST THE START OF A VERY DARK PATH.
DON'T DO THIS.
DEE DEEP DEE DEEP
STAND DOWN. PLEASE. YOU ARE NOT THE SHIELD.
DEE DEEP DEE DEEP
DEE DEEP DEE DEEP
NO, I'M NOT.
BECAUSE WE ARE ALL THE SHIELD.

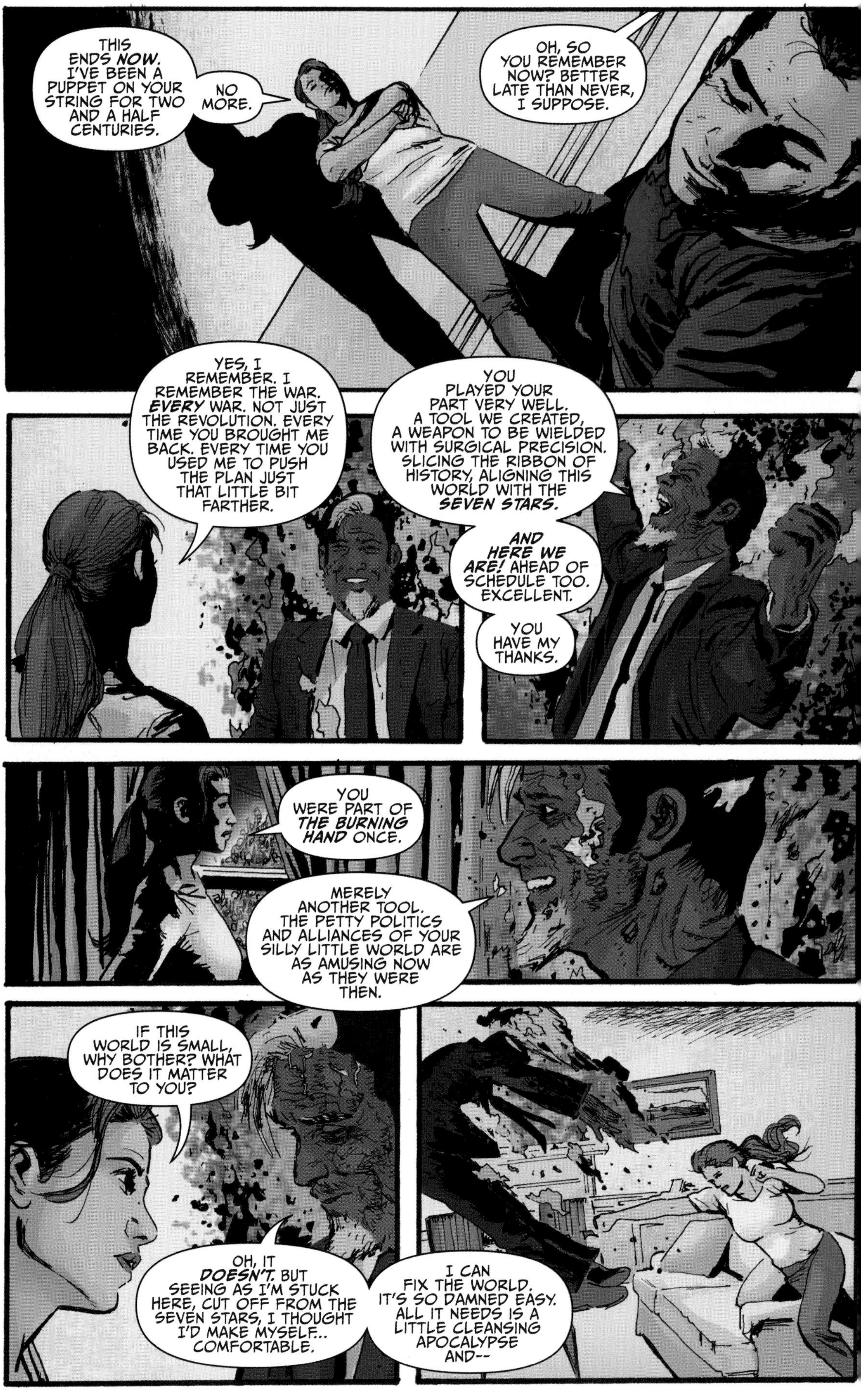
THIS ENDS NOW. I'VE BEEN A PUPPET ON YOUR STRING FOR TWO AND A HALF CENTURIES.
NO MORE.
OH, SO YOU REMEMBER NOW? BETTER LATE THAN NEVER, I SUPPOSE.
YES, I REMEMBER. I REMEMBER THE WAR. EVERY WAR. NOT JUST THE REVOLUTION. EVERY TIME YOU BROUGHT ME BACK. EVERY TIME YOU USED ME TO PUSH THE PLAN JUST THAT LITTLE BIT FARTHER.
YOU PLAYED YOUR PART VERY WELL. A TOOL WE CREATED, A WEAPON TO BE WIELDED WITH SURGICAL PRECISION. SLICING THE RIBBON OF HISTORY, ALIGNING THIS WORLD WITH THE SEVEN STARS.
AND HERE WE ARE! AHEAD OF SCHEDULE TOO. EXCELLENT.
YOU HAVE MY THANKS.
YOU WERE PART OF THE BURNING HAND ONCE.
MERELY ANOTHER TOOL. THE PETTY POLITICS AND ALLIANCES OF YOUR SILLY LITTLE WORLD ARE AS AMUSING NOW AS THEY WERE THEN.
IF THIS WORLD IS SMALL, WHY BOTHER? WHAT DOES IT MATTER TO YOU?
OH, IT DOESN'T. BUT SEEING AS I'M STUCK HERE, CUT OFF FROM THE SEVEN STARS, I THOUGHT I'D MAKE MYSELF... COMFORTABLE.
I CAN FIX THE WORLD. IT'S SO DAMNED EASY. ALL IT NEEDS IS A LITTLE CLEANSING APOCALYPSE AND--

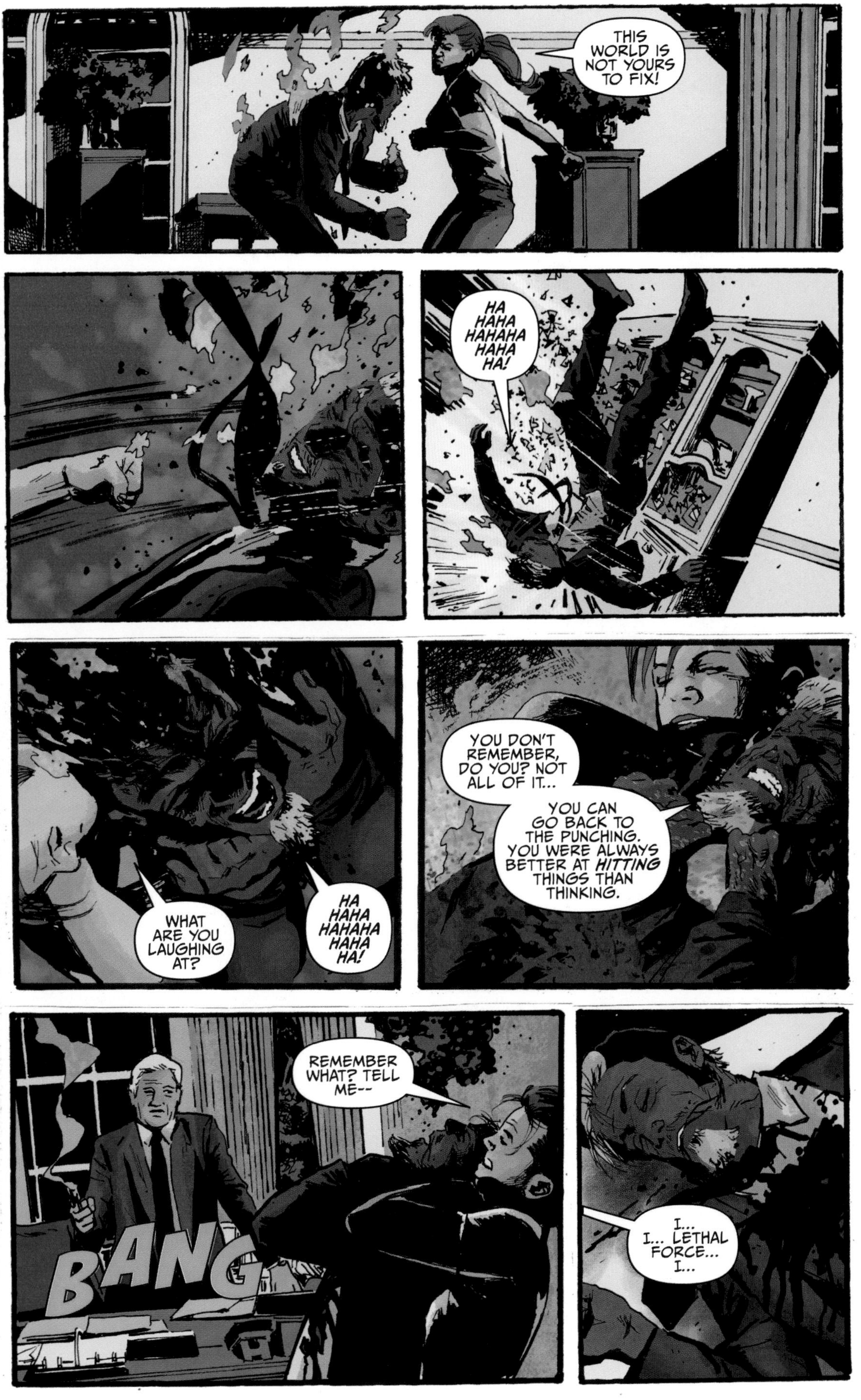

THIS WORLD IS NOT YOURS TO FIX!
HA HAHA HAHAHA HAHA HA!
WHAT ARE YOU LAUGHING AT?
HA HAHA HAHAHA HAHA HA!
YOU DON'T REMEMBER, DO YOU? NOT ALL OF IT...
YOU CAN GO BACK TO THE PUNCHING. YOU WERE ALWAYS BETTER AT *HITTING* THINGS THAN THINKING.
REMEMBER WHAT? TELL ME--
BANG
I... I... LETHAL FORCE... I...

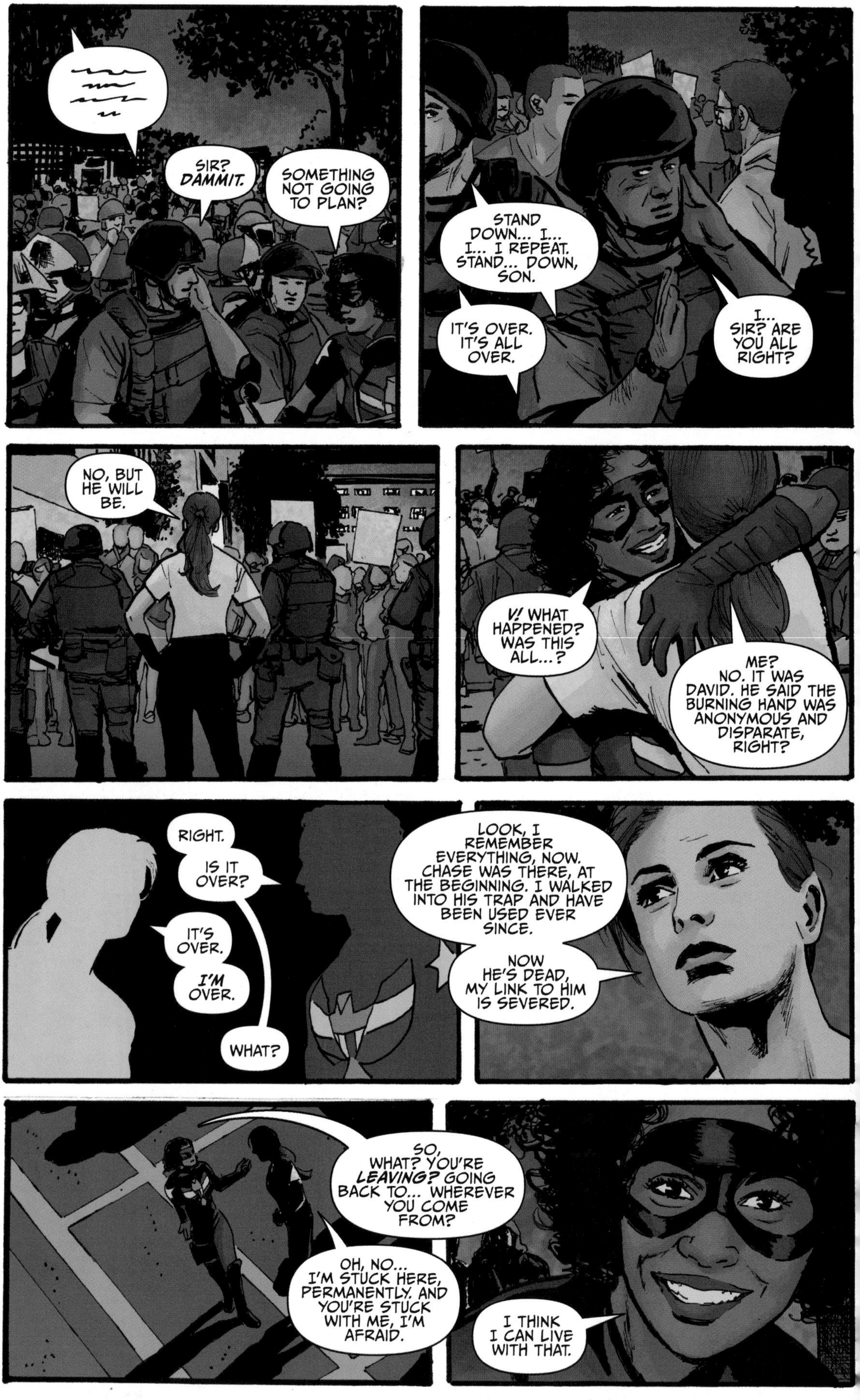

SIR? DAMMIT.
SOMETHING NOT GOING TO PLAN?
STAND DOWN... I... I... I REPEAT. STAND... DOWN, SON.
IT'S OVER. IT'S ALL OVER.
I... SIR? ARE YOU ALL RIGHT?
NO, BUT HE WILL BE.
V! WHAT HAPPENED? WAS THIS ALL...?
ME? NO. IT WAS DAVID. HE SAID THE BURNING HAND WAS ANONYMOUS AND DISPARATE, RIGHT?
RIGHT.
IS IT OVER?
IT'S OVER.
I'M OVER.
WHAT?
LOOK, I REMEMBER EVERYTHING, NOW. CHASE WAS THERE, AT THE BEGINNING. I WALKED INTO HIS TRAP AND HAVE BEEN USED EVER SINCE.
NOW HE'S DEAD, MY LINK TO HIM IS SEVERED.
SO, WHAT? YOU'RE LEAVING? GOING BACK TO... WHEREVER YOU COME FROM?
OH, NO... I'M STUCK HERE, PERMANENTLY. AND YOU'RE STUCK WITH ME, I'M AFRAID.
I THINK I CAN LIVE WITH THAT.

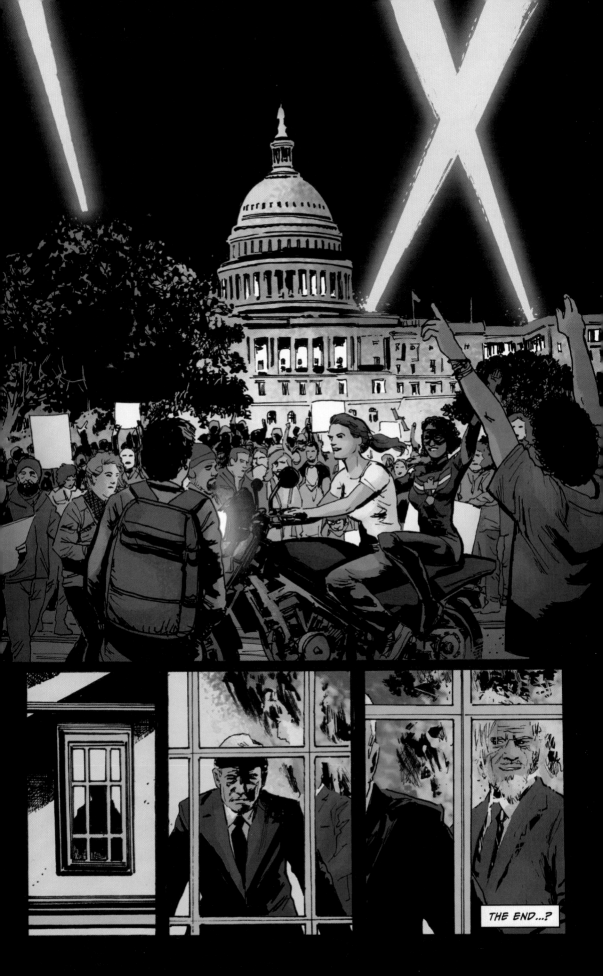

THE END...?

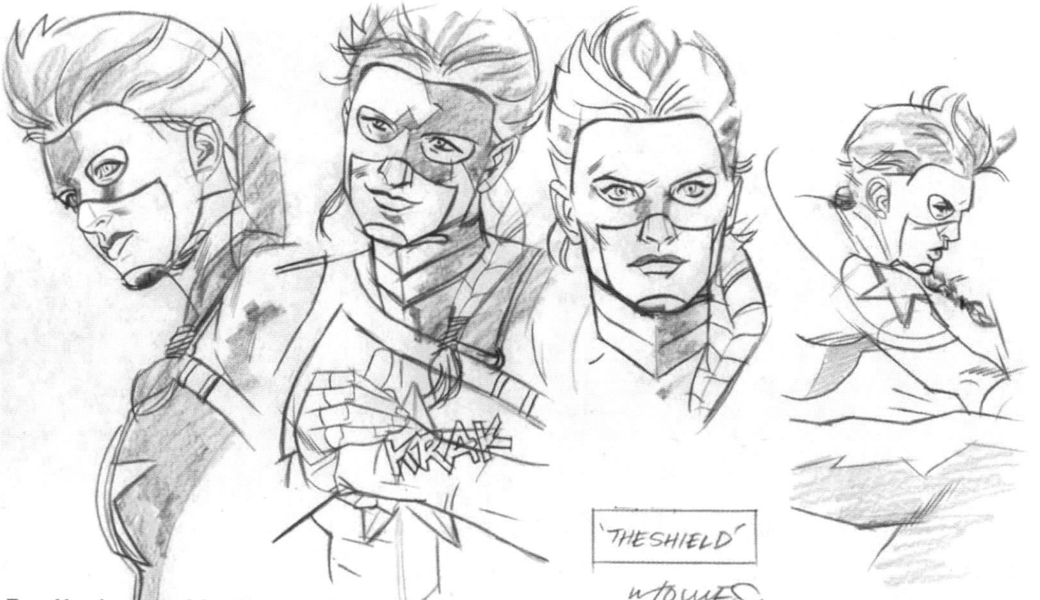
KRAK
'THE SHIELD'
WTORRES.

Preliminary Character Designs

Art by: Wilfredo Torres

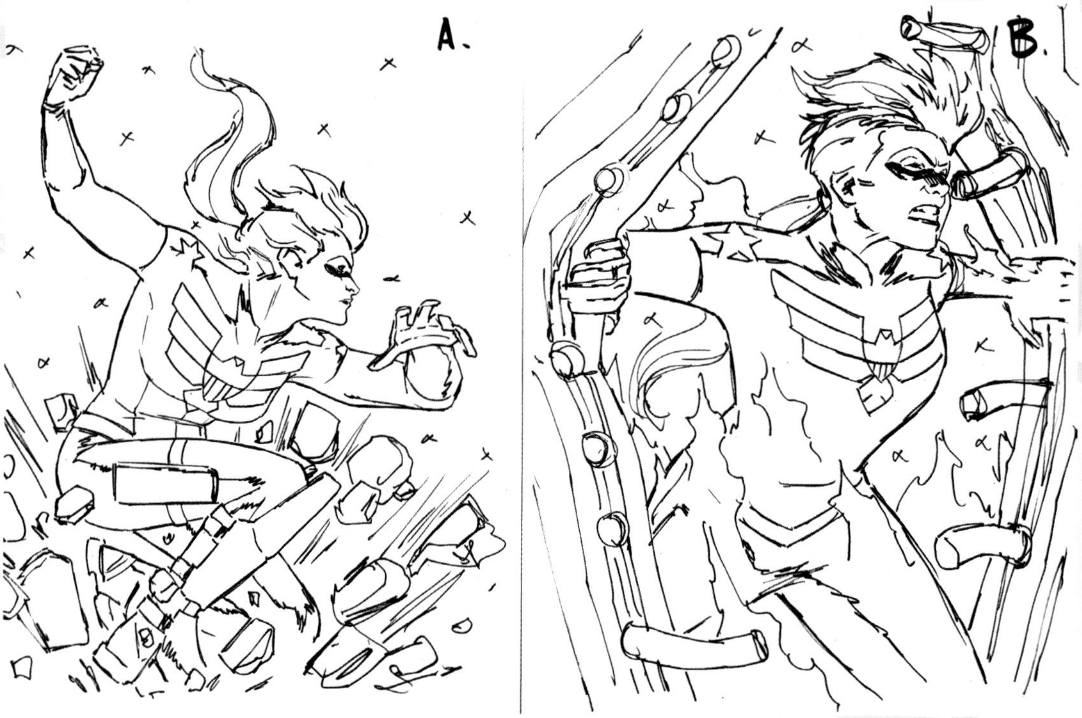
A.
B.

Art by: David Williams

CHARACTER CONCEPTS

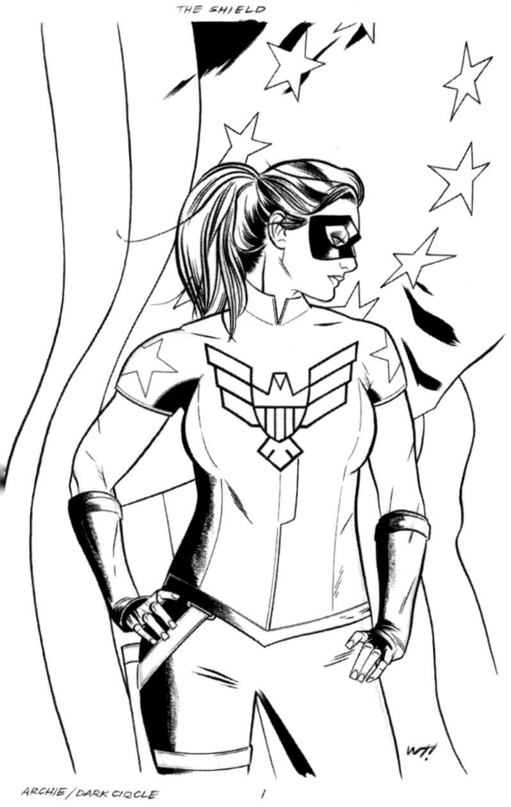
THE SHIELD
ARCHIE / DARK CIRCLE

Art by: Wilfredo Torres

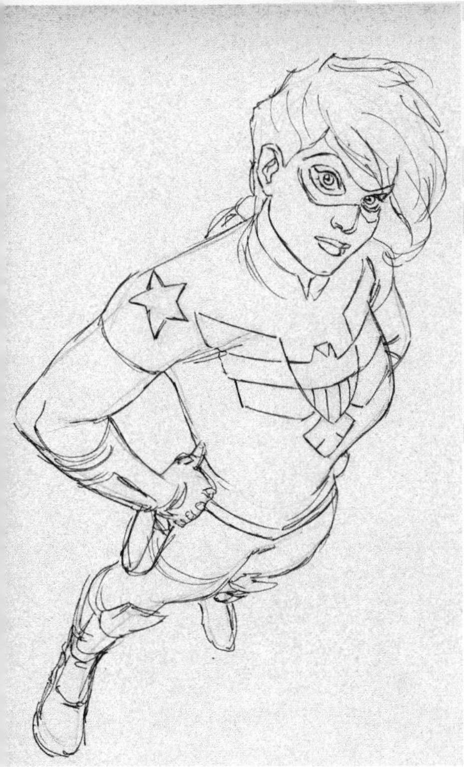

Art by: David Williams

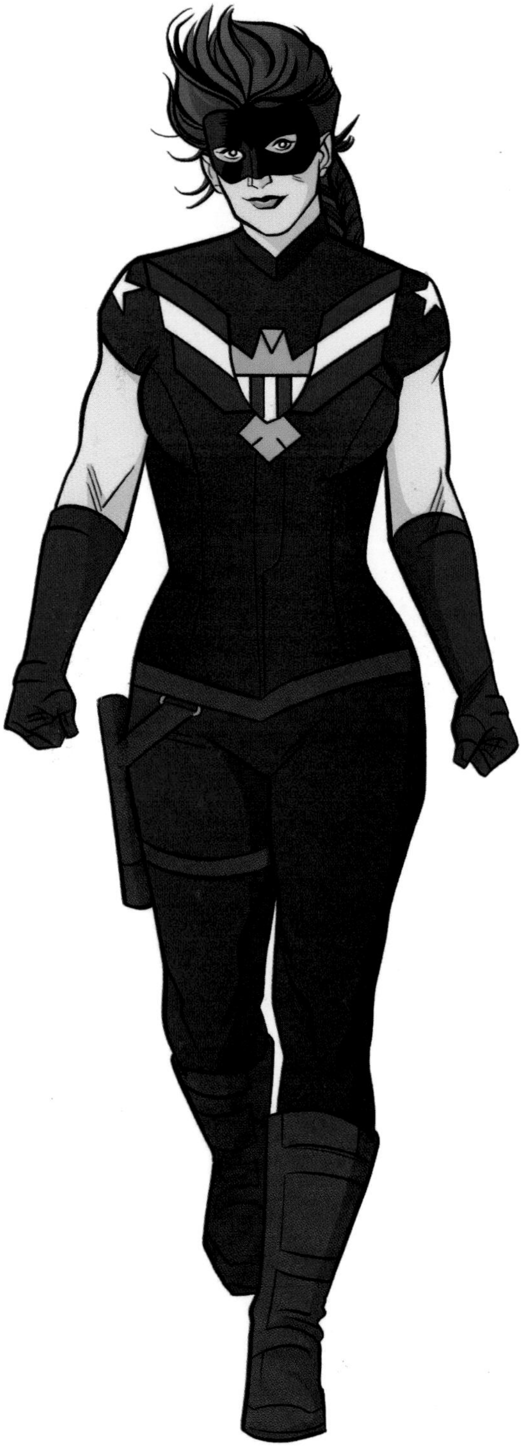

Art by: Wilfredo Torres

ISSUE ONE VARIANT COVER

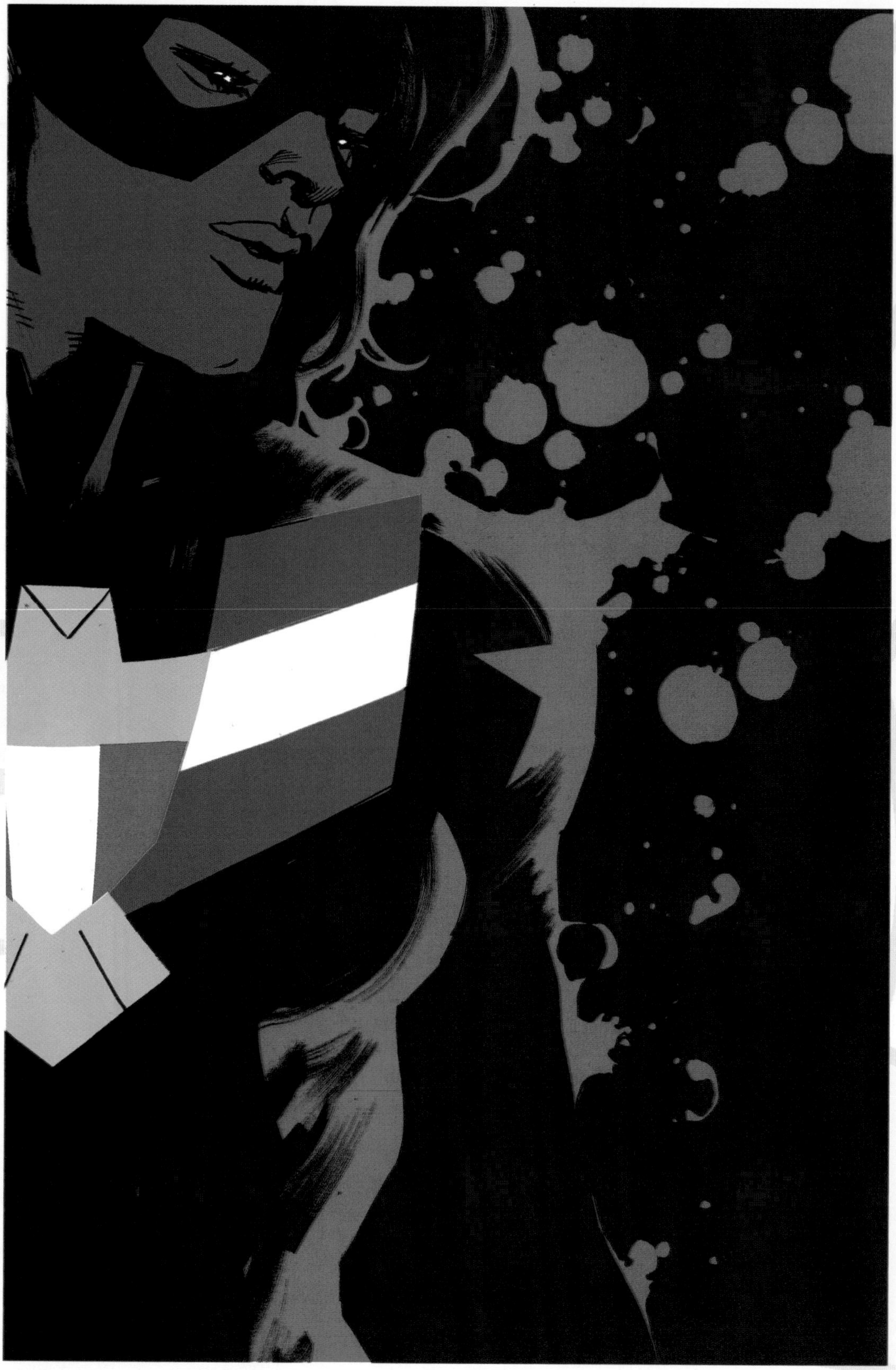

Art by: Rafael Albuquerque

ISSUE ONE VARIANT COVER

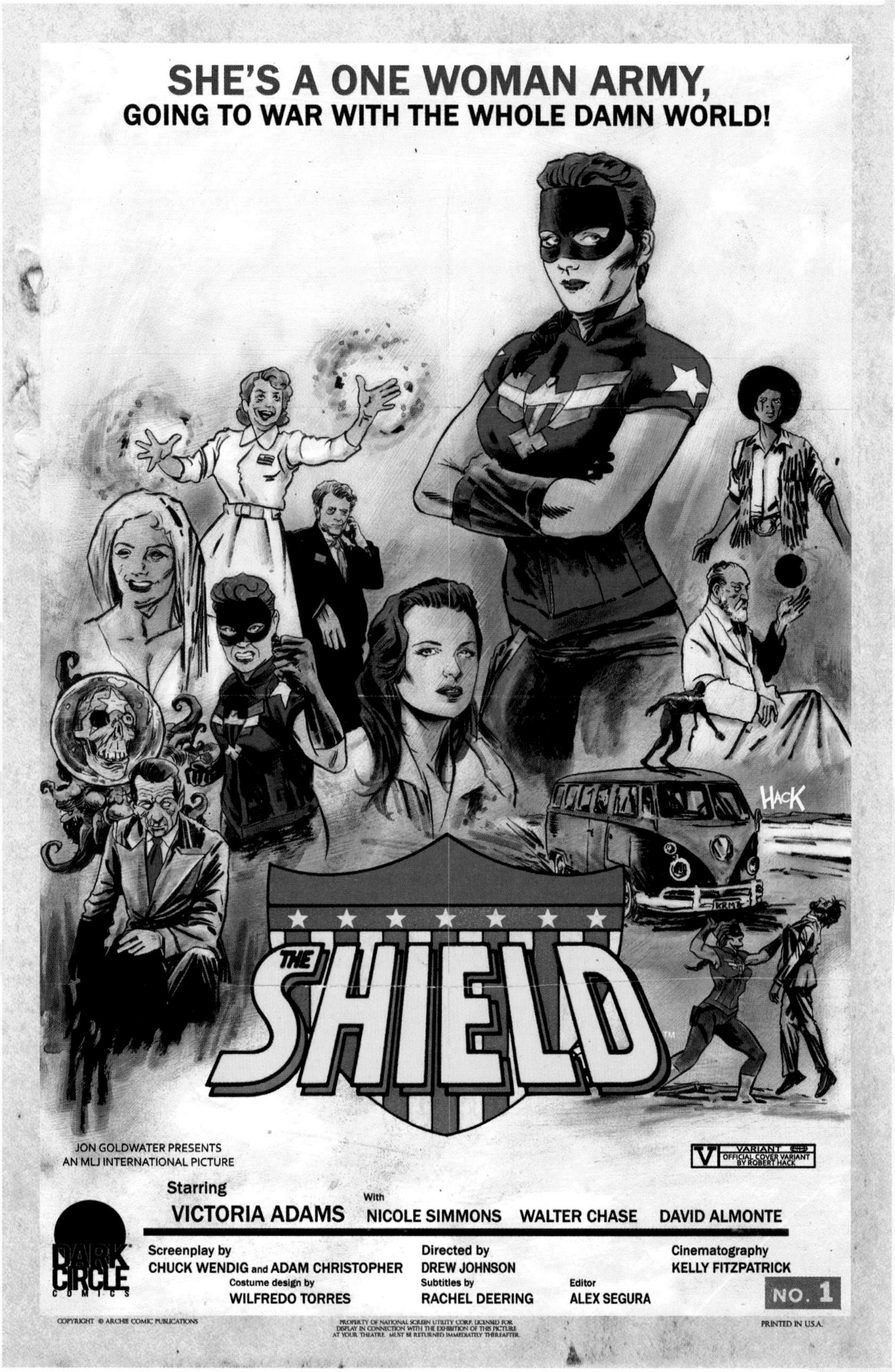
SHE'S A ONE WOMAN ARMY,
GOING TO WAR WITH THE WHOLE DAMN WORLD!
HACK
THE SHIELD
JON GOLDWATER PRESENTS
AN MLJ INTERNATIONAL PICTURE
VARIANT
OFFICIAL COVER VARIANT BY ROBERT HACK
Starring
VICTORIA ADAMS
With
NICOLE SIMMONS
WALTER CHASE
DAVID ALMONTE
DARK CIRCLE COMICS
Screenplay by
CHUCK WENDIG and ADAM CHRISTOPHER
Directed by
DREW JOHNSON
Cinematography
KELLY FITZPATRICK
Costume design by
WILFREDO TORRES
Subtitles by
RACHEL DEERING
Editor
ALEX SEGURA
NO. 1
COPYRIGHT © ARCHIE COMIC PUBLICATIONS
PROPERTY OF NATIONAL SCREEN UTILITY CORP. LICENSED FOR DISPLAY IN CONNECTION WITH THE EXHIBITION OF THIS PICTURE AT YOUR THEATRE. MUST BE RETURNED IMMEDIATELY THEREAFTER.
PRINTED IN U.S.A.

Art by: Robert Hack

ISSUE ONE VARIANT COVER

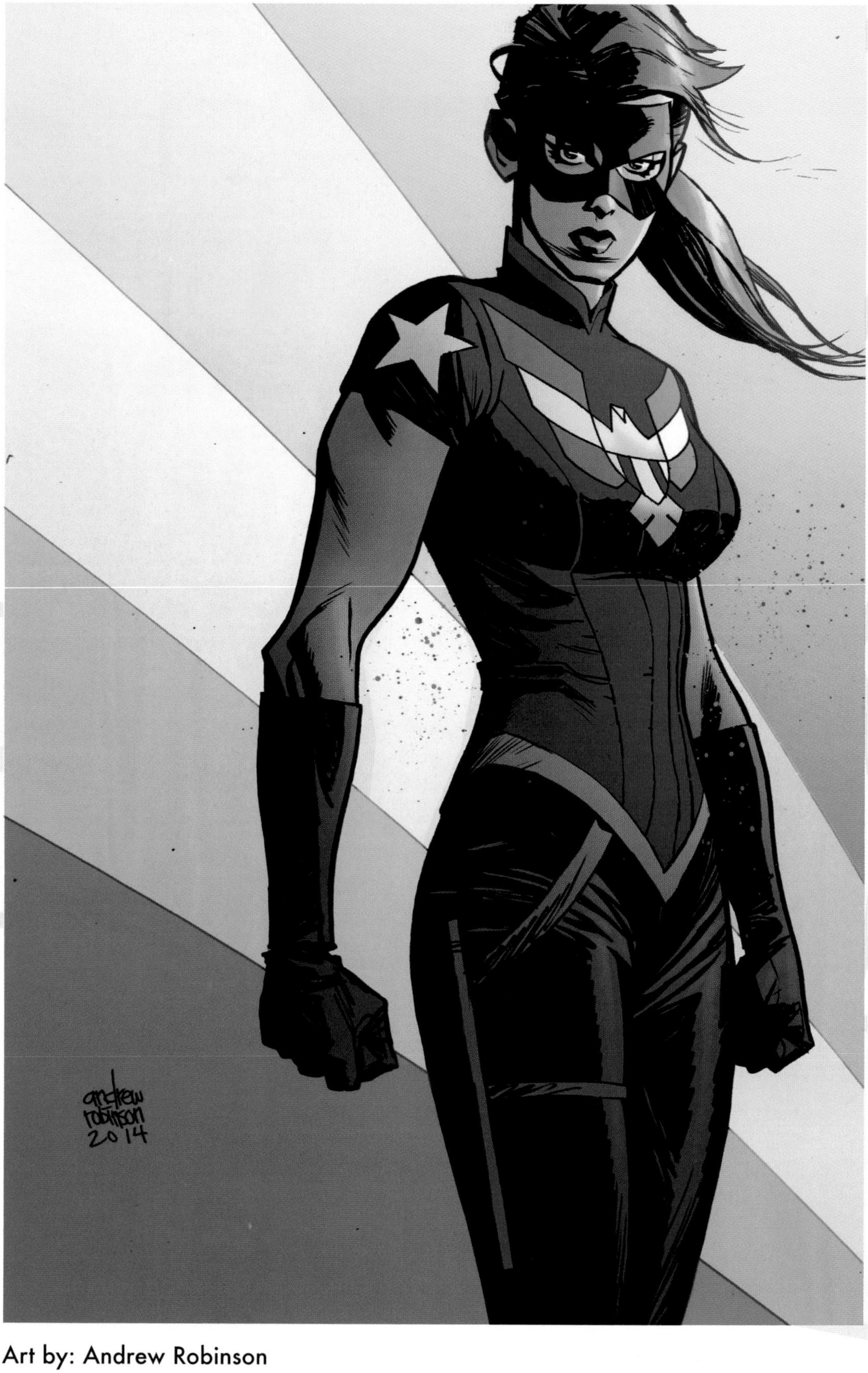
andrew robinson 2014

Art by: Andrew Robinson

ISSUE ONE VARIANT COVER

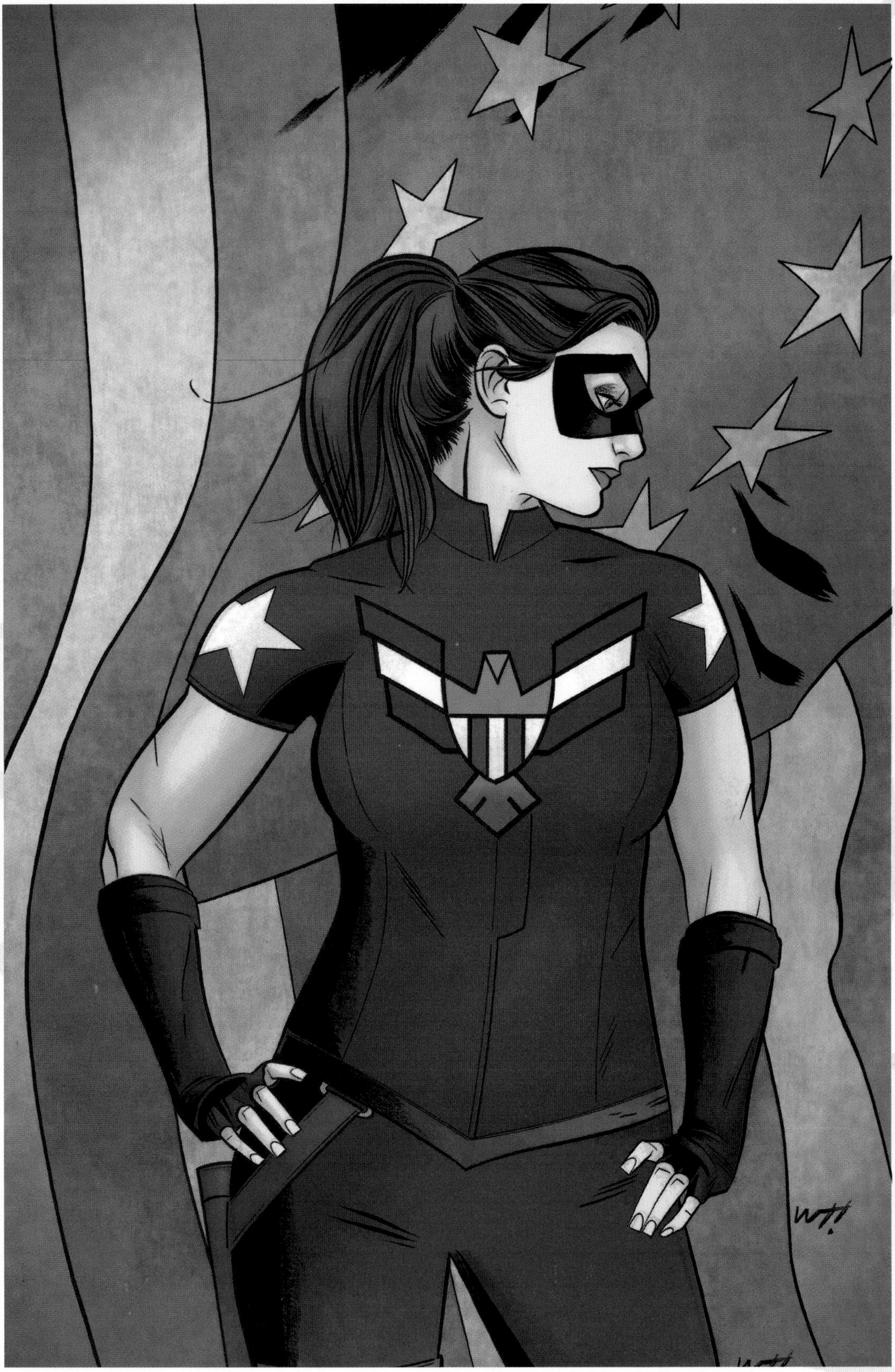
WT!

Art by: Wilfredo Torres

ISSUE ONE LOCAL COMIC SHOP DAY COVER

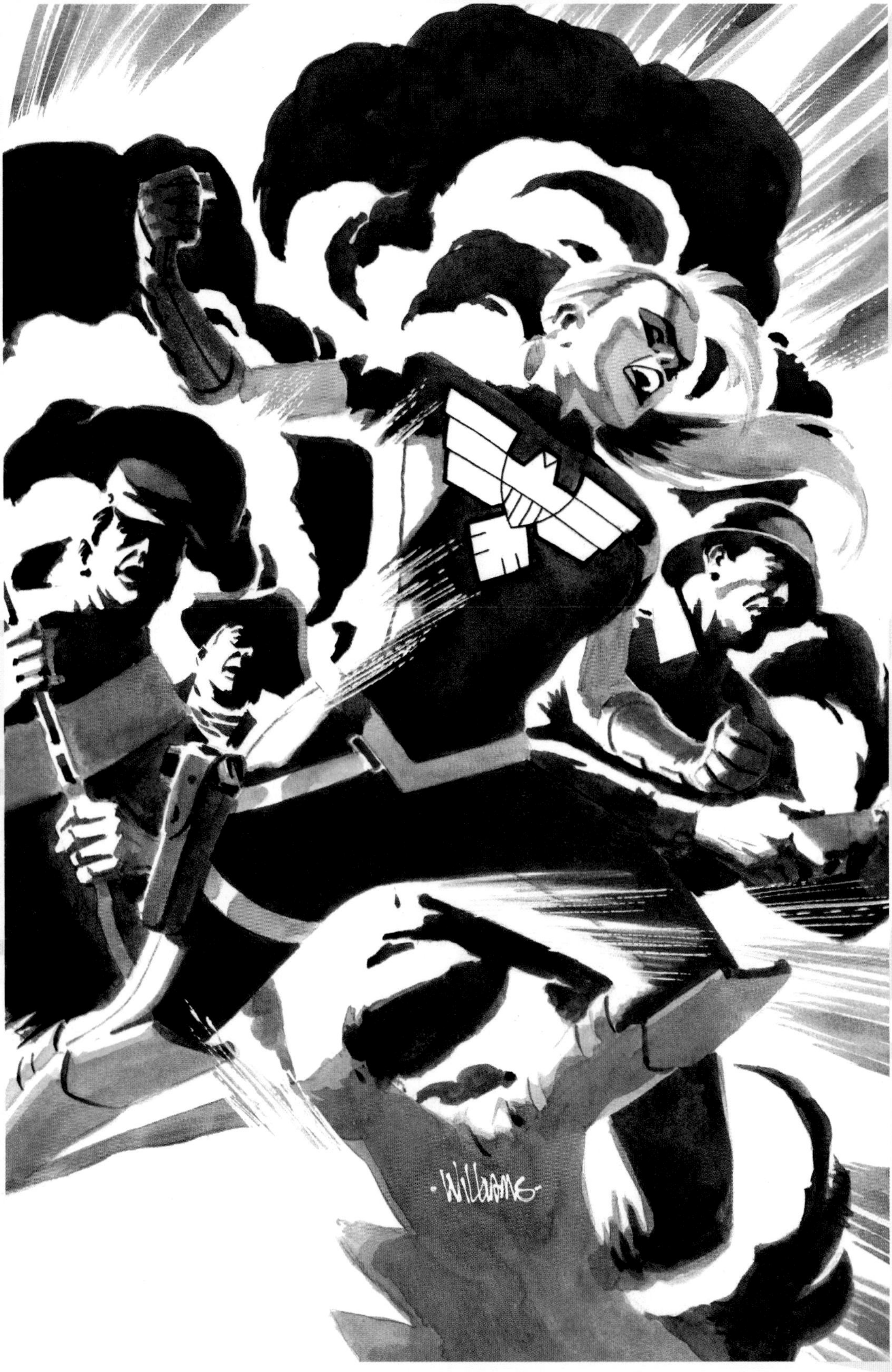

Williams

Art by: David Williams

ISSUE TWO VARIANT COVER

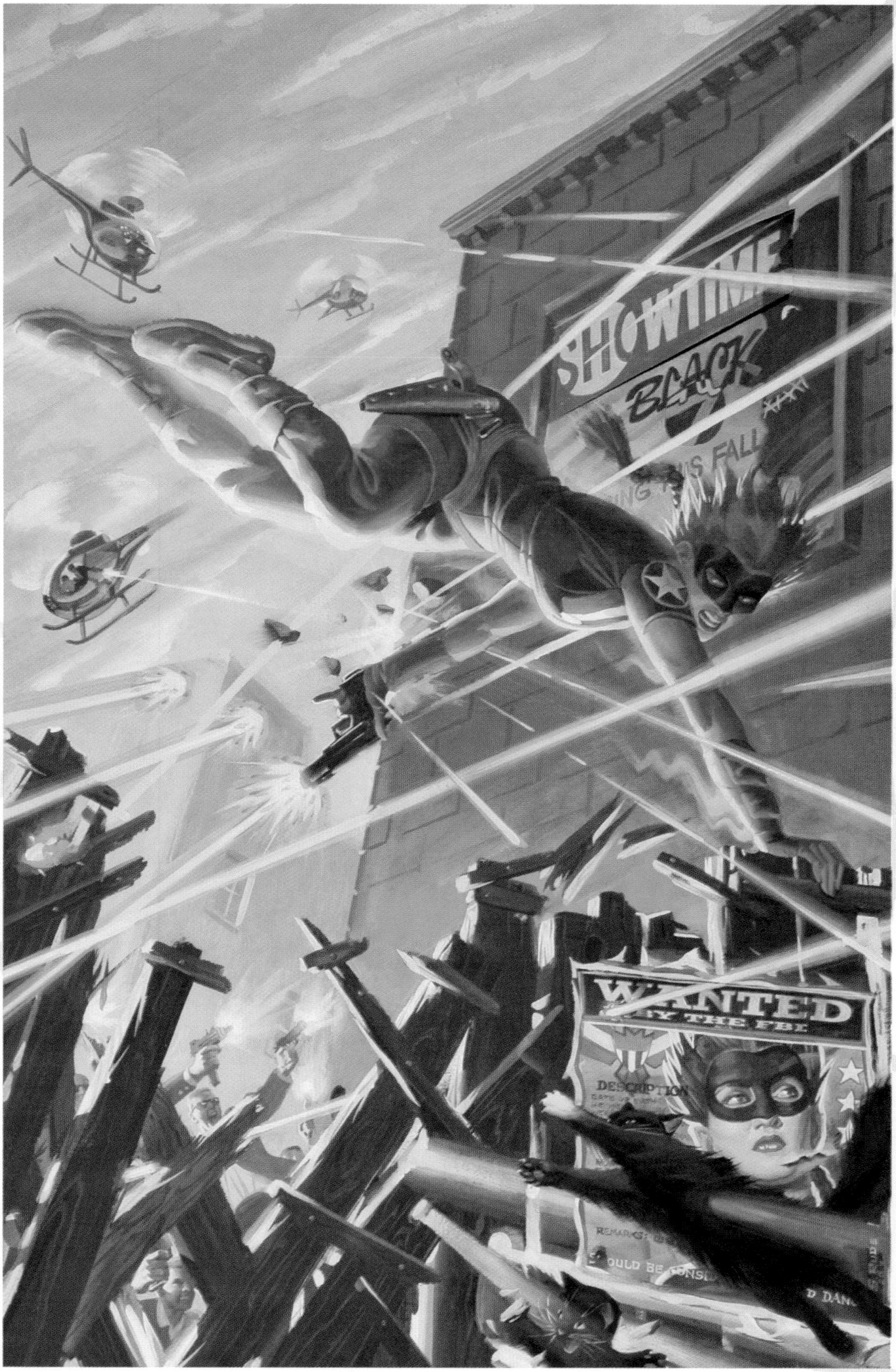
BLACK
WANTED
DESCRIPTION

Art by: Steve Rude

ISSUE TWO VARIANT COVER

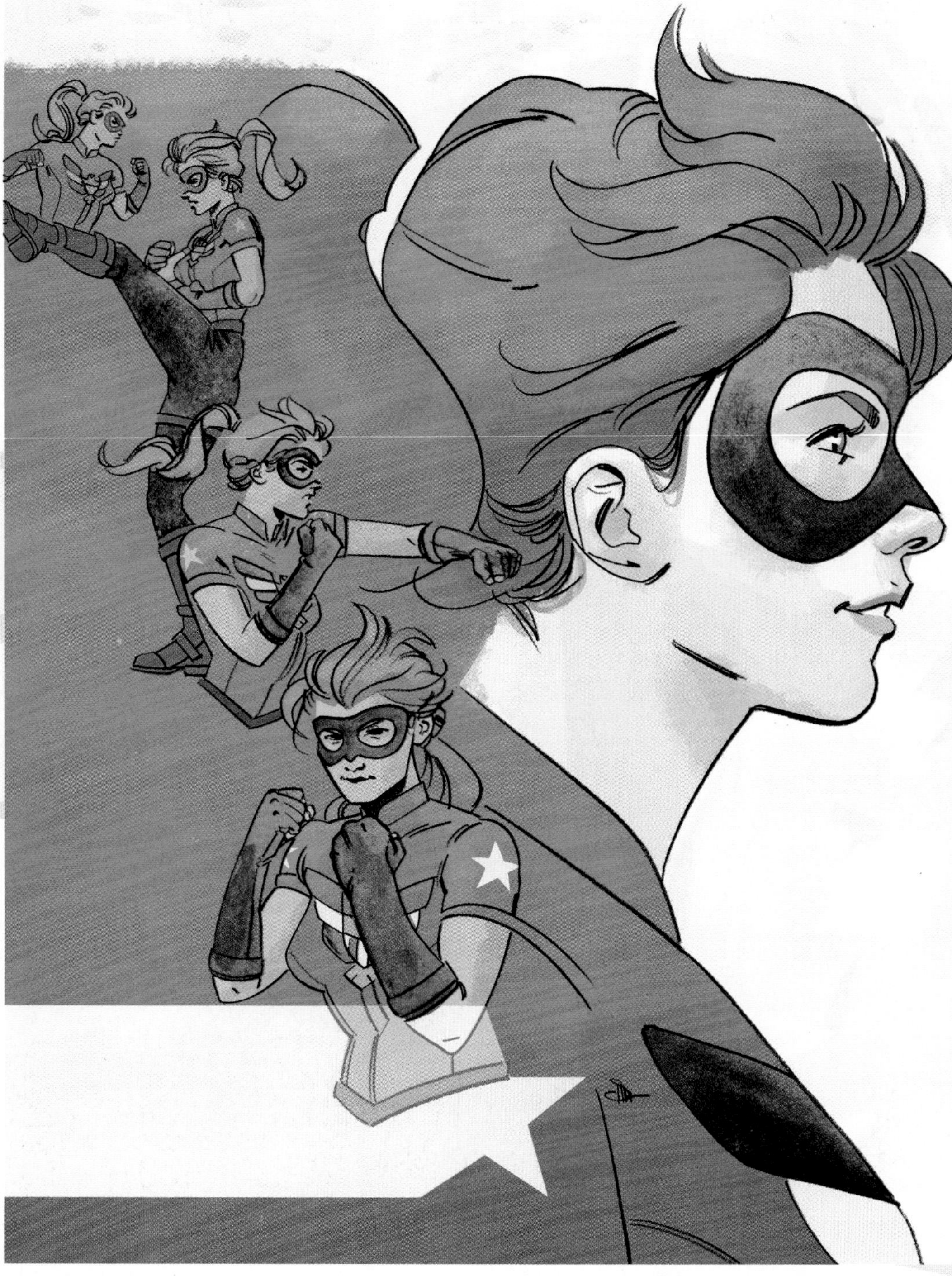

Art by: Evan Shaner

ISSUE TWO VARIANT COVER

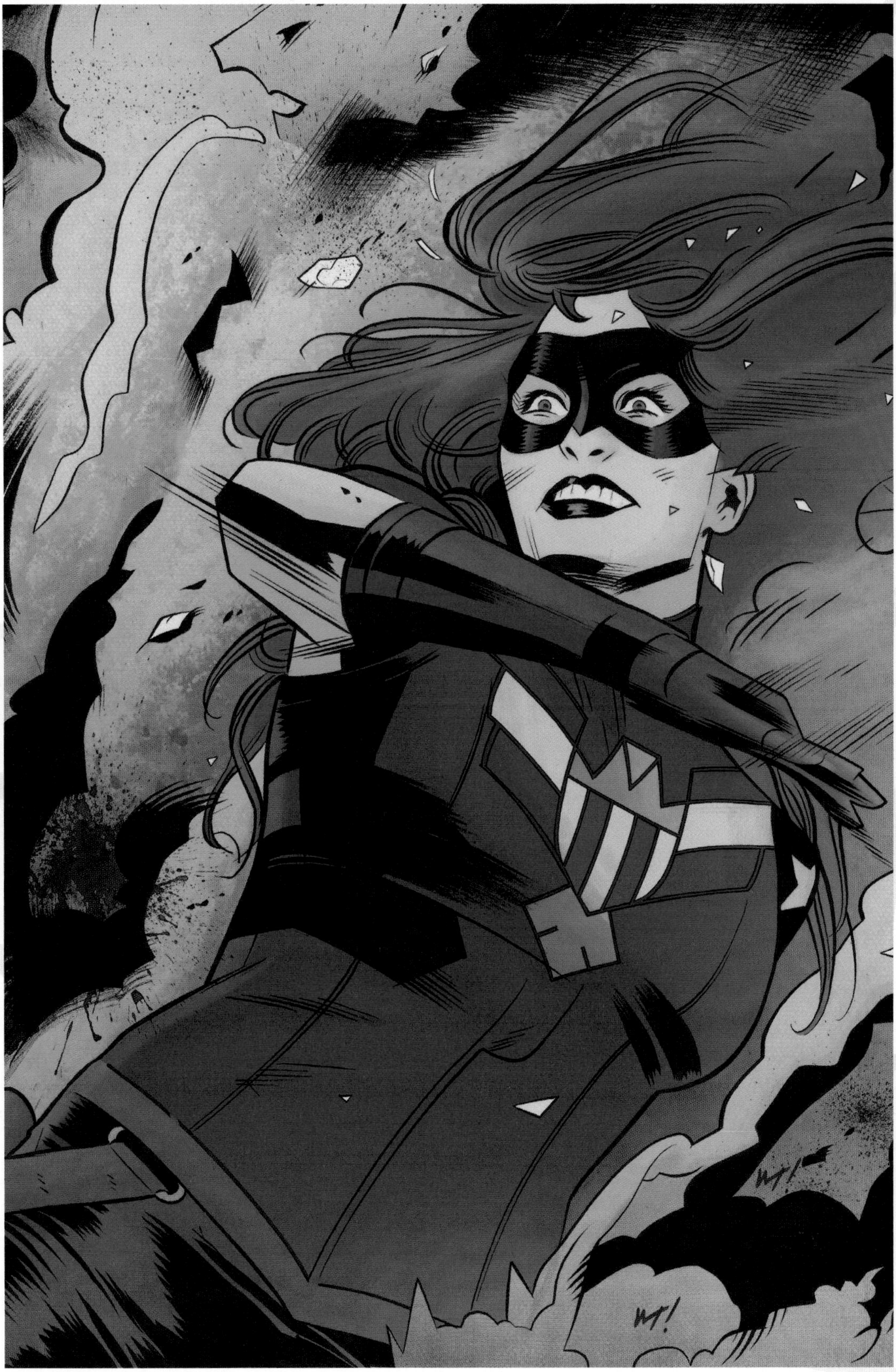

Art by: Wilfredo Torres

ISSUE TWO VARIANT COVER

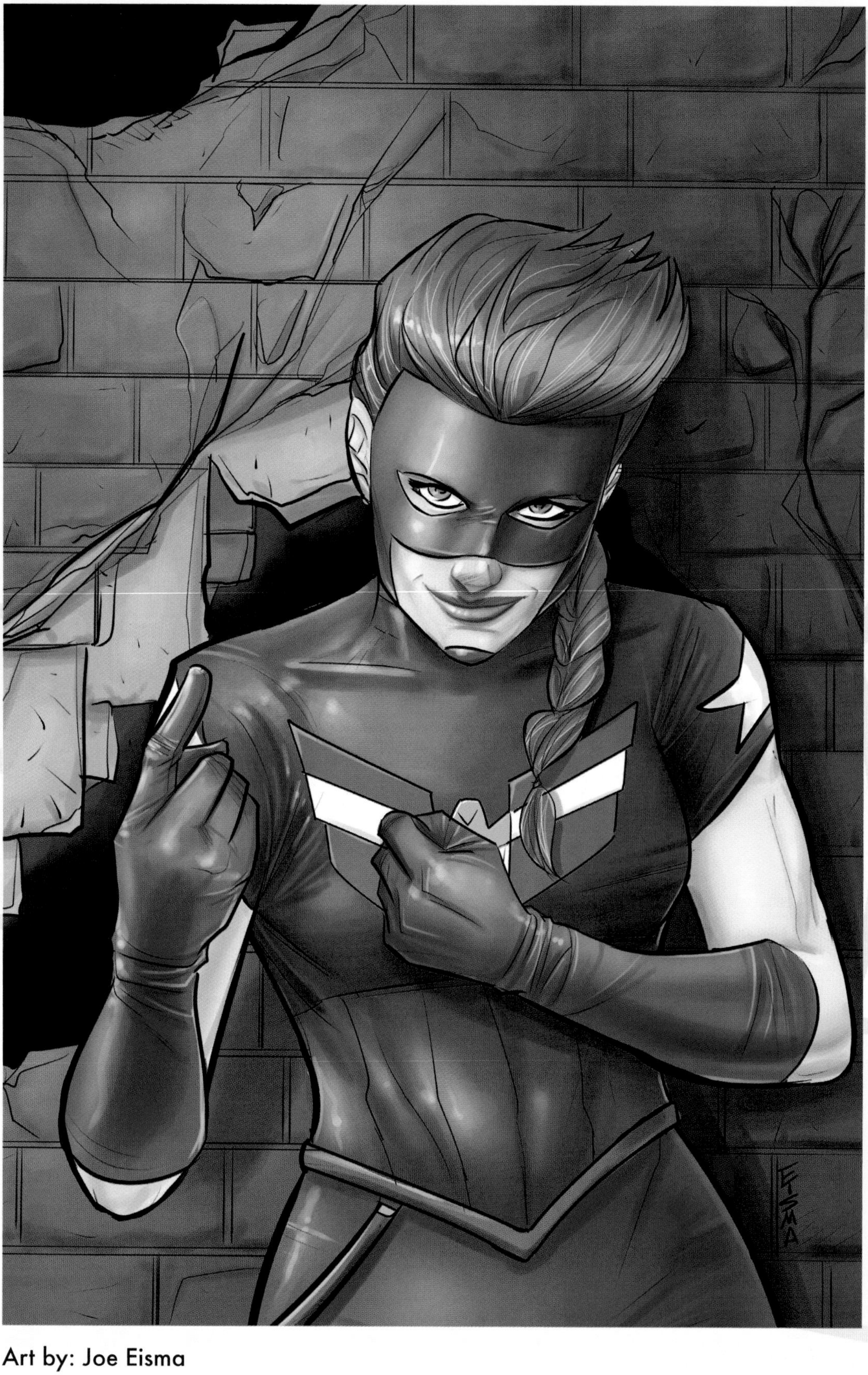
EISMA

Art by: Joe Eisma

ISSUE THREE VARIANT COVER

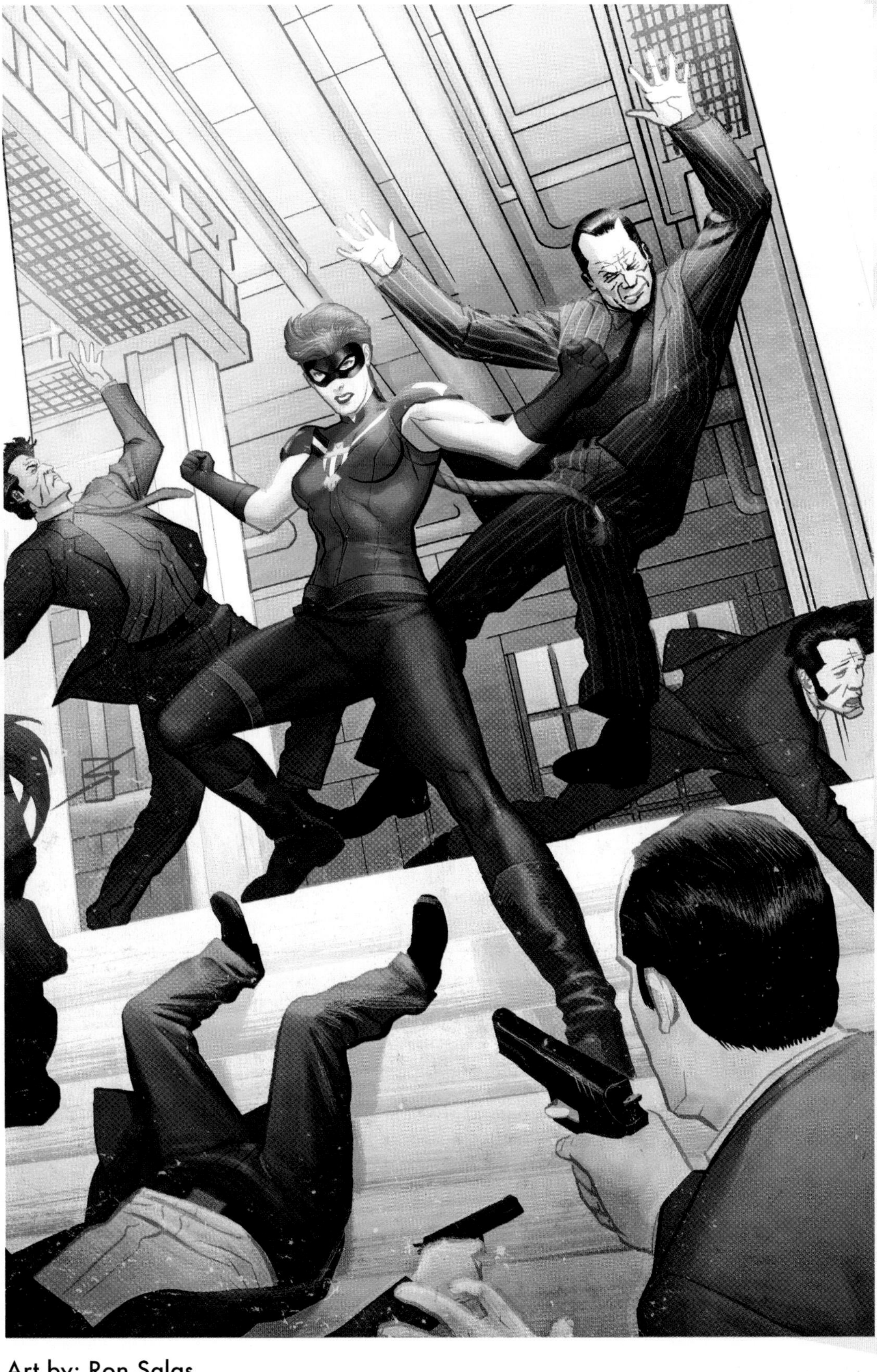

Art by: Ron Salas

ISSUE THREE VARIANT COVER

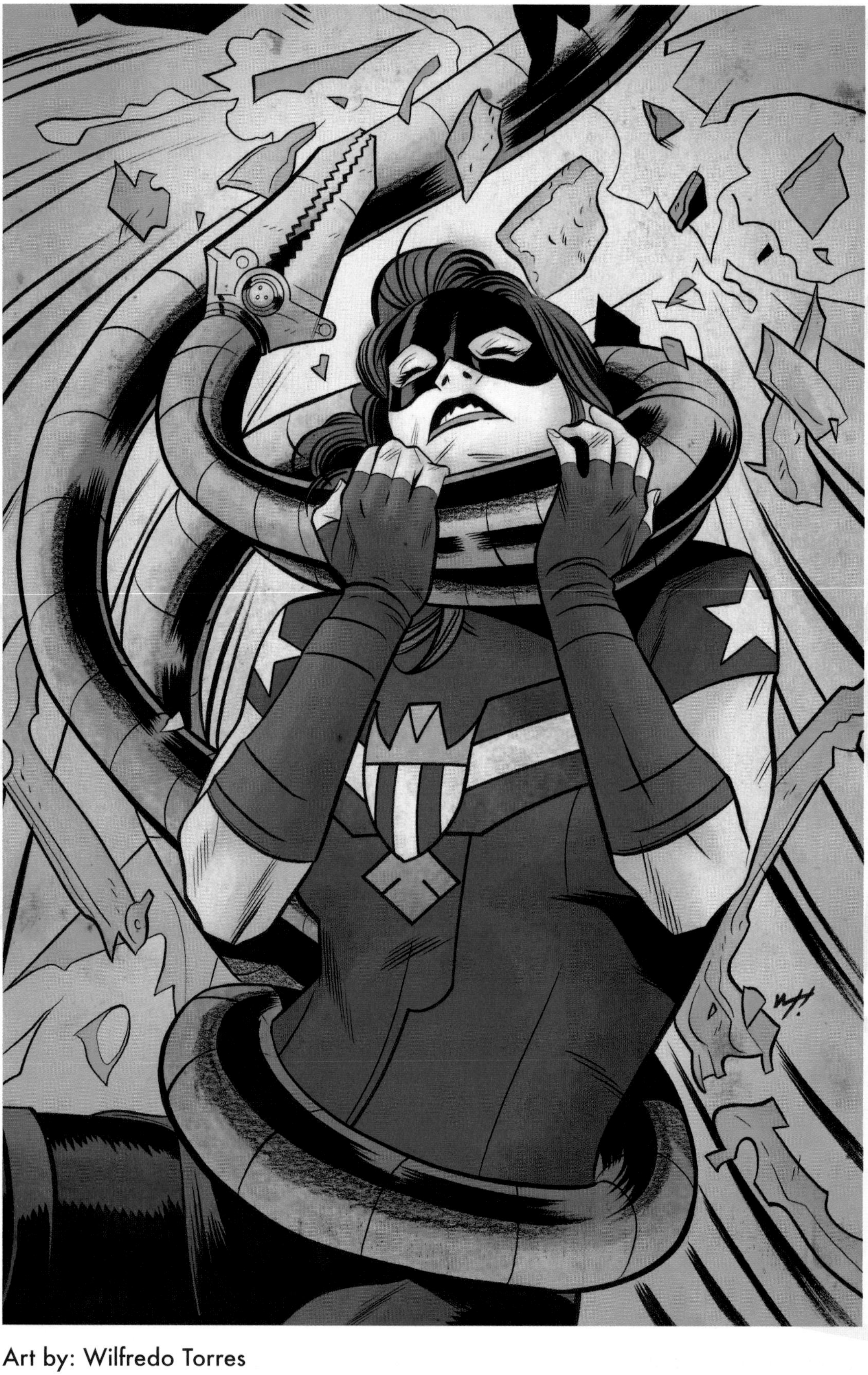

Art by: Wilfredo Torres

ISSUE FOUR VARIANT COVER

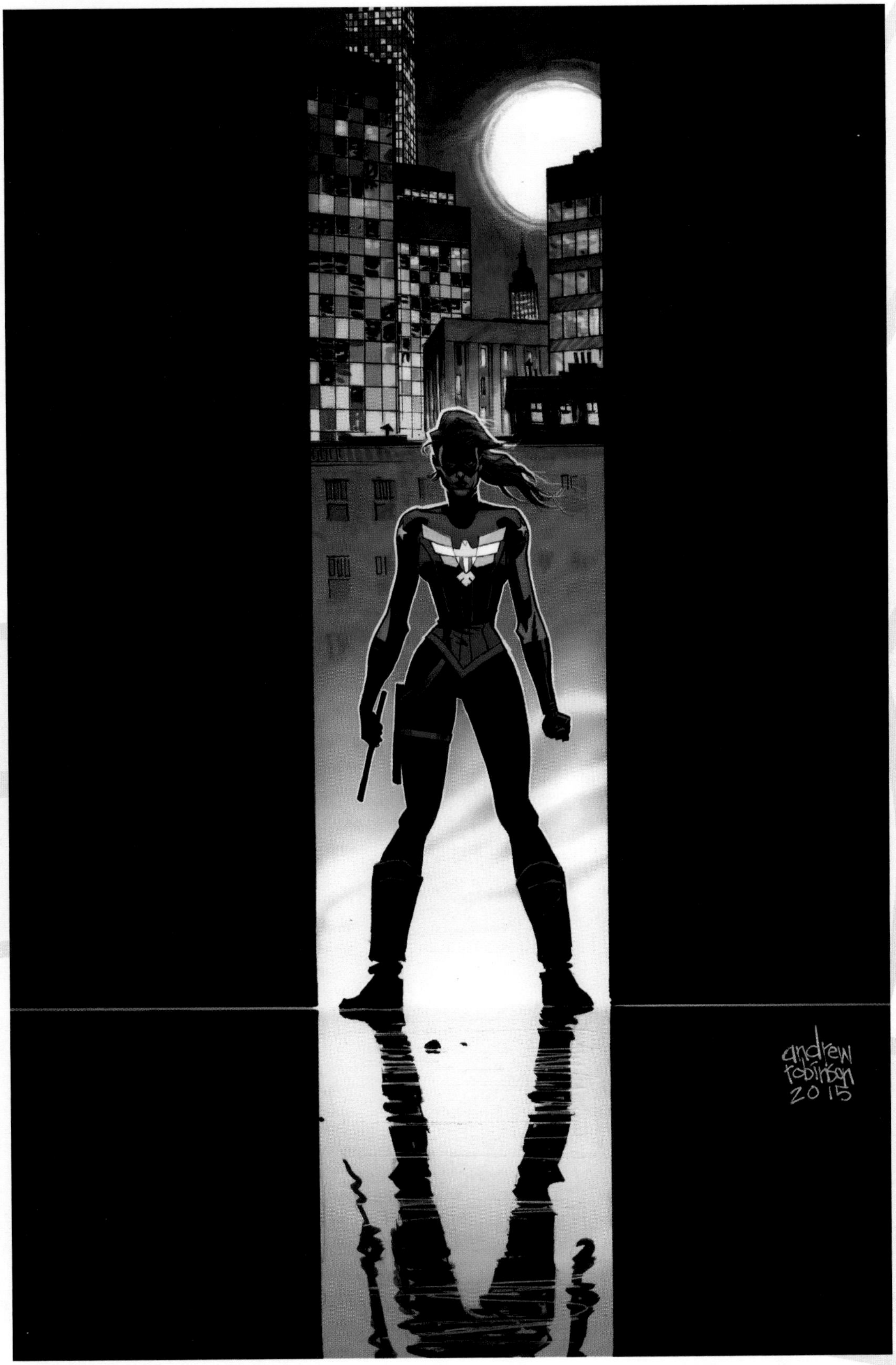
andrew robinson 2015

Art by: Andrew Robinson

UNRELEASED COVER

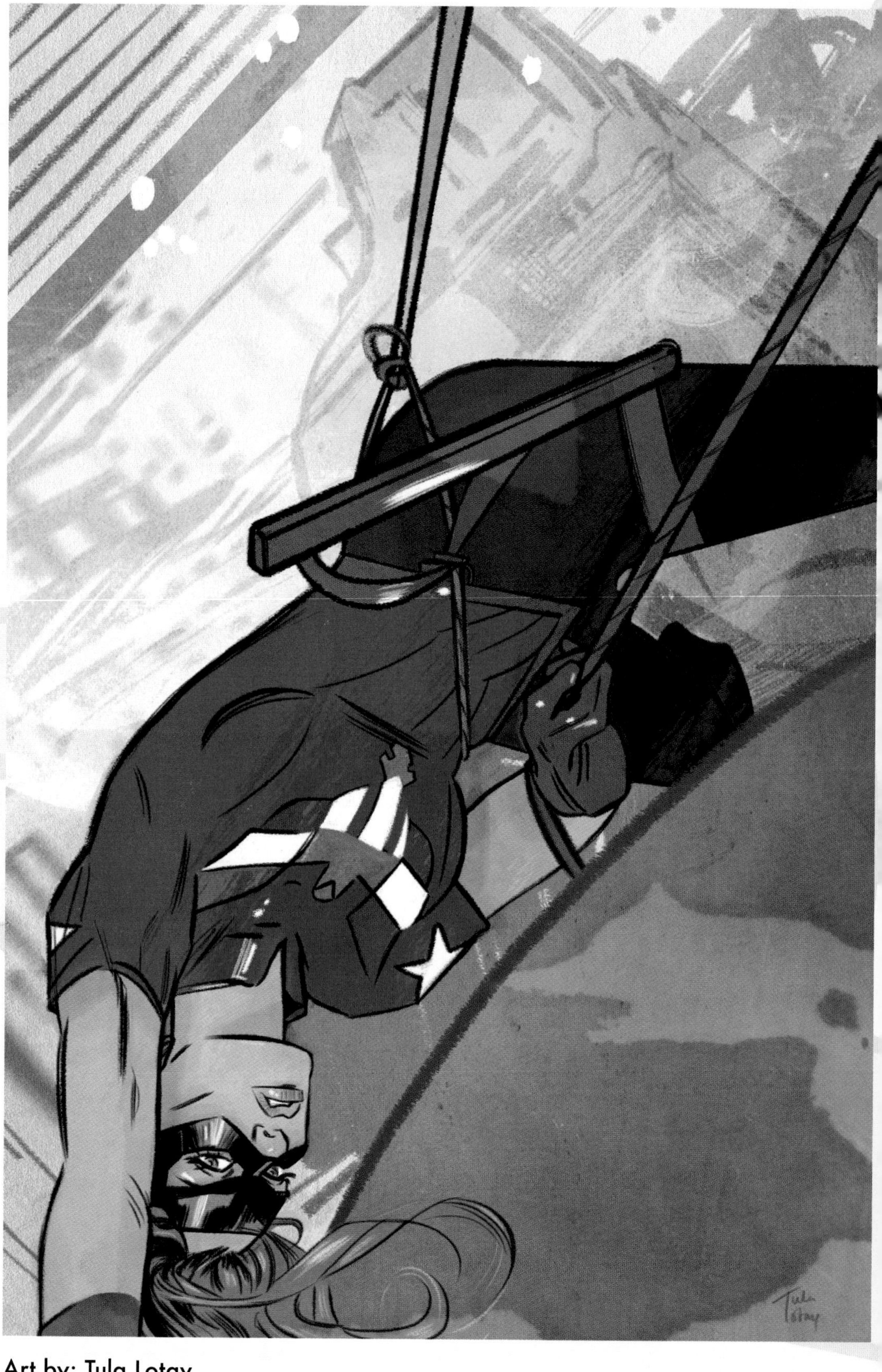

Art by: Tula Lotay

UNRELEASED COVER

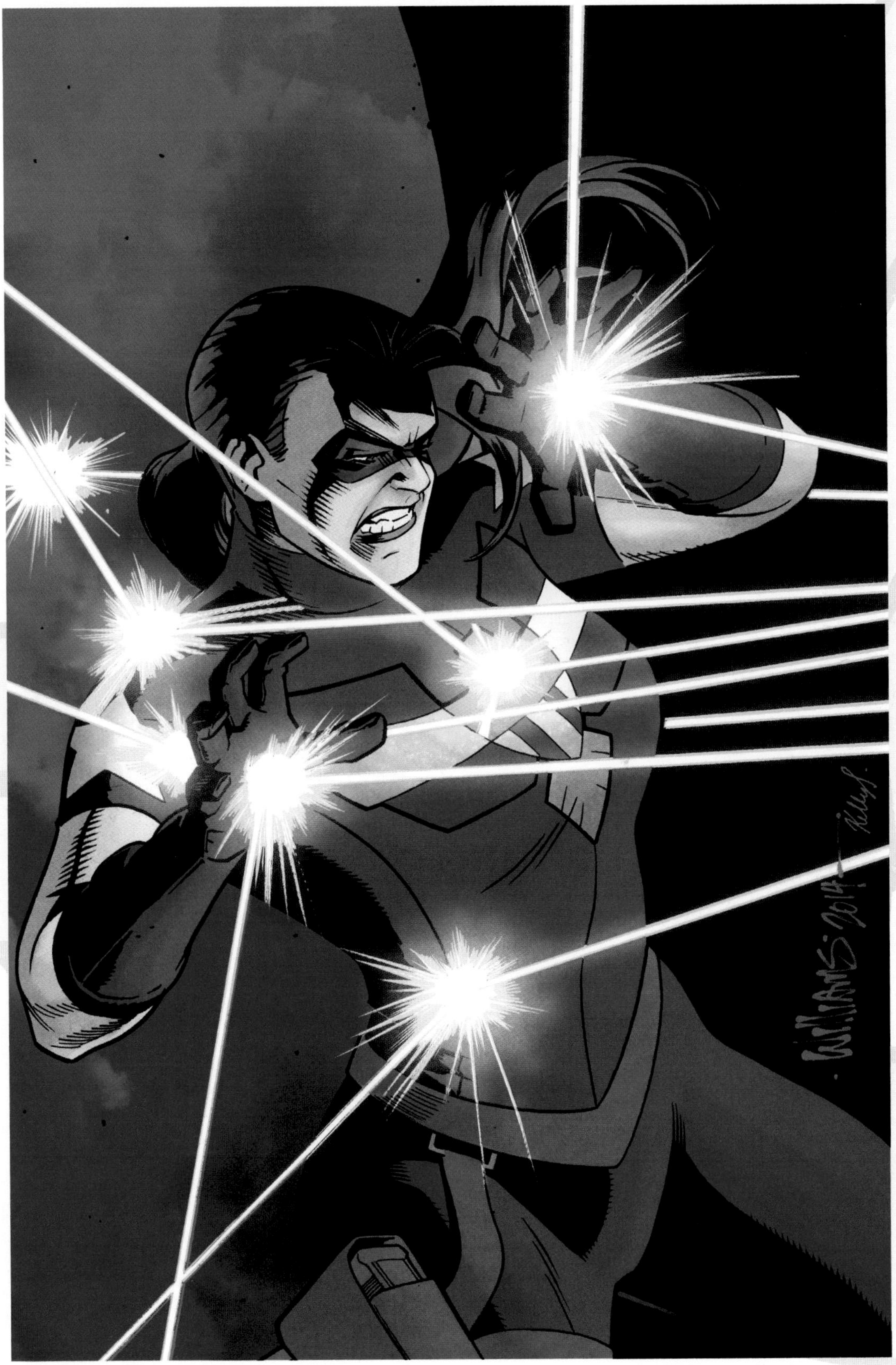

Art by: David Williams
with Kelly Fitzpatrick

UNRELEASED COVER

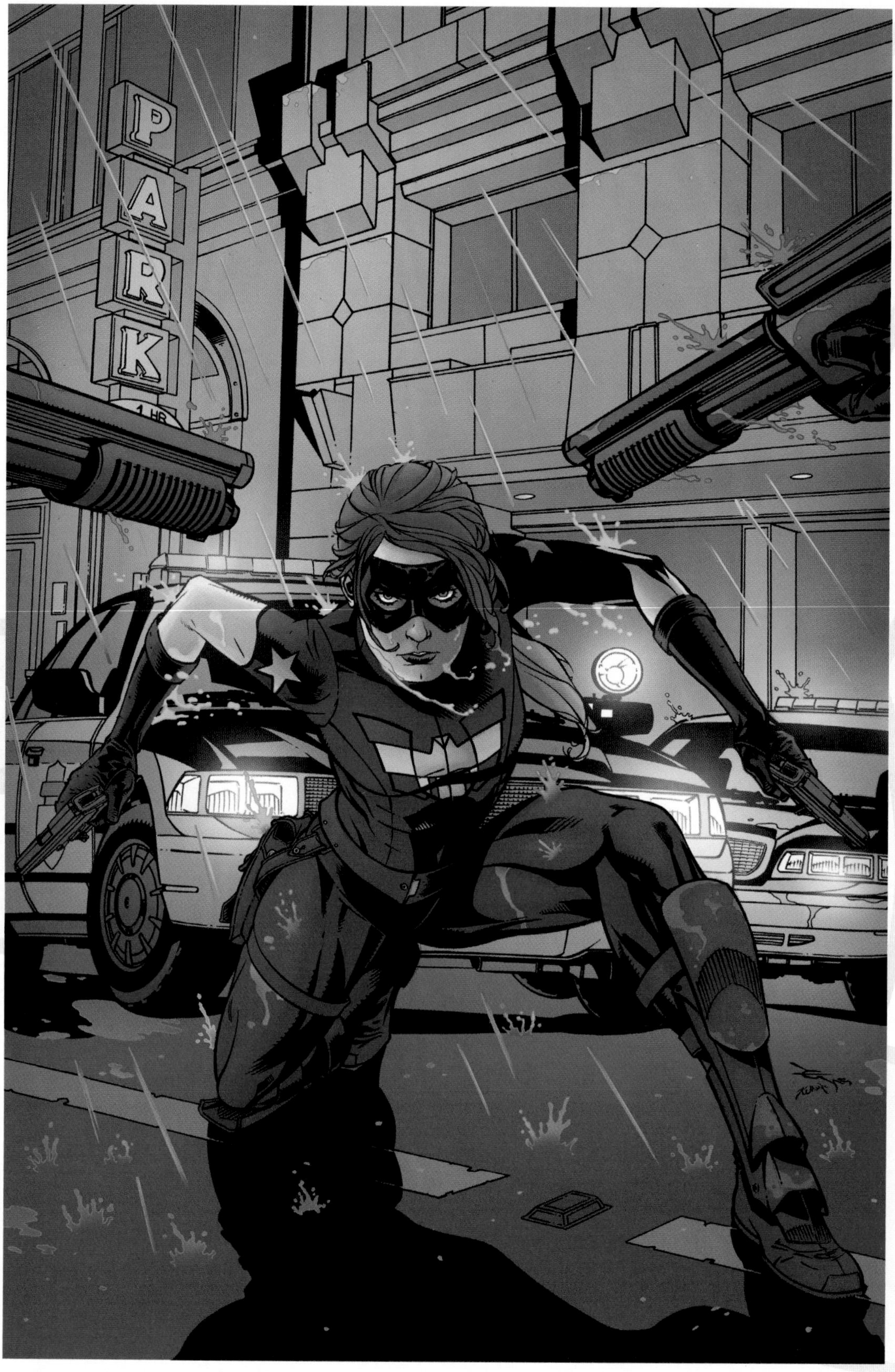
PARK
1 HR

Art by: Drew Johnson
with Kelly Fitzpatrick

UNRELEASED COVER

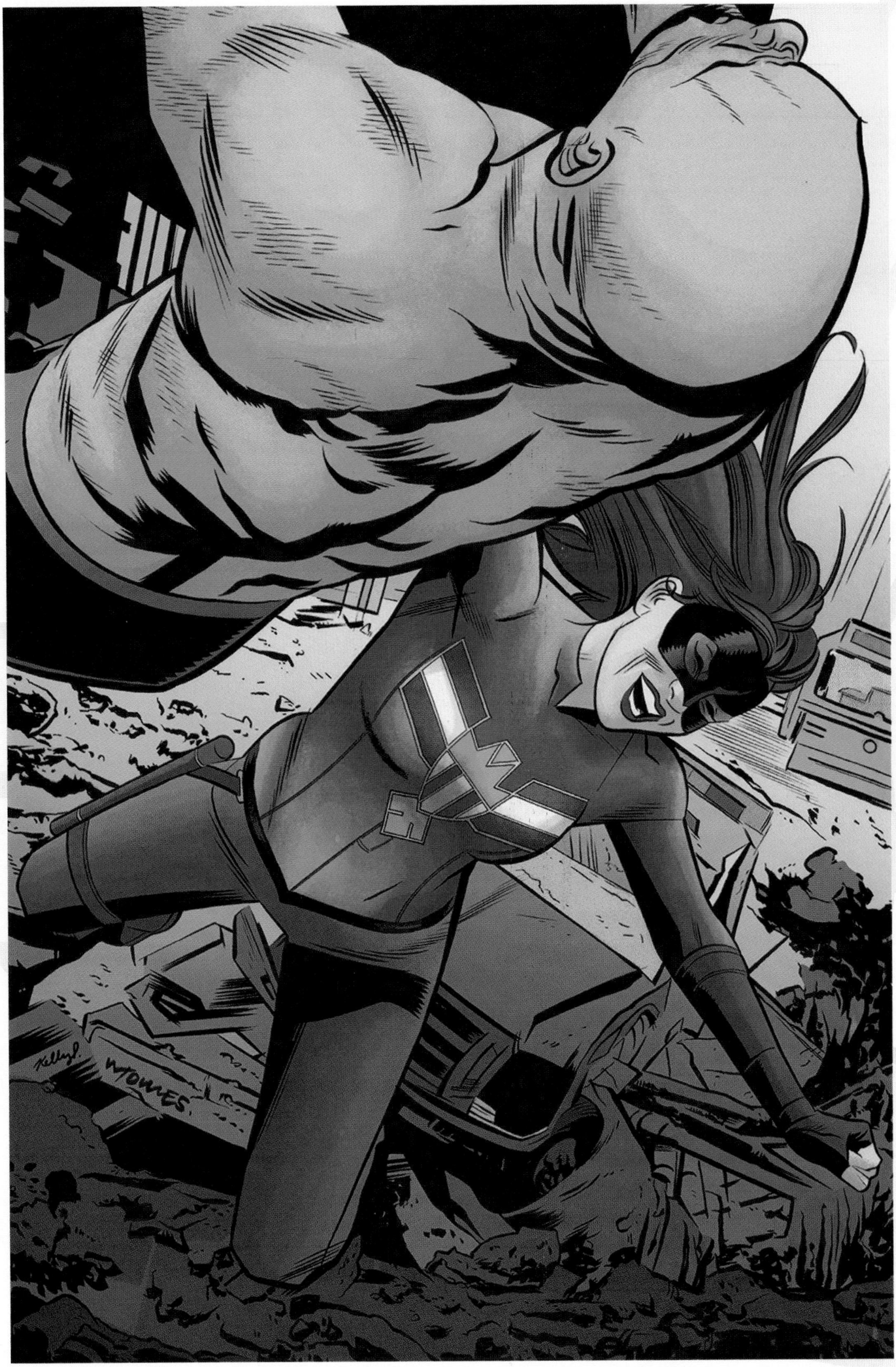

Art by: Wilfredo Torres

THE SHIELD RETURNS IN THE PAGES OF...

THE MIGHTY
CRUSADERS

DARK CIRCLE COMICS PRESENTS AN ALL-NEW ONGOING SER
FROM SUPERSTARS IAN FLYNN (WRITER) & KELSEY SHANNON (AR

SPECIAL PREVIEW

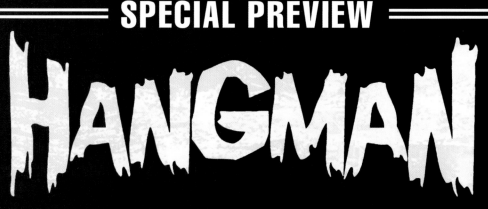

HANGMAN

They say HANGMAN is nothing more than an urban legend. A spook story told to scare criminals straight. But those who encounter him know different.

They know that when he comes for you... you're dead already.

Experience a taste of this tale of horror, the supernatural and violence.

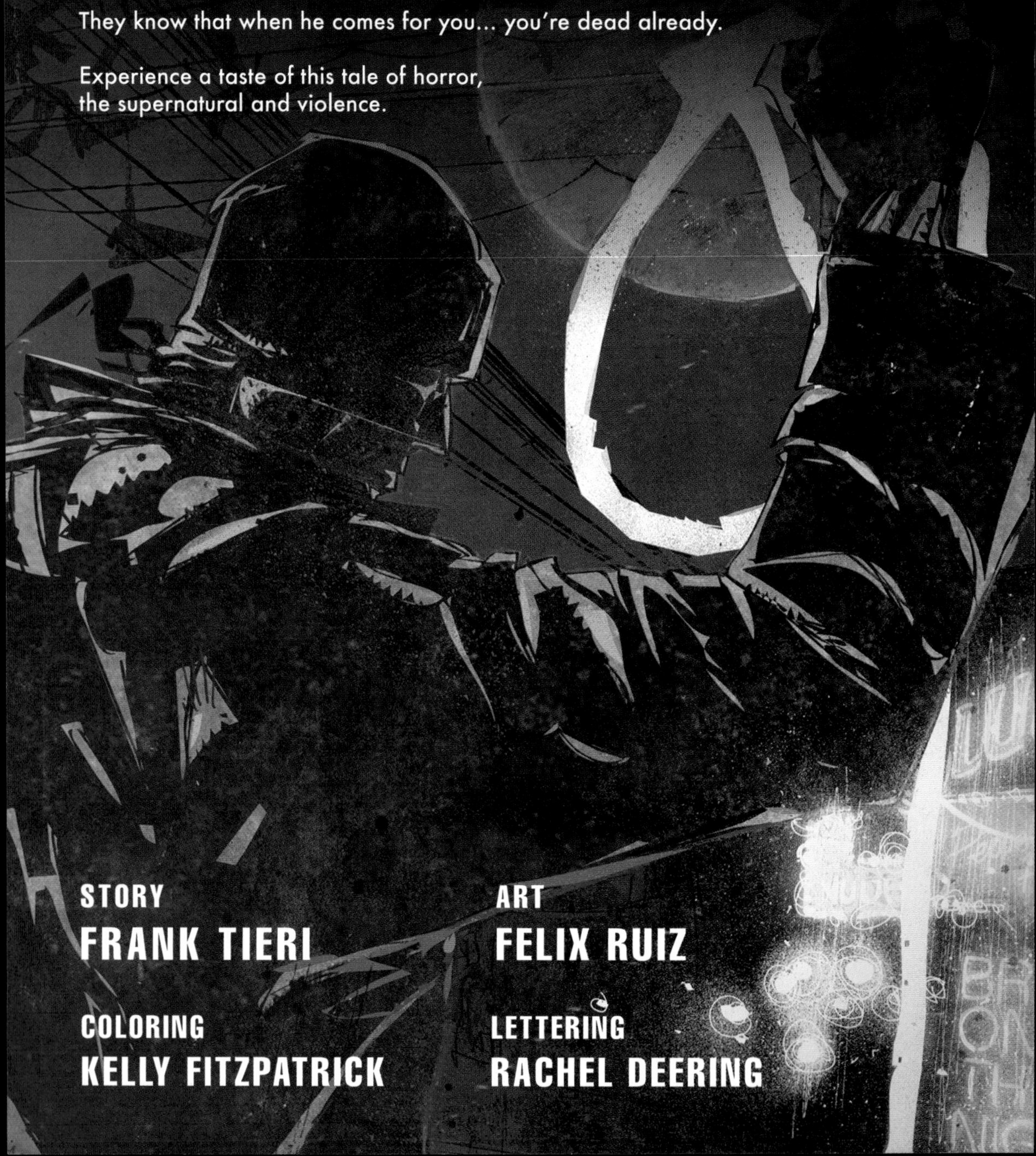

STORY
FRANK TIERI

ART
FELIX RUIZ

COLORING
KELLY FITZPATRICK

LETTERING
RACHEL DEERING

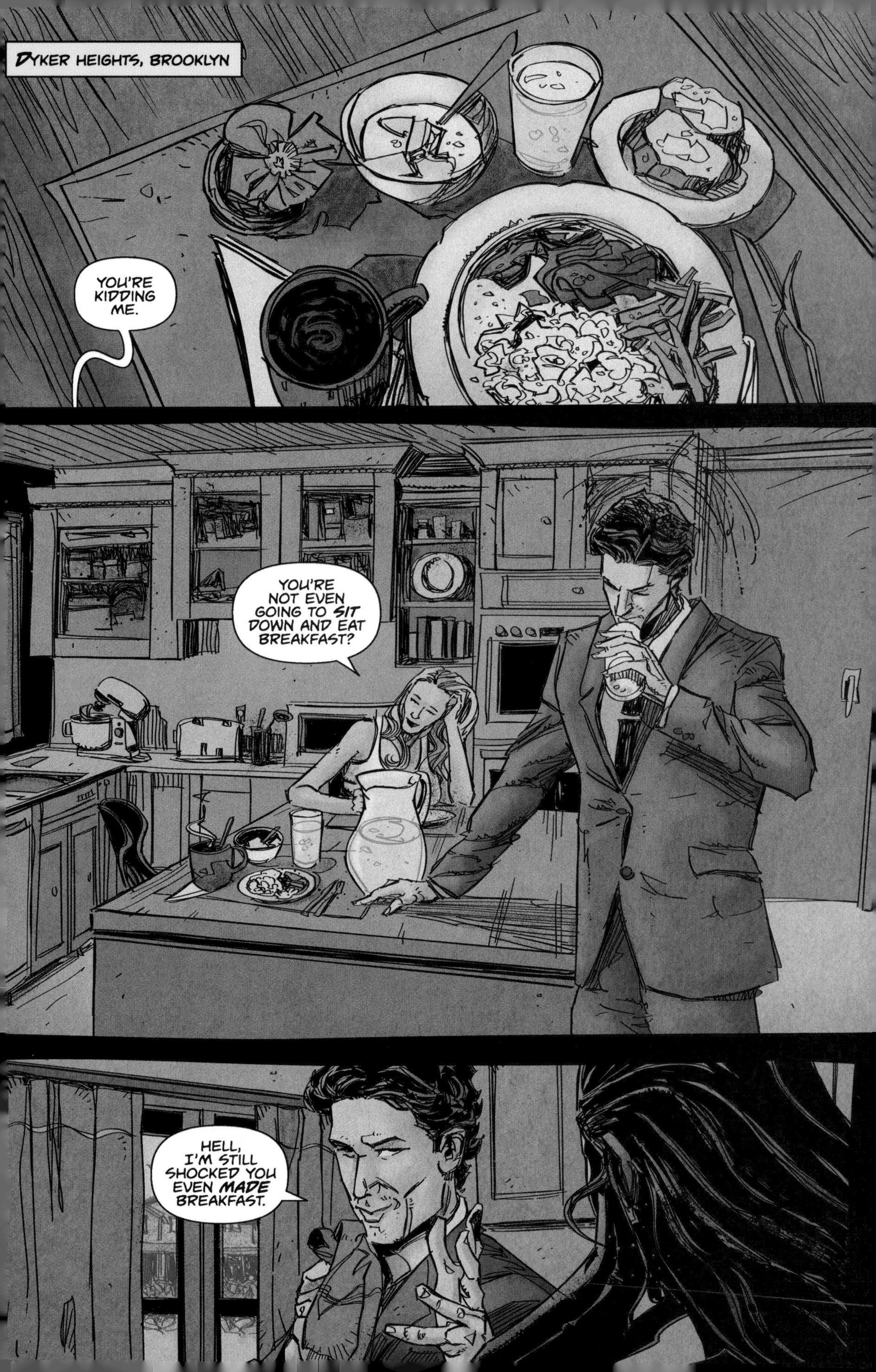
DYKER HEIGHTS, BROOKLYN
YOU'RE KIDDING ME.
YOU'RE NOT EVEN GOING TO SIT DOWN AND EAT BREAKFAST?
HELL, I'M STILL SHOCKED YOU EVEN MADE BREAKFAST.

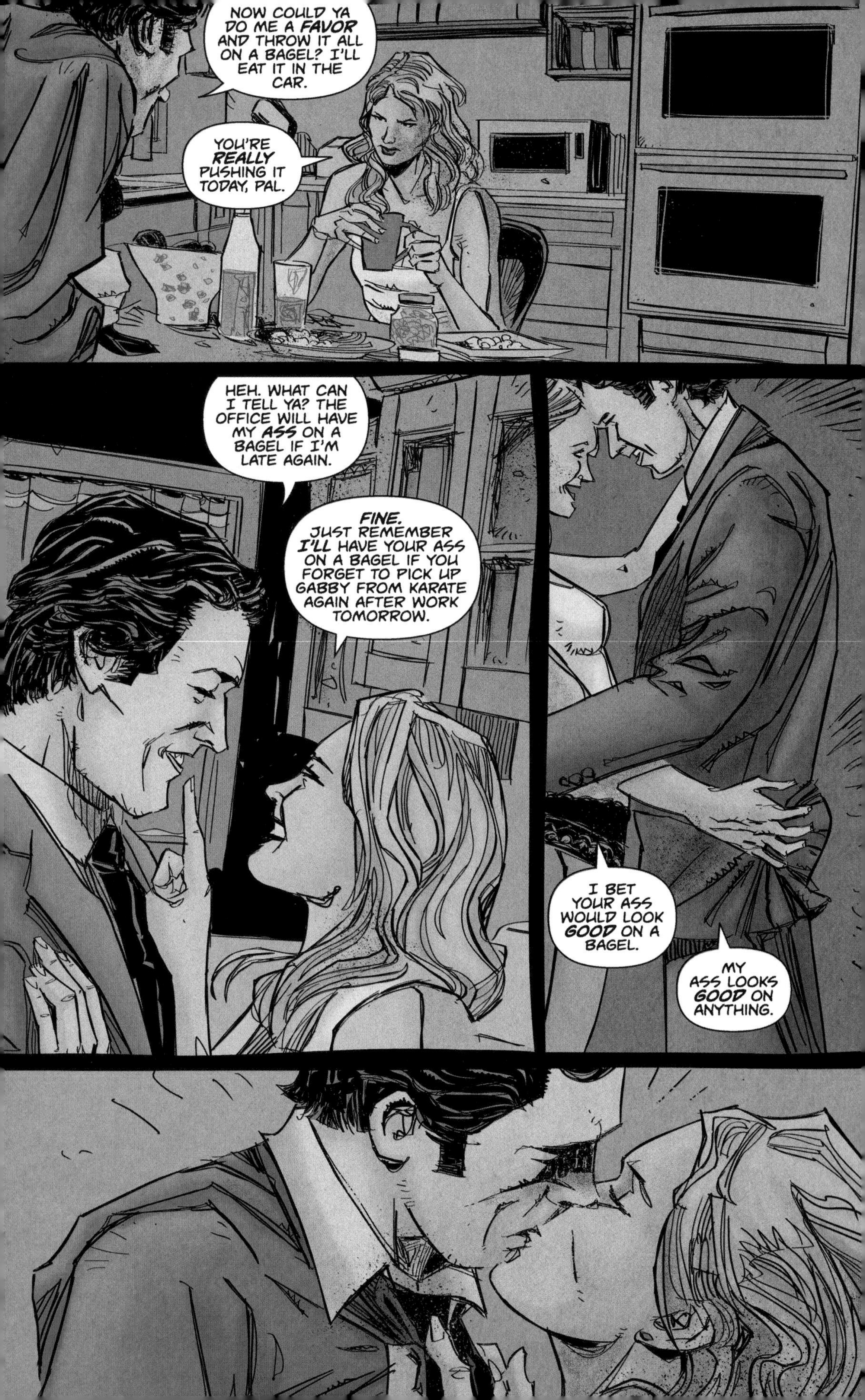
NOW COULD YA DO ME A FAVOR AND THROW IT ALL ON A BAGEL? I'LL EAT IT IN THE CAR.
YOU'RE REALLY PUSHING IT TODAY, PAL.
HEH. WHAT CAN I TELL YA? THE OFFICE WILL HAVE MY ASS ON A BAGEL IF I'M LATE AGAIN.
FINE. JUST REMEMBER I'LL HAVE YOUR ASS ON A BAGEL IF YOU FORGET TO PICK UP GABBY FROM KARATE AGAIN AFTER WORK TOMORROW.
I BET YOUR ASS WOULD LOOK GOOD ON A BAGEL.
MY ASS LOOKS GOOD ON ANYTHING.

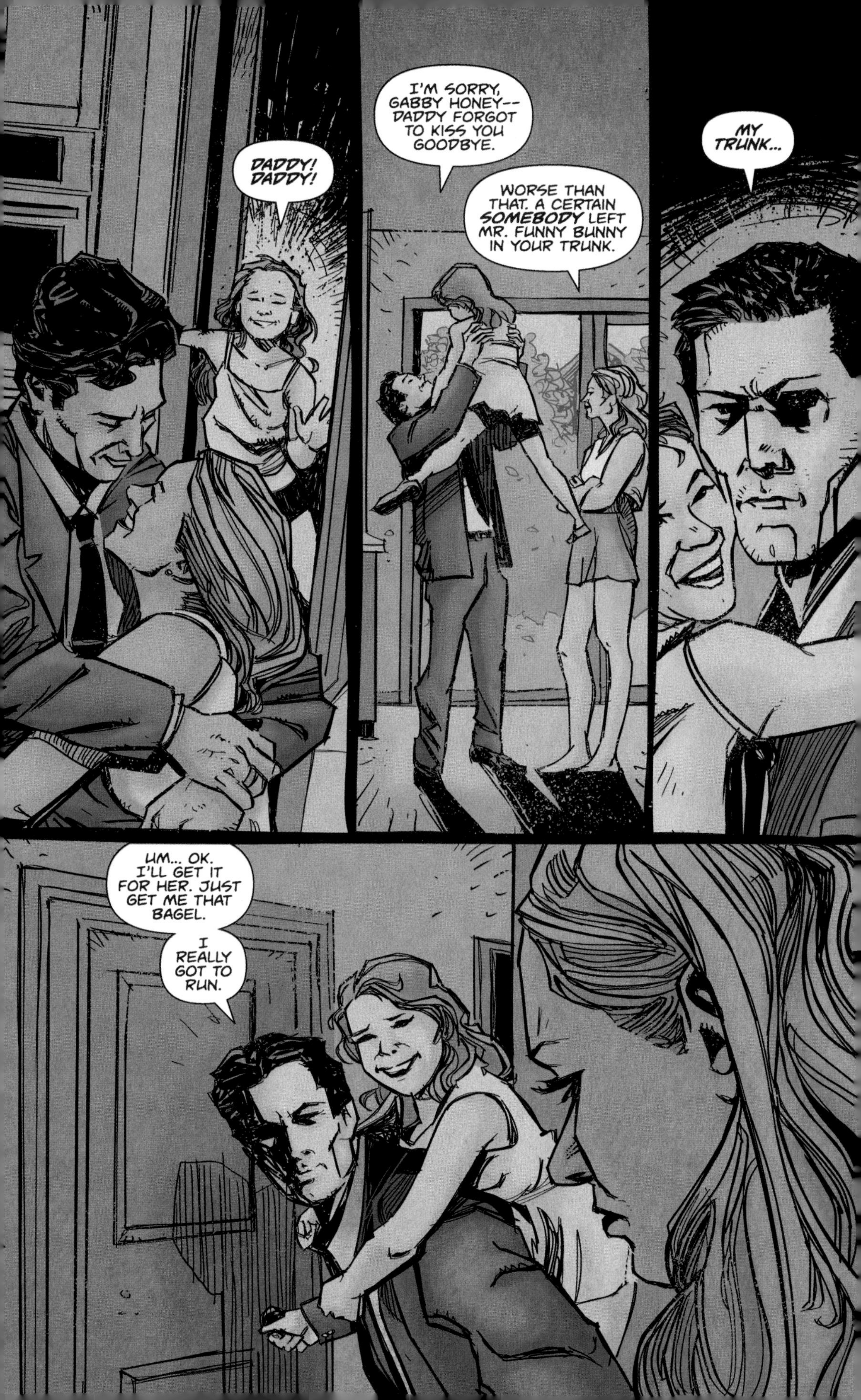
DADDY! DADDY!
I'M SORRY, GABBY HONEY-- DADDY FORGOT TO KISS YOU GOODBYE.
WORSE THAN THAT. A CERTAIN SOMEBODY LEFT MR. FUNNY BUNNY IN YOUR TRUNK.
MY TRUNK...
UM... OK. I'LL GET IT FOR HER. JUST GET ME THAT BAGEL.
I REALLY GOT TO RUN.

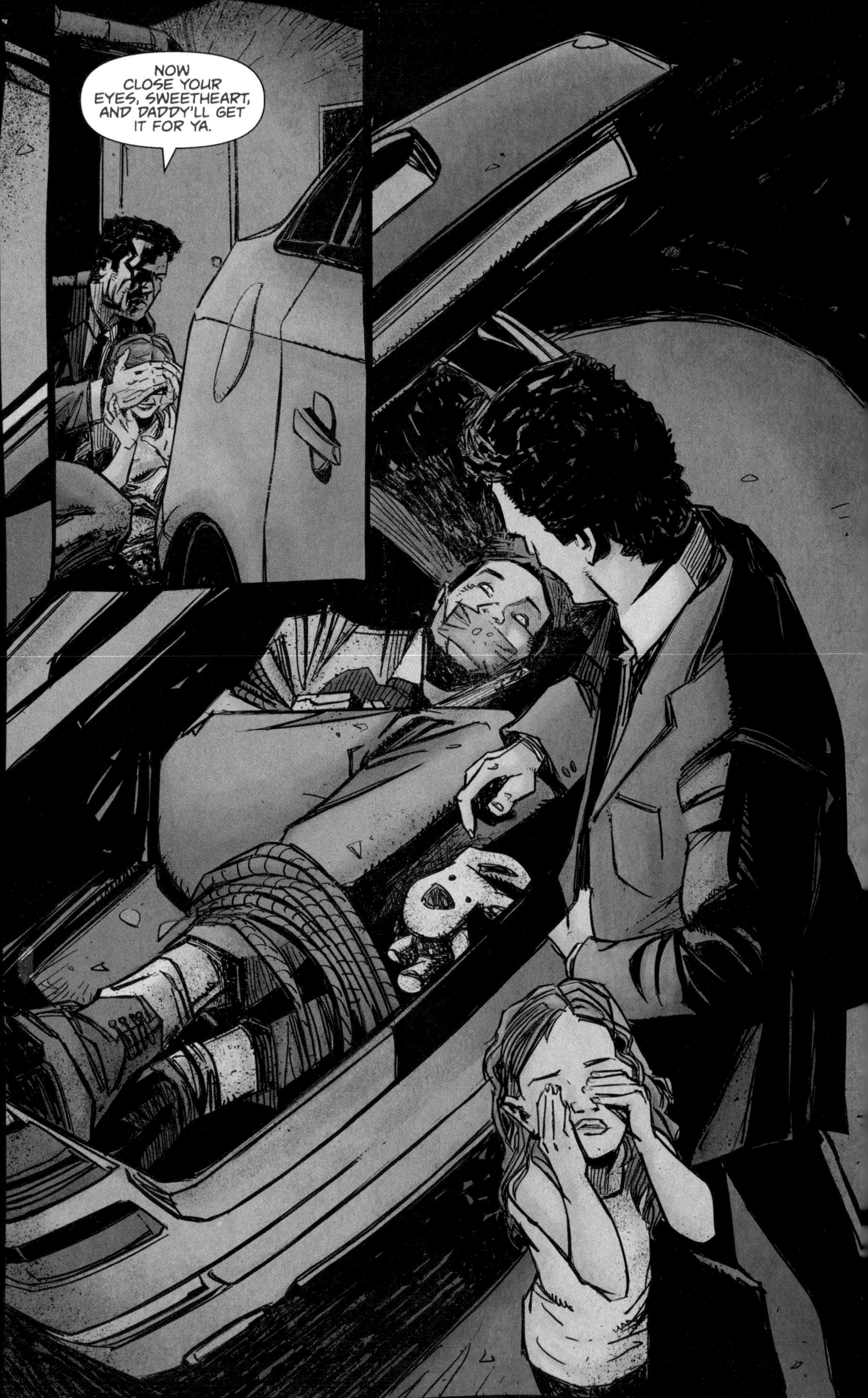
NOW CLOSE YOUR EYES, SWEETHEART, AND DADDY'LL GET IT FOR YA.

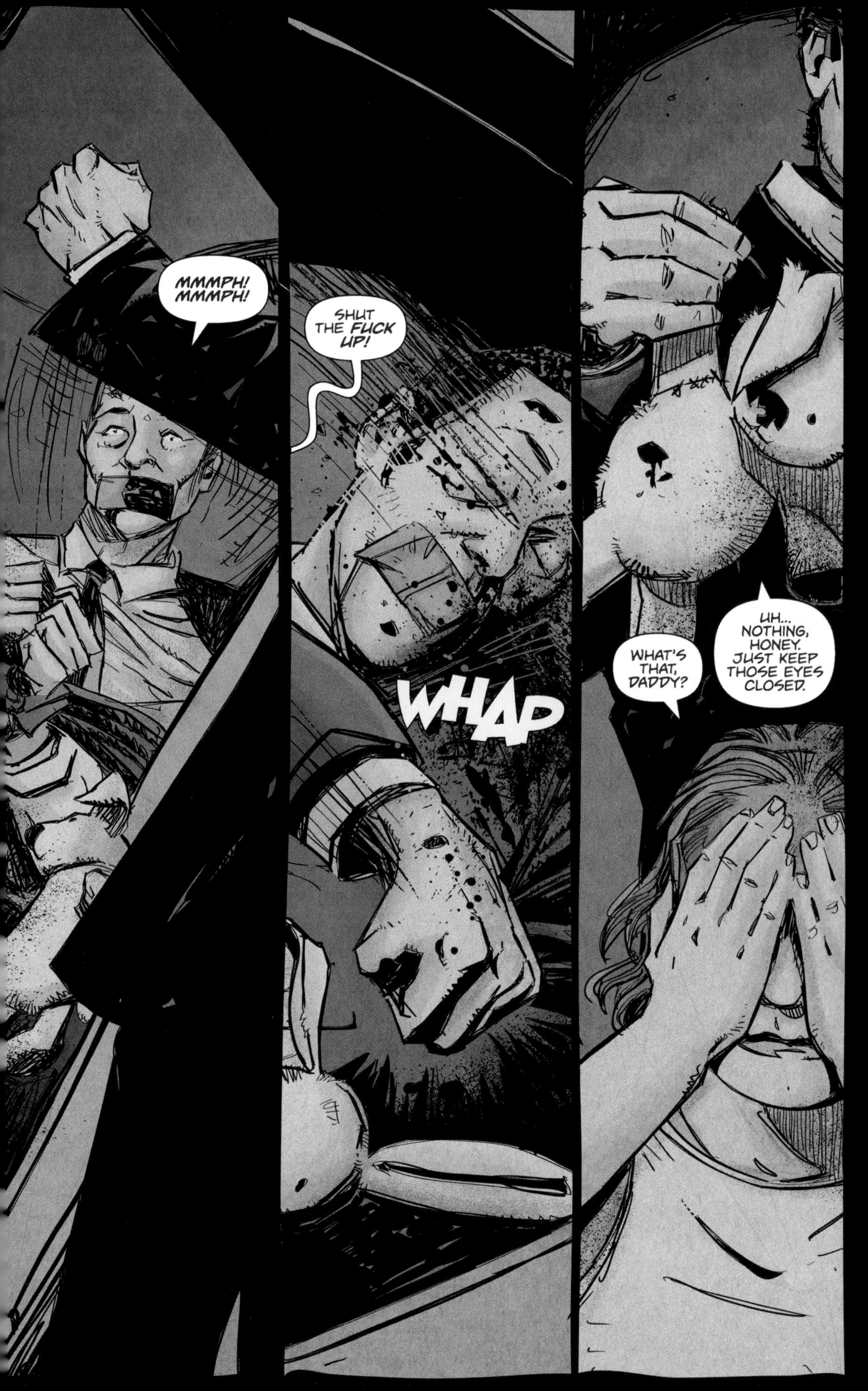
MMMPH! MMMPH!
SHUT THE FUCK UP!
WHAP
WHAT'S THAT, DADDY?
UH... NOTHING, HONEY. JUST KEEP THOSE EYES CLOSED.

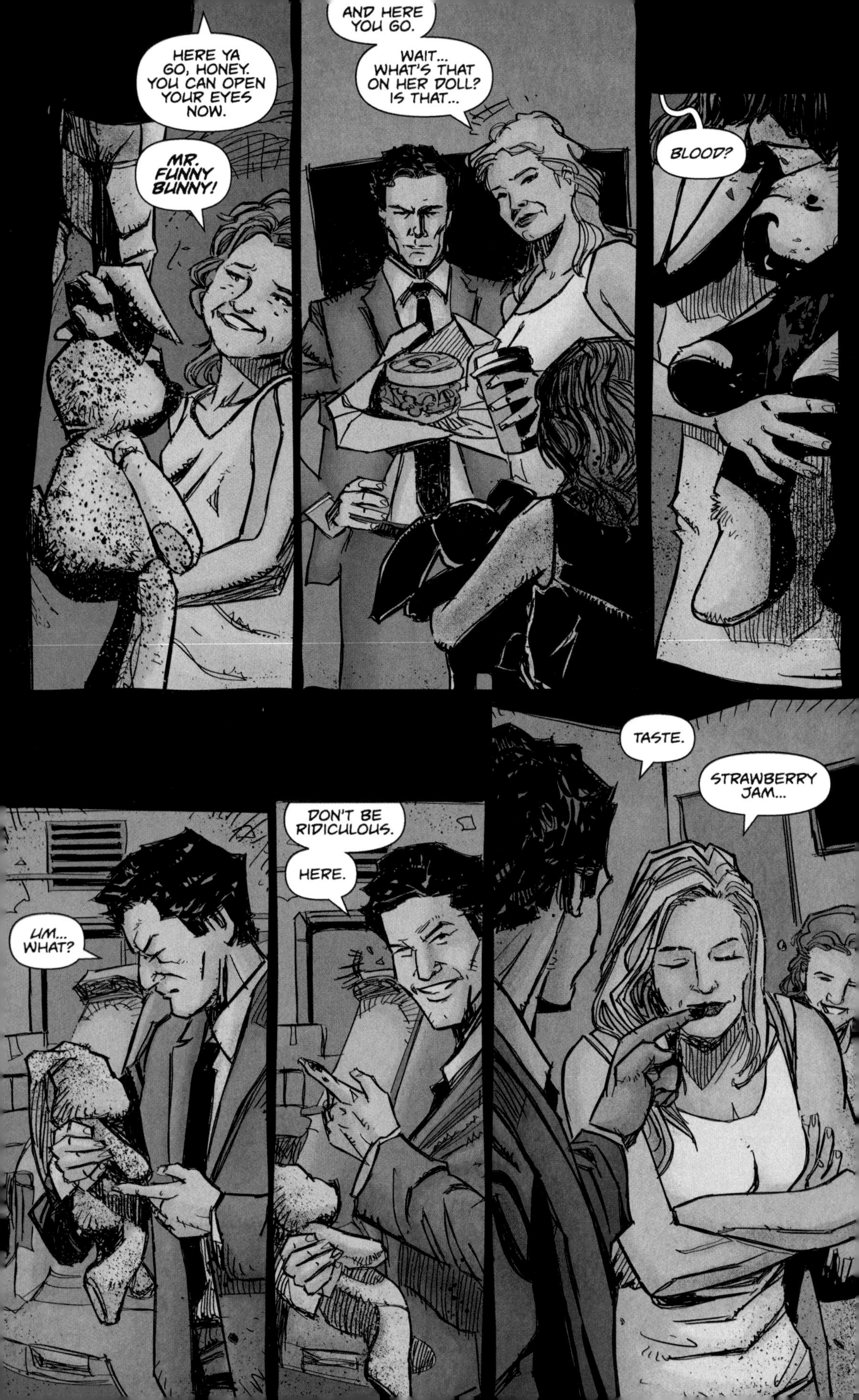
HERE YA GO, HONEY. YOU CAN OPEN YOUR EYES NOW.
MR. FUNNY BUNNY!
AND HERE YOU GO.
WAIT... WHAT'S THAT ON HER DOLL? IS THAT...
BLOOD?
UM... WHAT?
DON'T BE RIDICULOUS.
HERE.
TASTE.
STRAWBERRY JAM...

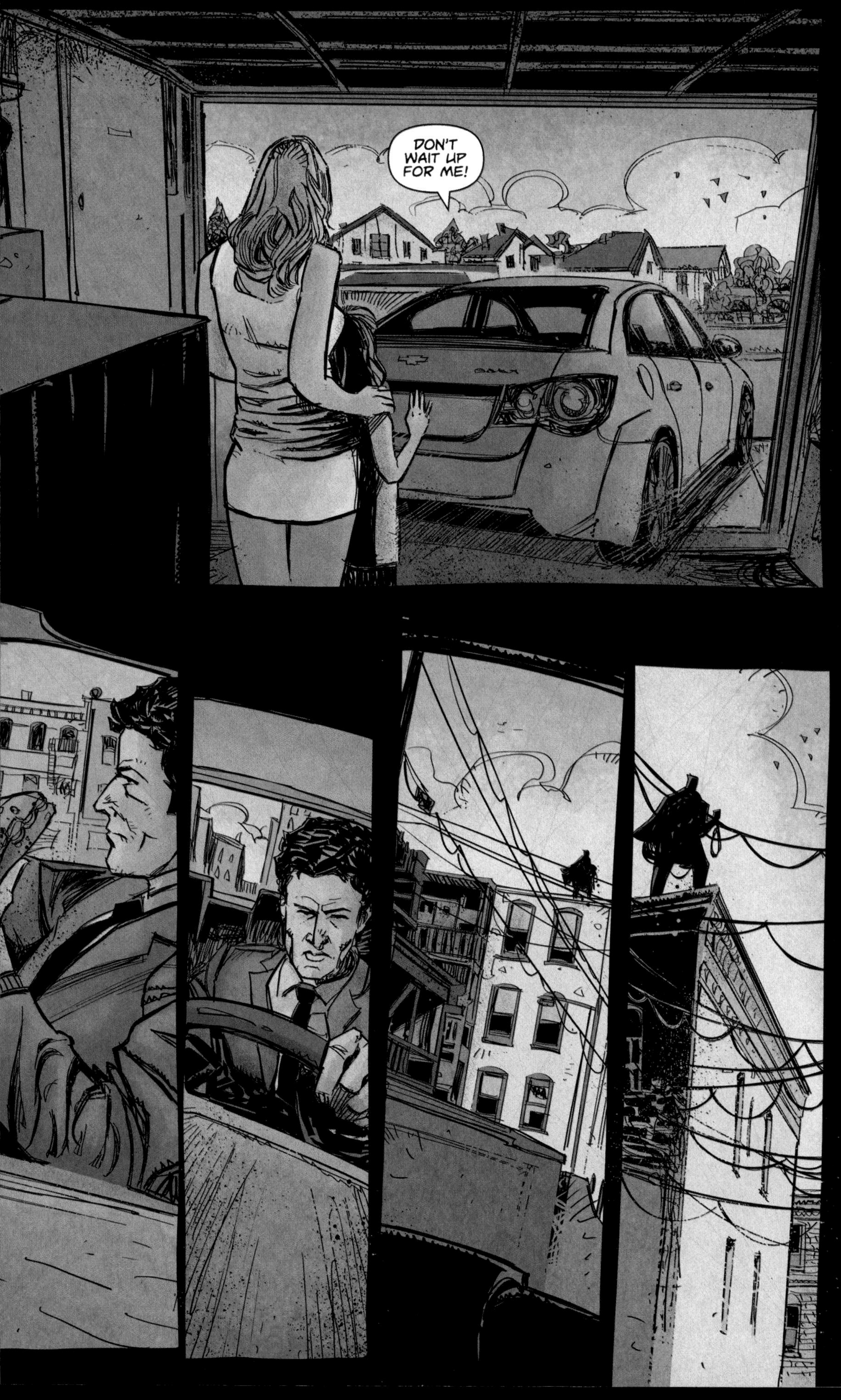
DON'T WAIT UP FOR ME!

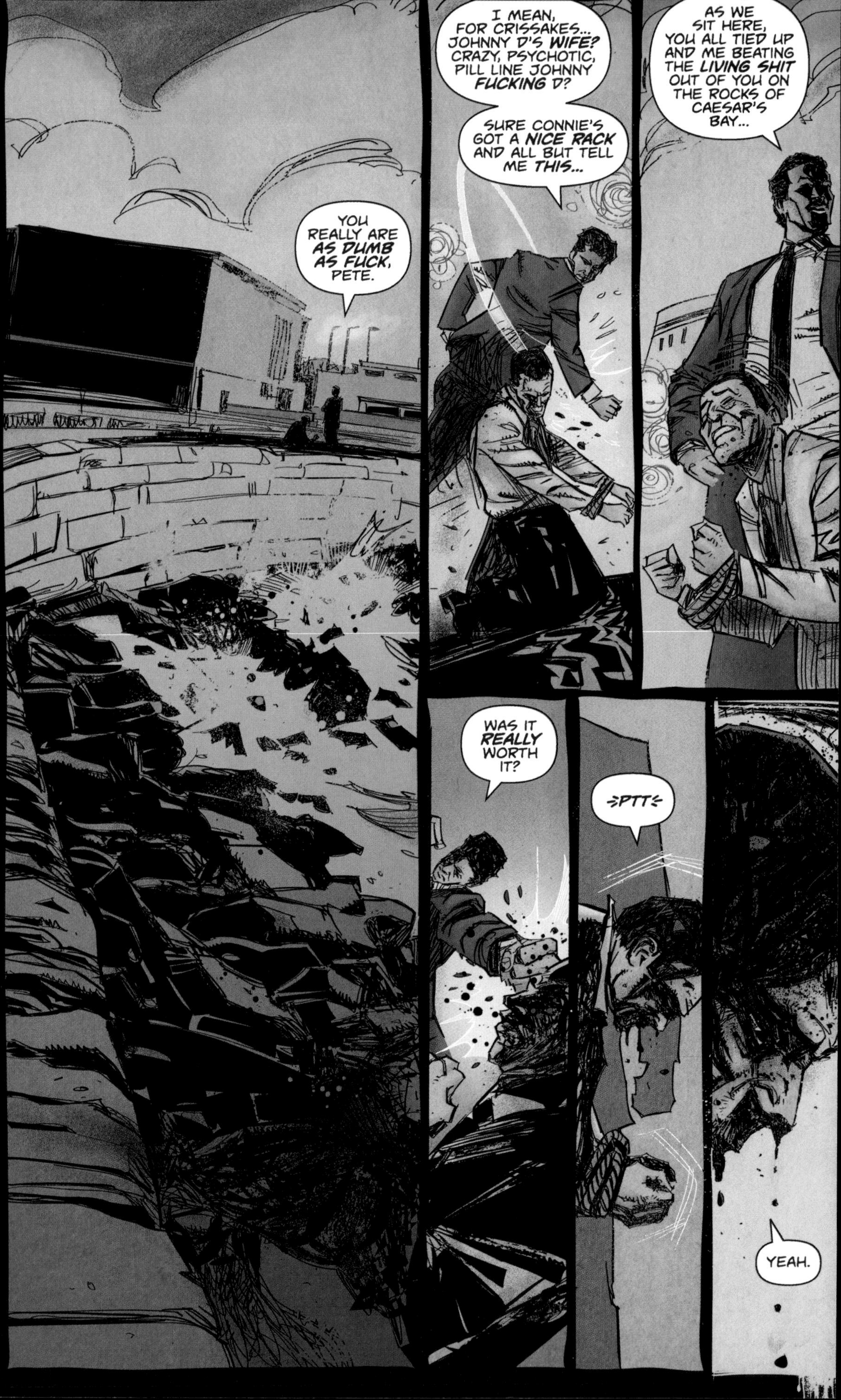
YOU REALLY ARE AS DUMB AS FUCK, PETE.
I MEAN, FOR CRISSAKES... JOHNNY D'S WIFE? CRAZY, PSYCHOTIC, PILL LINE JOHNNY FUCKING D?
SURE CONNIE'S GOT A NICE RACK AND ALL BUT TELL ME THIS...
AS WE SIT HERE, YOU ALL TIED UP AND ME BEATING THE LIVING SHIT OUT OF YOU ON THE ROCKS OF CAESAR'S BAY...
WAS IT REALLY WORTH IT?
PTT
YEAH.

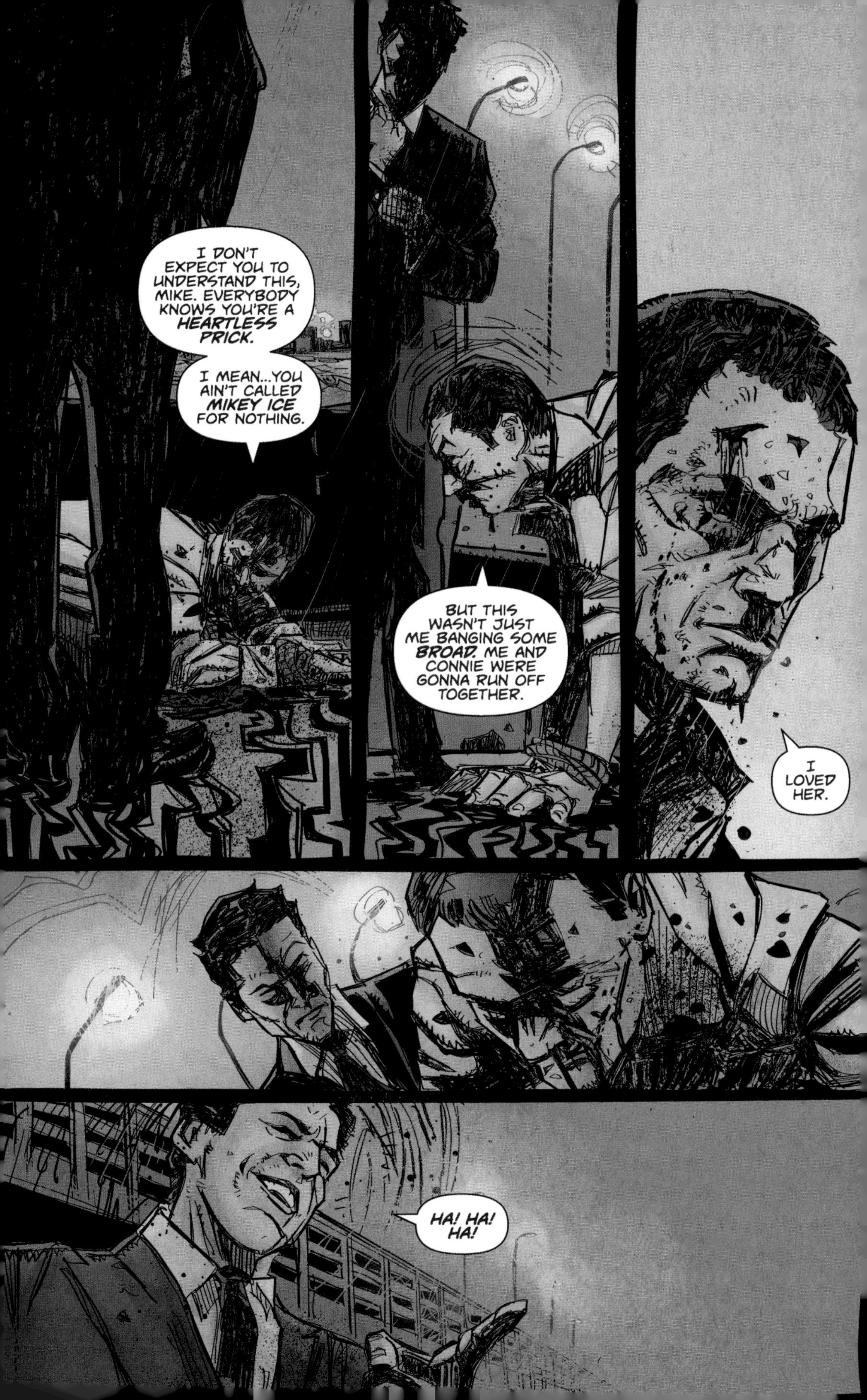
I DON'T EXPECT YOU TO UNDERSTAND THIS, MIKE. EVERYBODY KNOWS YOU'RE A HEARTLESS PRICK.
I MEAN...YOU AIN'T CALLED MIKEY ICE FOR NOTHING.
BUT THIS WASN'T JUST ME BANGING SOME BROAD. ME AND CONNIE WERE GONNA RUN OFF TOGETHER.
I LOVED HER.
HA! HA! HA!

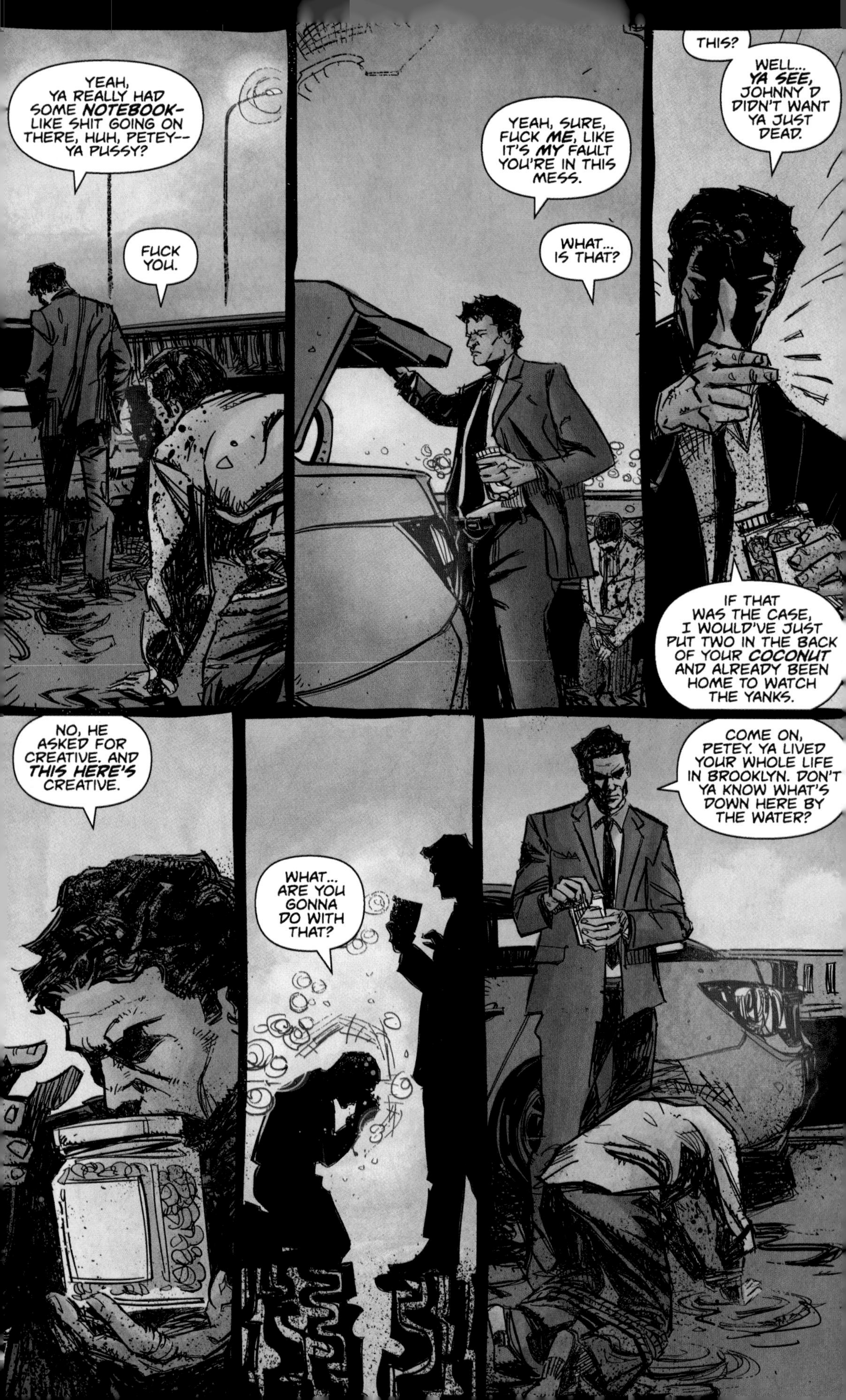
YEAH, YA REALLY HAD SOME NOTEBOOK-LIKE SHIT GOING ON THERE, HUH, PETEY--YA PUSSY?
FUCK YOU.
YEAH, SURE, FUCK ME, LIKE IT'S MY FAULT YOU'RE IN THIS MESS.
WHAT... IS THAT?
THIS?
WELL... YA SEE, JOHNNY D DIDN'T WANT YA JUST DEAD.
IF THAT WAS THE CASE, I WOULD'VE JUST PUT TWO IN THE BACK OF YOUR COCONUT AND ALREADY BEEN HOME TO WATCH THE YANKS.
NO, HE ASKED FOR CREATIVE. AND THIS HERE'S CREATIVE.
WHAT... ARE YOU GONNA DO WITH THAT?
COME ON, PETEY. YA LIVED YOUR WHOLE LIFE IN BROOKLYN. DON'T YA KNOW WHAT'S DOWN HERE BY THE WATER?

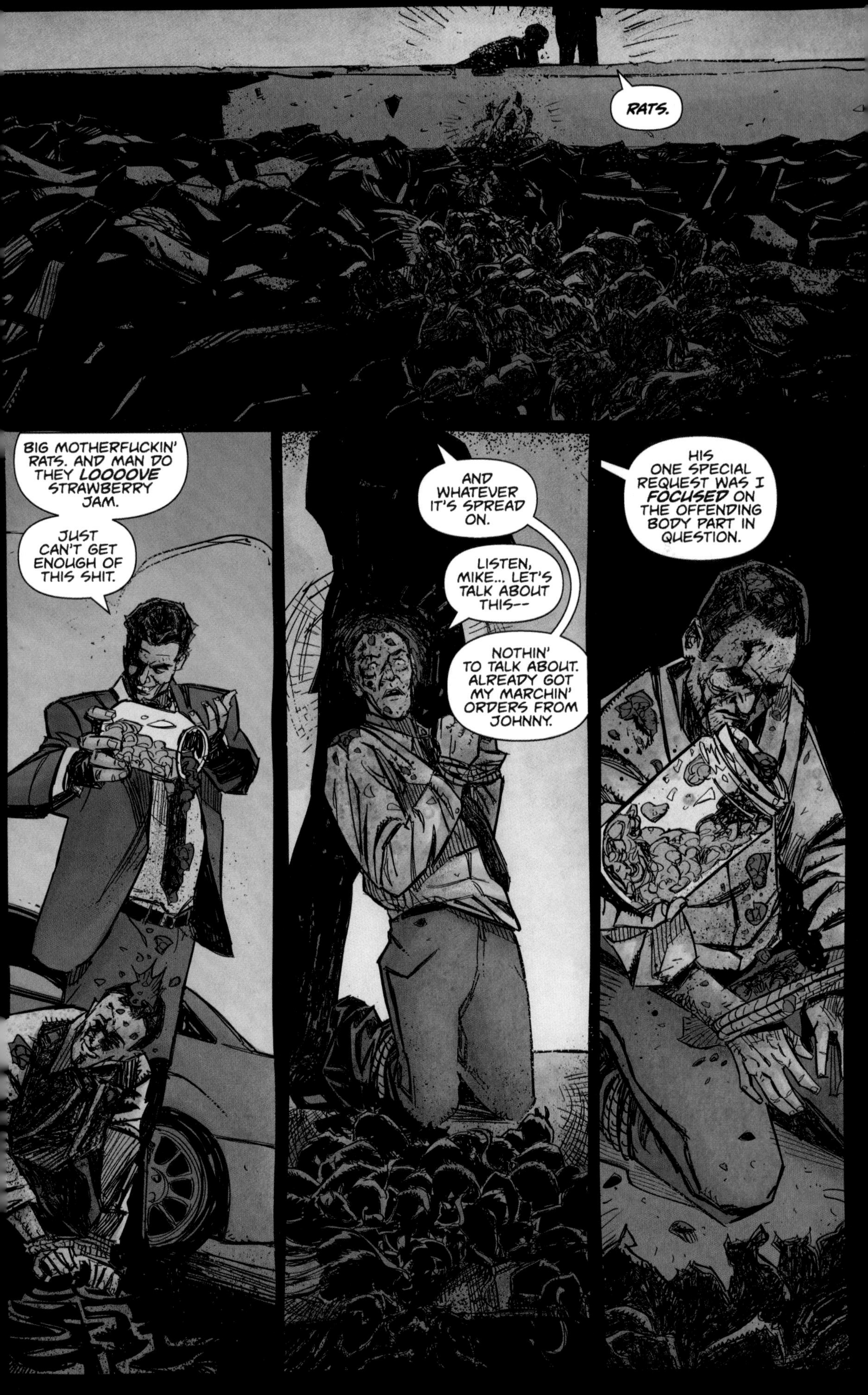
RATS.
BIG MOTHERFUCKIN' RATS. AND MAN DO THEY LOOOOVE STRAWBERRY JAM.
JUST CAN'T GET ENOUGH OF THIS SHIT.
AND WHATEVER IT'S SPREAD ON.
LISTEN, MIKE... LET'S TALK ABOUT THIS--
NOTHIN' TO TALK ABOUT. ALREADY GOT MY MARCHIN' ORDERS FROM JOHNNY.
HIS ONE SPECIAL REQUEST WAS I FOCUSED ON THE OFFENDING BODY PART IN QUESTION.

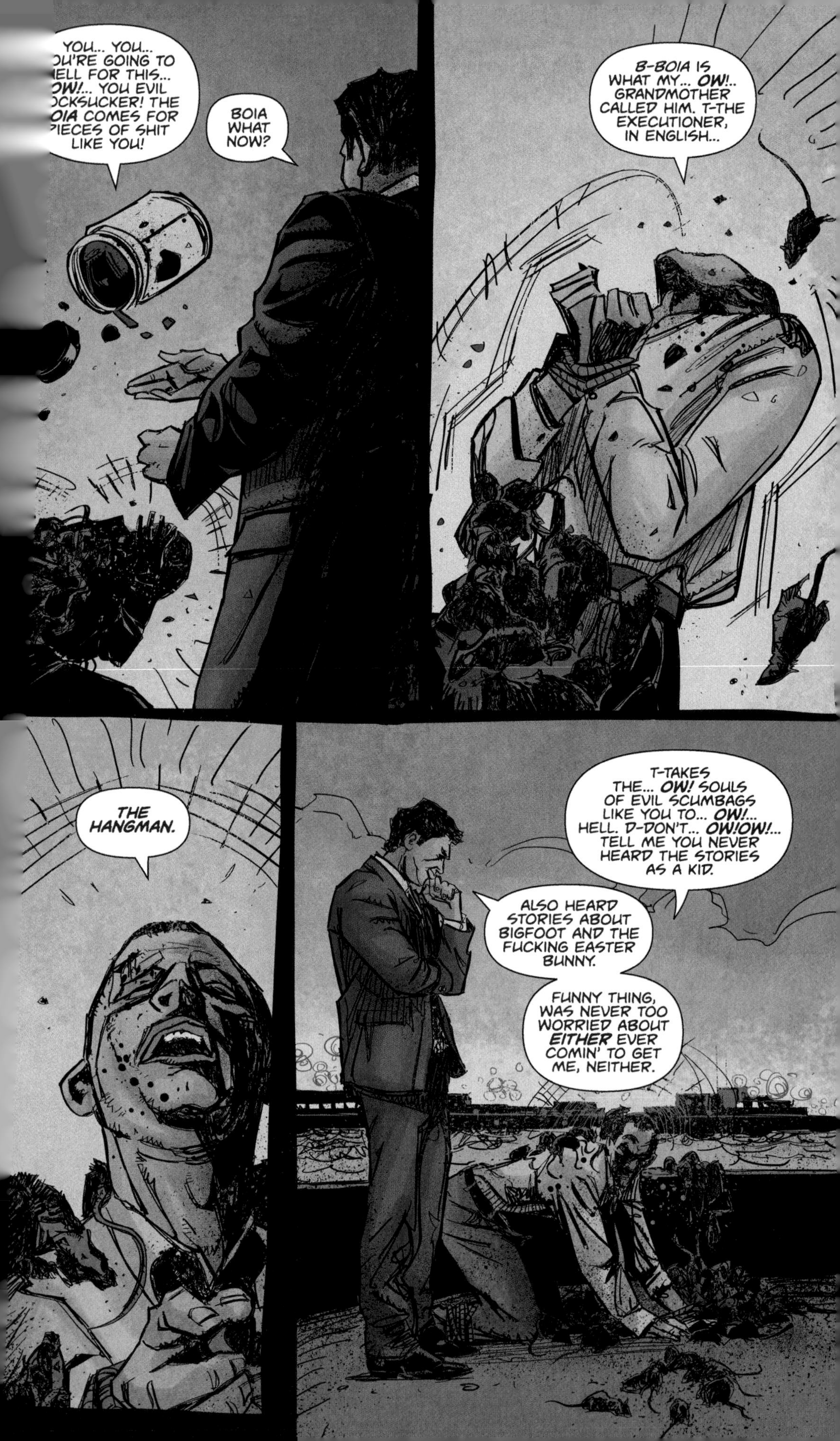
YOU... YOU... OU'RE GOING TO ELL FOR THIS... OW!... YOU EVIL OCKSUCKER! THE OIA COMES FOR IECES OF SHIT LIKE YOU!
BOIA WHAT NOW?
B-BOIA IS WHAT MY... OW!.. GRANDMOTHER CALLED HIM. T-THE EXECUTIONER, IN ENGLISH...
THE HANGMAN.
T-TAKES THE... OW! SOULS OF EVIL SCUMBAGS LIKE YOU TO... OW!... HELL. D-DON'T... OW!OW!... TELL ME YOU NEVER HEARD THE STORIES AS A KID.
ALSO HEARD STORIES ABOUT BIGFOOT AND THE FUCKING EASTER BUNNY.
FUNNY THING, WAS NEVER TOO WORRIED ABOUT EITHER EVER COMIN' TO GET ME, NEITHER.

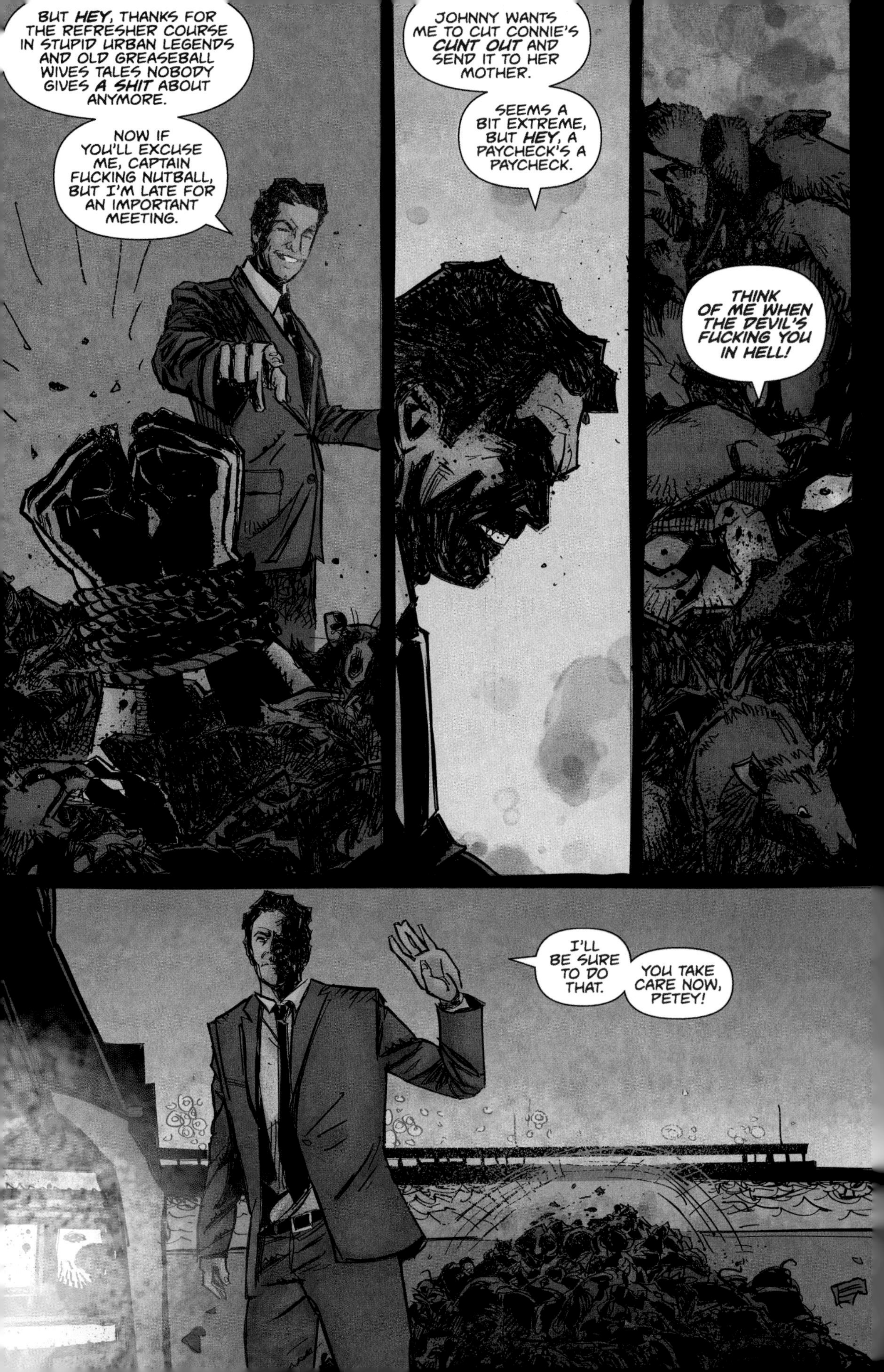
BUT HEY, THANKS FOR THE REFRESHER COURSE IN STUPID URBAN LEGENDS AND OLD GREASEBALL WIVES TALES NOBODY GIVES A SHIT ABOUT ANYMORE.
NOW IF YOU'LL EXCUSE ME, CAPTAIN FUCKING NUTBALL, BUT I'M LATE FOR AN IMPORTANT MEETING.
JOHNNY WANTS ME TO CUT CONNIE'S CUNT OUT AND SEND IT TO HER MOTHER.
SEEMS A BIT EXTREME, BUT HEY, A PAYCHECK'S A PAYCHECK.
THINK OF ME WHEN THE DEVIL'S FUCKING YOU IN HELL!
I'LL BE SURE TO DO THAT.
YOU TAKE CARE NOW, PETEY!

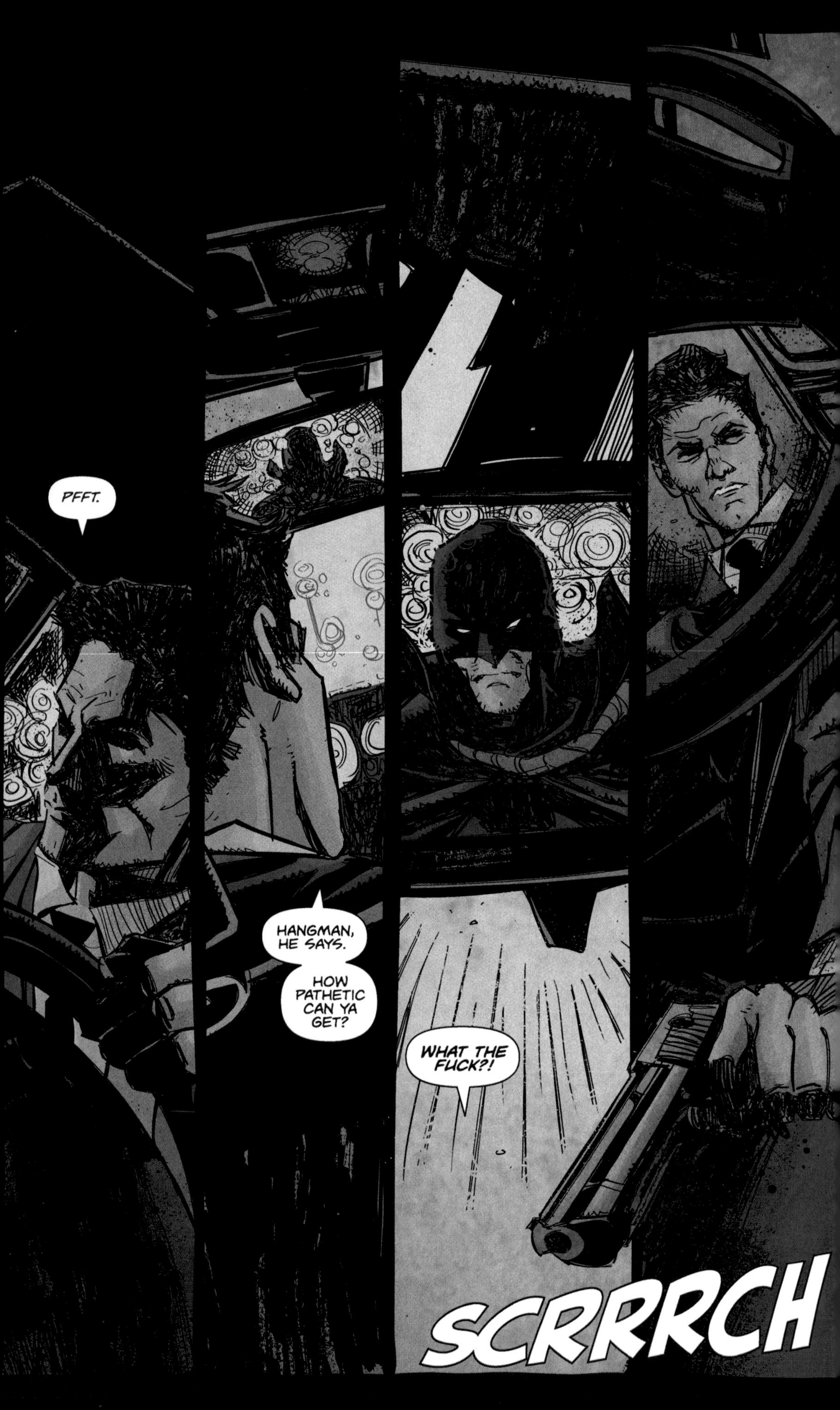
PFFT.
HANGMAN, HE SAYS.
HOW PATHETIC CAN YA GET?
WHAT THE FUCK?!
SCRRRCH

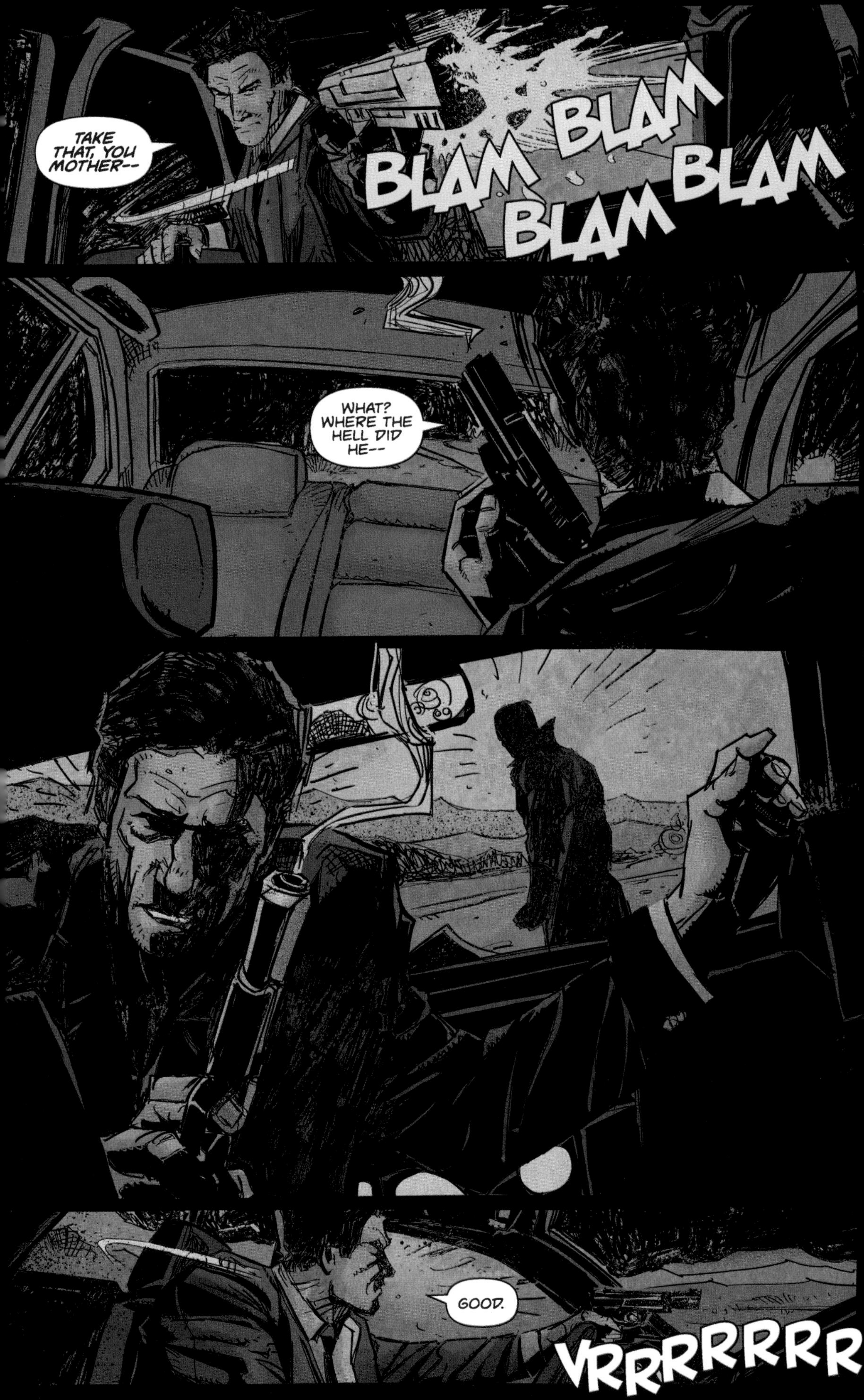
TAKE THAT, YOU MOTHER--
BLAM BLAM
BLAM BLAM
BLAM
WHAT? WHERE THE HELL DID HE--
GOOD.
VRRRRRRR

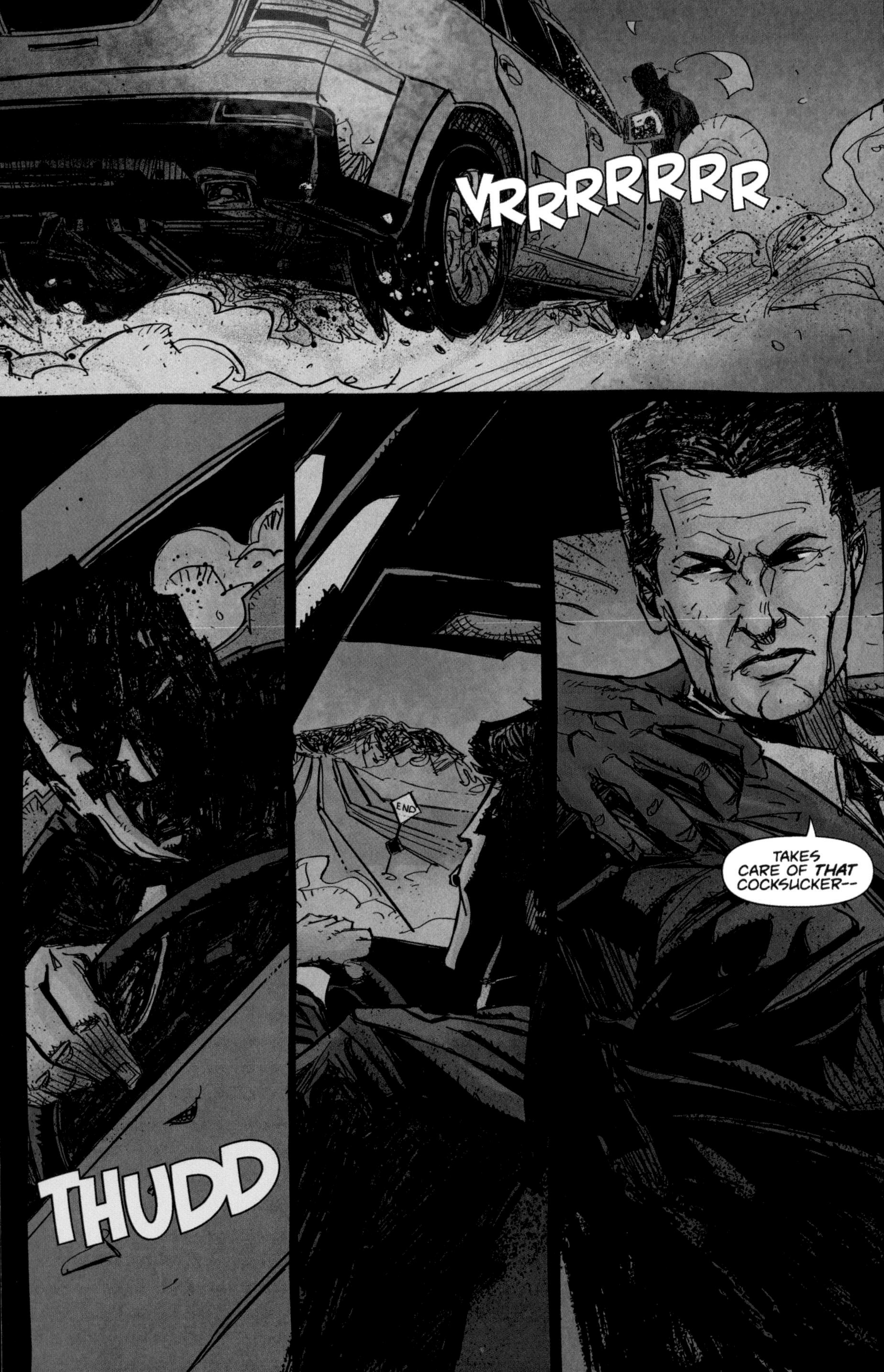
VRRRRRRR
END
TAKES CARE OF THAT COCKSUCKER--
THUDD

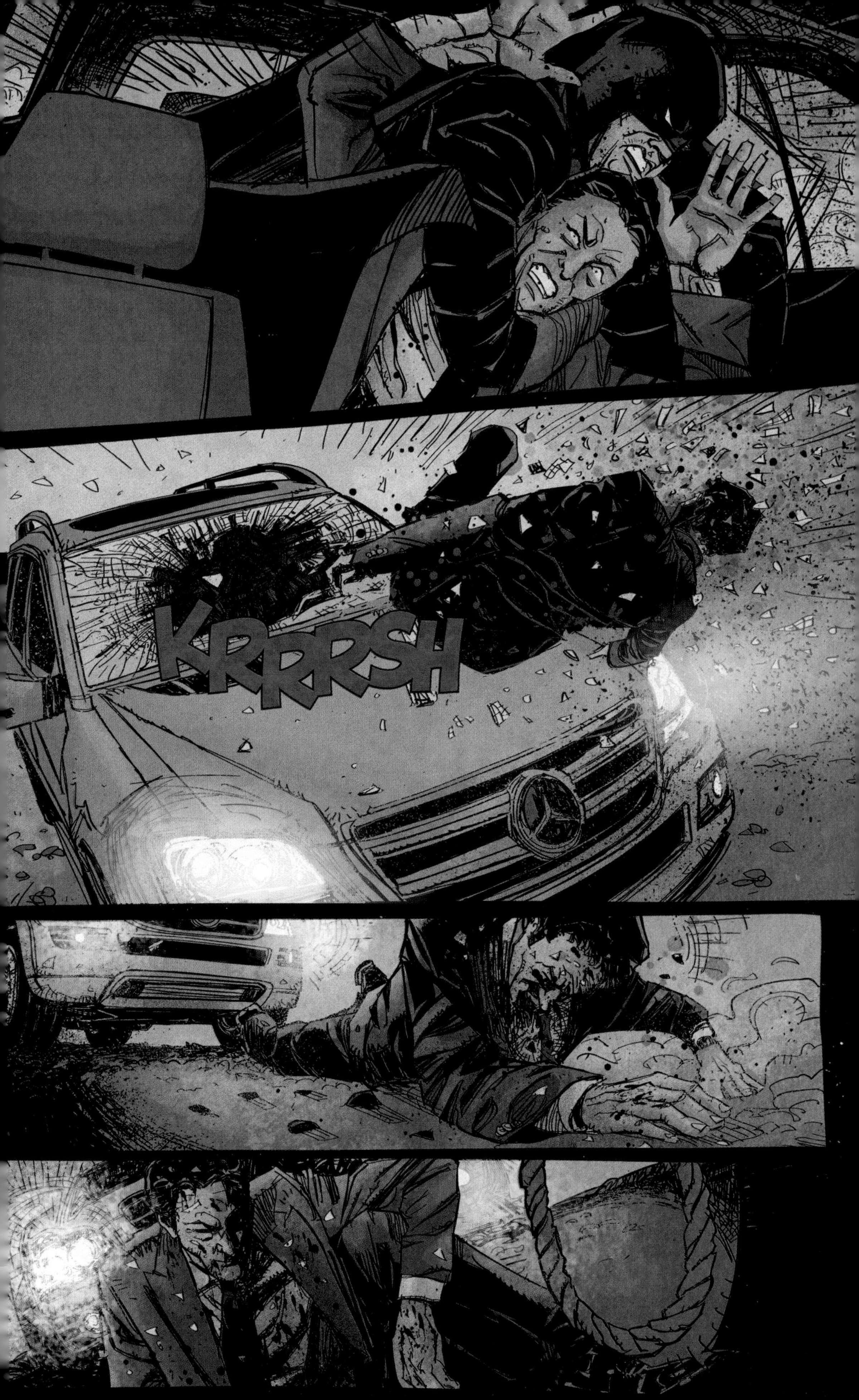
KRRRSH

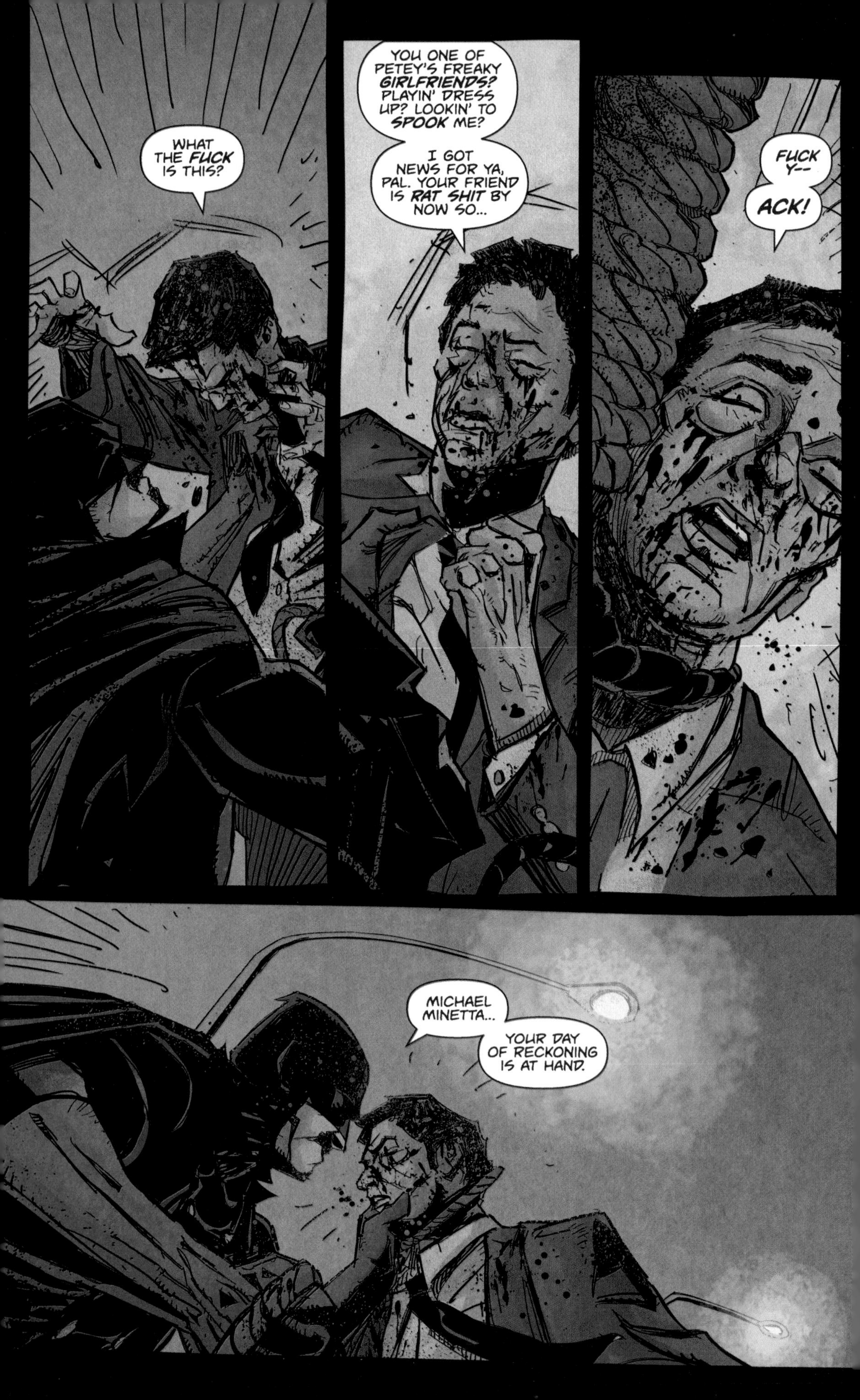
WHAT THE FUCK IS THIS?
YOU ONE OF PETEY'S FREAKY GIRLFRIENDS? PLAYIN' DRESS UP? LOOKIN' TO SPOOK ME?
I GOT NEWS FOR YA, PAL. YOUR FRIEND IS RAT SHIT BY NOW SO...
FUCK Y--
ACK!
MICHAEL MINETTA...
YOUR DAY OF RECKONING IS AT HAND.

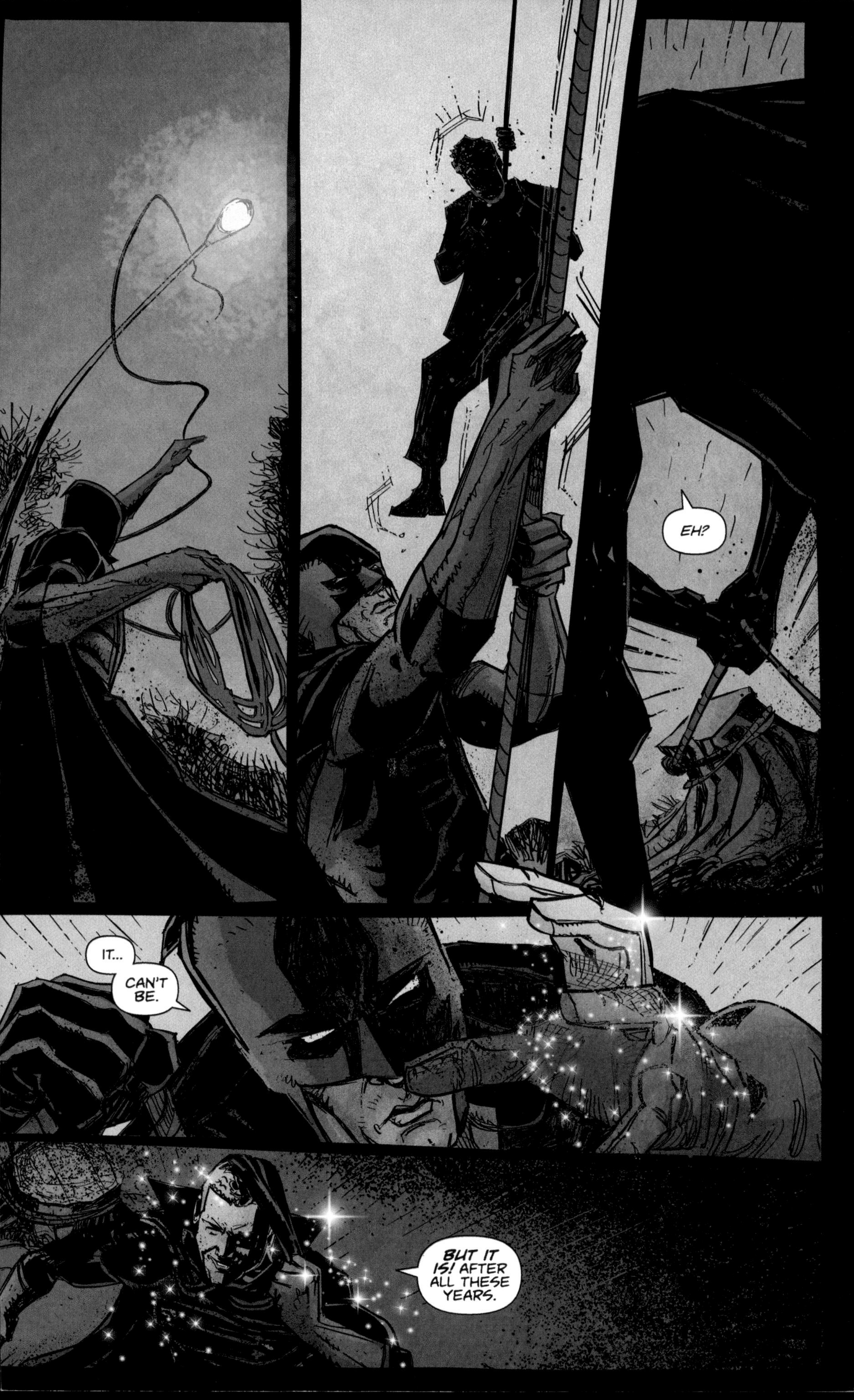
EH?
IT...
CAN'T BE.
BUT IT IS! AFTER ALL THESE YEARS.

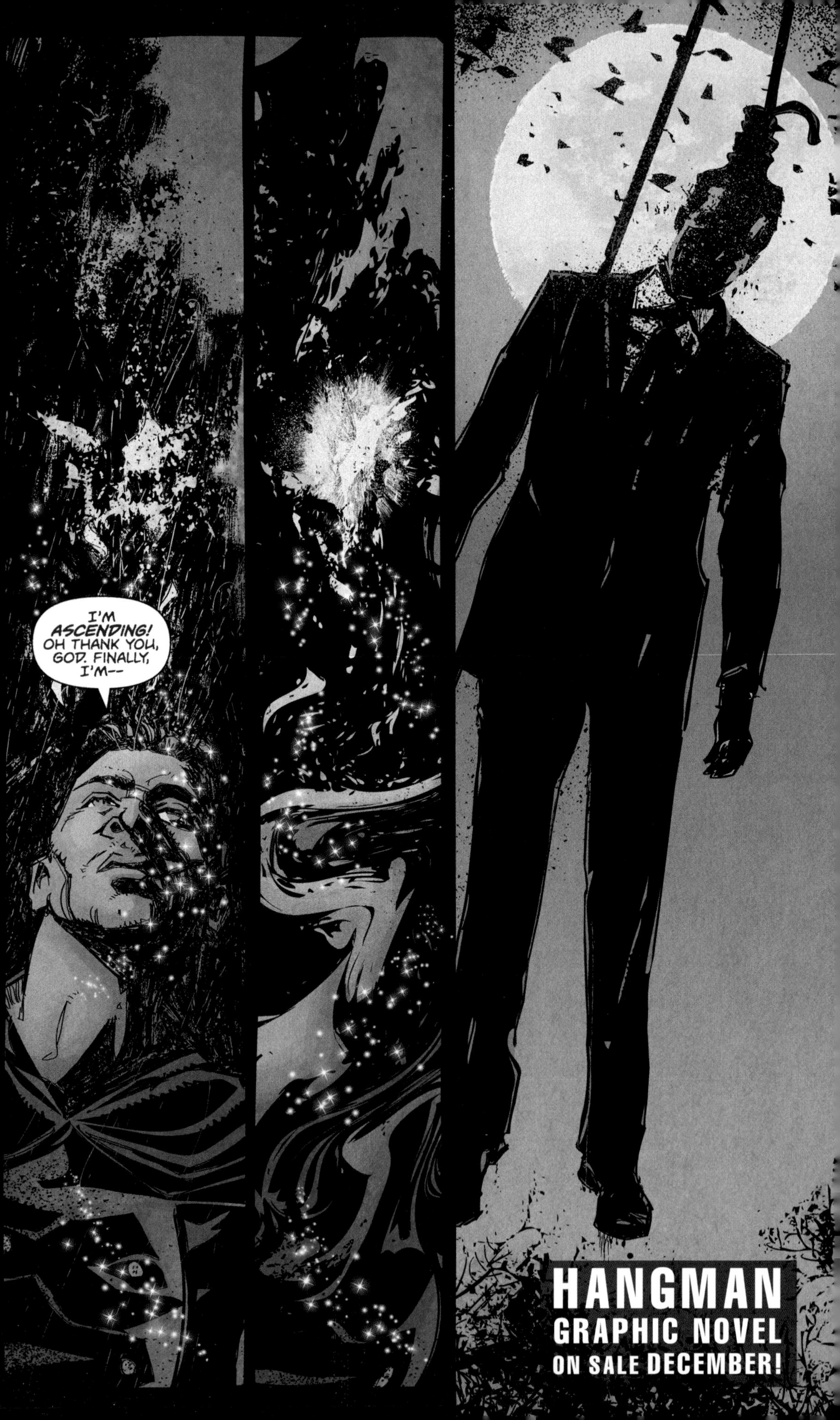
I'M ASCENDING! OH THANK YOU, GOD. FINALLY, I'M--
HANGMAN
GRAPHIC NOVEL
ON SALE DECEMBER!